SIGMA LENSES

THE EXPANDED GUIDE

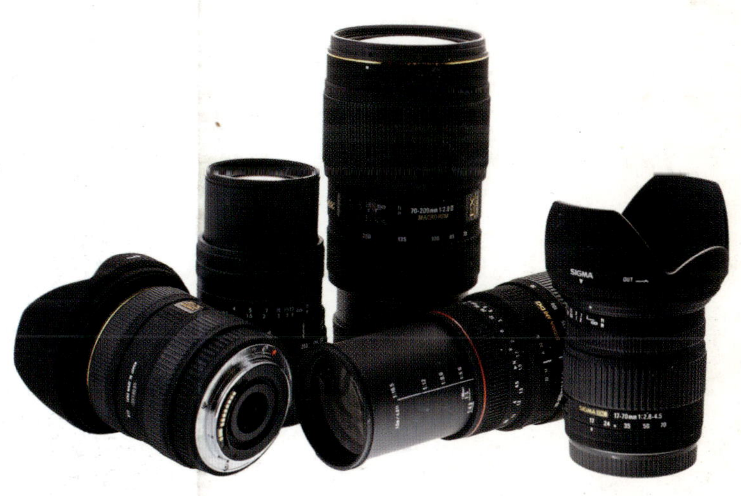

AF476869

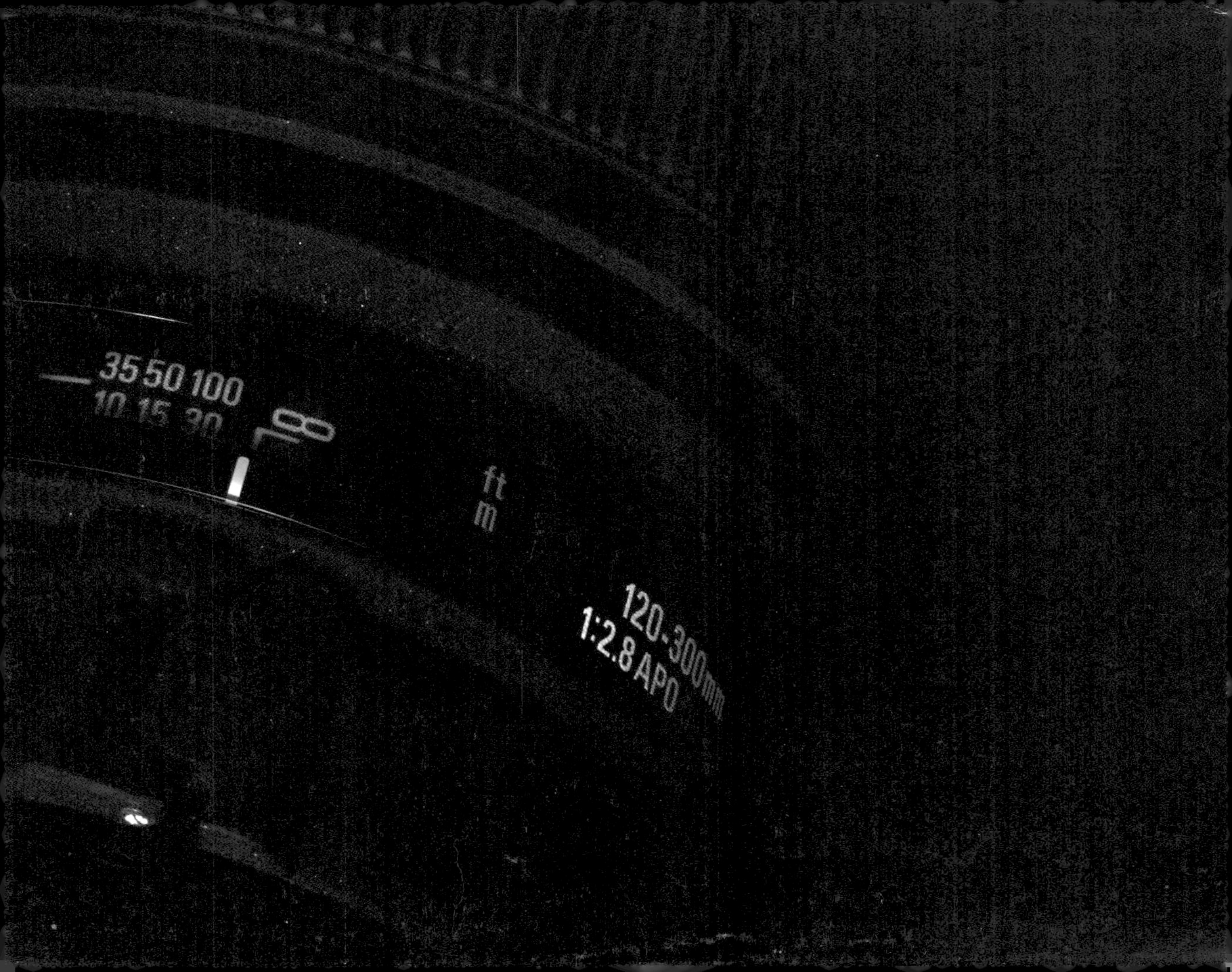

35 50 100
10 15 30
ft
m
120-300mm
1:2.8 APO

SIGMA LENSES

THE EXPANDED GUIDE

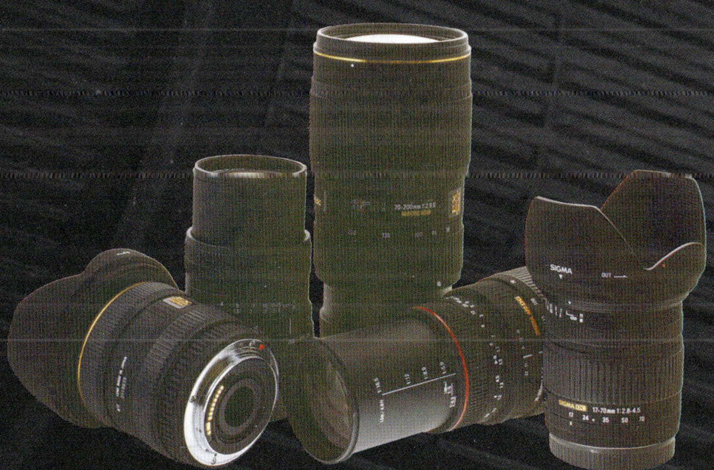

Andy Stansfield

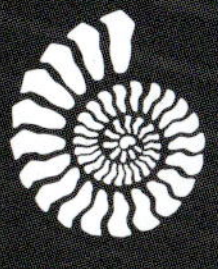

AMMONITE
PRESS

First published 2010 by
Ammonite Press
an imprint of AE Publications Ltd
166 High Street, Lewes, East Sussex, BN7 1XU

Text © AE Publications Ltd
Product photography © Sigma
Illustrative photography © Andy Stansfield
© Copyright in the Work AE Publications Ltd, 2010

ISBN 978-1906672-45-4

All rights reserved

The right of Andy Stansfield to be identified as the author of this work has been asserted in accordance with the Copyright, Designs, and Patents Act 1988, sections 77 and 78.

No part of this publication may be reproduced, stored in a retrieval system, or transmitted in any form or by any means without the prior permission of the publisher and copyright owner.

This book is sold subject to the condition that all designs are copyright and are not for commercial reproduction without the permission of the designer and copyright owner.

The publishers and author can accept no legal responsibility for any consequences arising from the application of information, advice, or instructions given in this publication.

A catalog record for this book is available from the British Library.

Editor: Tom Mugridge
Design: Fineline Studios

Set in Frutiger and Palatino
Color origination by GMC Reprographics
Printed and bound in China by Hung Hing

Contents

<table>
<tr><td>Lenses included in this book</td><td>Page</td></tr>
</table>

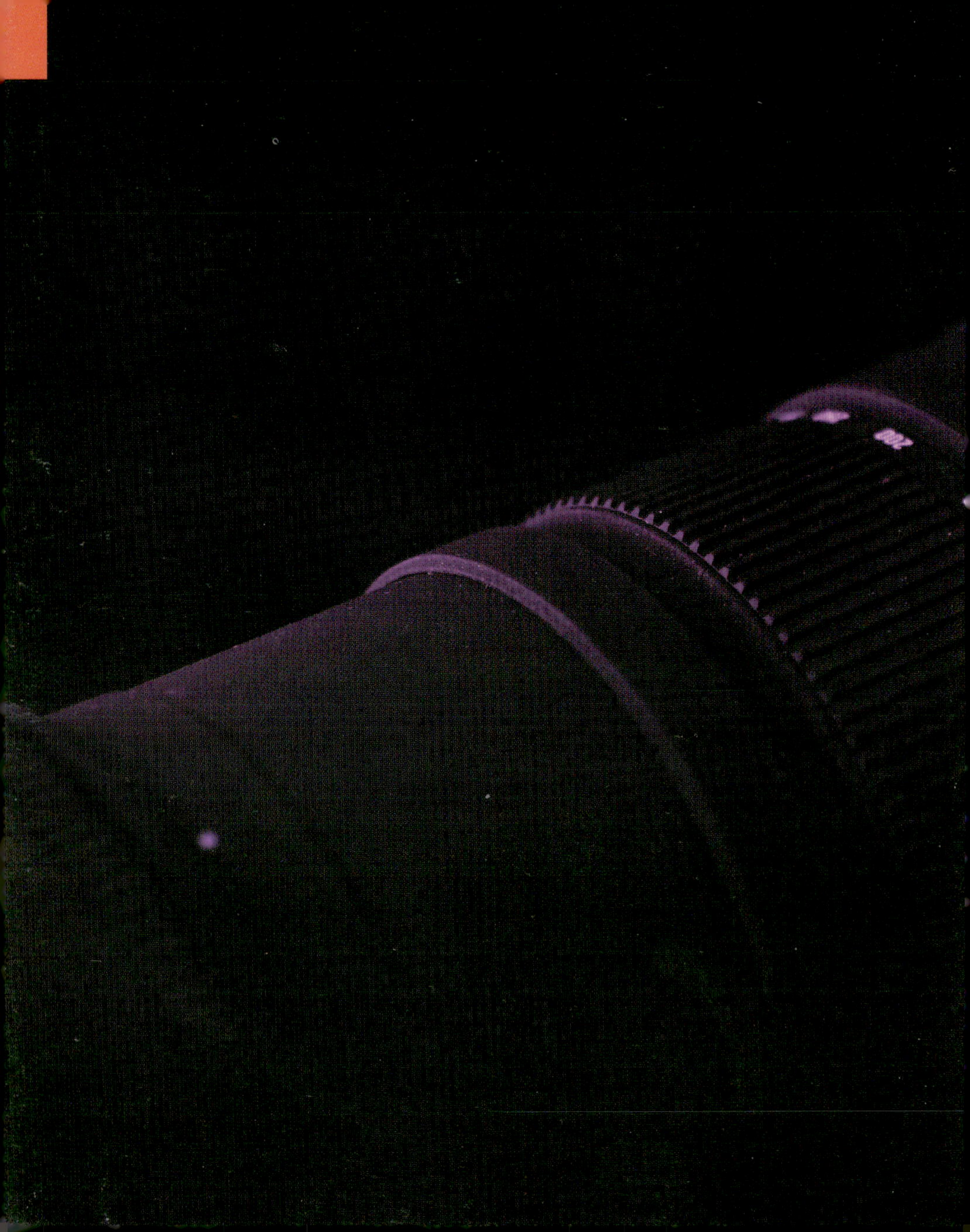

Chapter **1**

Overview

With so much attention often focused on the rollercoaster development of camera technology, it has been a refreshing change to be able to write about lenses, the opportunities they open up, and the fun that can be had with them. This is perhaps the first time that a book has been devoted solely to the complete range of lenses available from an independent manufacturer, and its preparation has been rewarding in itself. It has been a glorious excuse to illustrate the joys of using different optics.

This guide could not have been compiled without the extraordinary assistance of Sigma Imaging (UK) Limited, and their help is indicative of their desire to back up their products with service and integrity. Sigma provided me with every single lens in their range, plus several discontinued lenses that were also of interest—46 in total, with some costing as much as a small car. I am immensely grateful for that support. Nevertheless, none of the Sigma products in this book has been accorded anything less than honest appraisal, with constructive criticism being leveled where it is due.

I have owned a number of Sigma lenses over the years, and I still use several firm favorites on a regular basis alongside Canon models. Indeed, with so many different lenses to cover, it has simply not

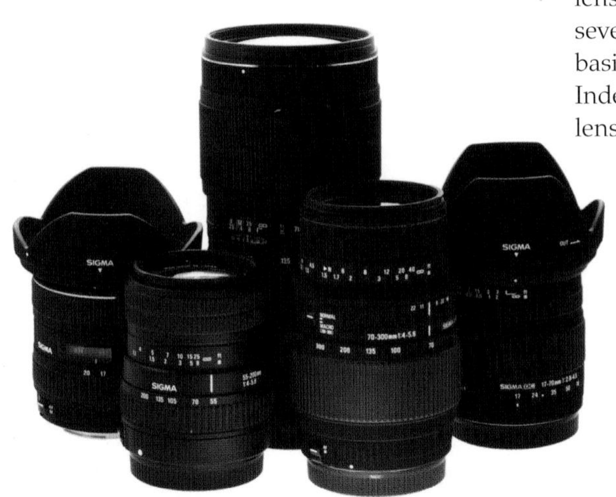

QUALITY CONTROL
Sigma lenses are assembled by hand in the company's factory in Aizu, Japan.

been possible to work with anything but the Canon versions of these lenses. My apologies to the owners of other makes, but they must take the descriptions of and comments upon each lens as being indicative of what to expect.

Which brings us to the primary purpose of this guide. It is intended as an introduction to Sigma's products, an opportunity to make comparisons and to narrow down the choices available. Also, to determine which lenses you want to explore further by researching technical reviews on the internet and examining the lenses for yourself at a reputable retail outlet. This guide is not intended to provide irrefutable technical analysis; as such, comments are unavoidably subjective, though they are based on a lifetime's experience of photography and many thousands of published images. Many of the lenses Sigma provided had previously been out on loan to the photographic press. How they were treated is an unknown factor so, while any criticism is usually constructive, in some cases it may apply solely to the lens supplied and not necessarily to every copy of that lens manufactured.

Finally, while the photographs shown alongside the descriptions of individual lenses have been captured with those same optics, the technique pages are illustrated with images from my files, which are intended to convey specific styles of photography, rather than images necessarily taken with Sigma products.

From a mountainside in Japan

Sigma was founded in 1961 by the current President, Mr. Michiro Yamaki, who has witnessed the factory he located on a quiet mountainside in Aizu, Japan develop into a base for the largest independent lens production facility in the world. Sigma have their own Research and Development division and subsidiaries in several European countries, Hong Kong, and the USA.

All lens components are produced by Sigma themselves whenever possible and each individual lens is assembled by hand at the Aizu factory. To quote company literature: "…when it comes to assembly of the latest products, nothing can beat the precision of a human being."

From the cutting, grinding, and polishing of lens elements to the production of sophisticated integrated circuit chips in the Sigma factory's "clean rooms," the company claim "no shortcut to excellence." Quality control has become a credo rather than merely a target, and this attention to detail was evident in all of the 46 different lenses that I examined during the writing of his book.

Lenses and sensor size

Many photographers don't realize that the image projected by the lens onto the film or camera sensor is circular rather than rectangular.

A full-frame sensor (below, left) is large enough to accommodate the maximum amount of the projected image circle. However, the smaller APS-C sensor (center) covers a smaller proportion of the image circle projected by a lens designed for 35mm film or a full-frame sensor. This is very useful in terms of absolute image quality, as it crops away the parts of the image circle where deterioration of the image is more likely. A lens designed solely for use with an APS-C sensor (right) has a smaller image circle, once again maximizing the sensor area. There is a great deal of confusion about the implications of this as regards lenses. This is largely because people insist on making comparisons such as saying that a 50mm lens on a camera with the smaller APS-C sensor is equivalent to an 80mm lens (i.e. 50mm × 1.6) with a full-frame sensor. Not true. A 50mm lens behaves like a 50mm lens no matter what camera it is on and the size of the projected image will always be the same, assuming identical camera-to-subject distance. The only thing that changes is the field of view.

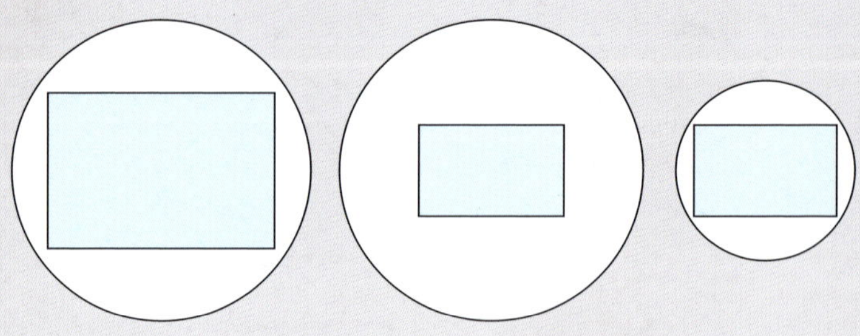

Lens designations

EX lenses

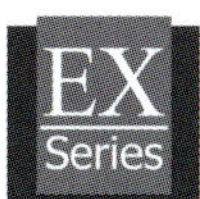

Sigma's EX lenses are the cream of the crop. The EX designation is only applied to the best of Sigma's extensive range and is reserved for those lenses that have a higher standard of construction, finish, and performance. Two-thirds of the current lineup are classified as EX lenses, including 23 full-frame DG lenses and seven DC lenses, the latter being designed solely for crop-sensor cameras.

There was a time when it was easier to tell an EX lens apart from a non-EX model. The obvious gold lettering has remained a constant, but in recent years the appearance of the non-EX lenses has improved significantly. However, construction, weight, and the use of plastics still

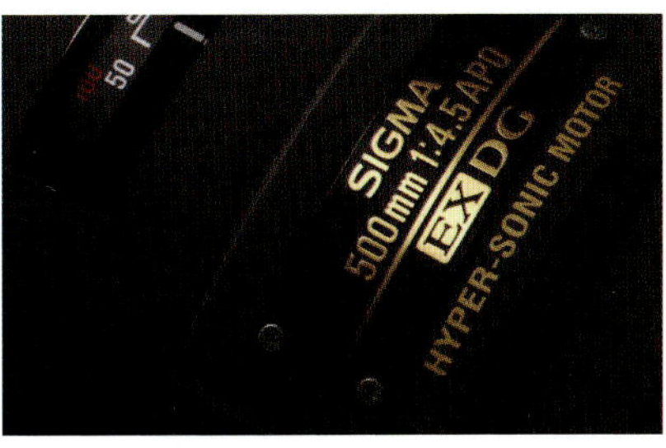

EX LENS BADGE
Sigma's flagship EX lenses can be identified by their distinctive gold lettering.

set them apart. All EX lenses come in a matte black finish and in a black fitted lens case. The smaller of these have belt loops, while the cases for the larger lenses have fittings for a shoulder strap, which is provided.

DG lenses

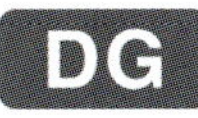

DG lenses are high-performance lenses that are optimized for digital cameras, but which can be used equally well on film cameras. They are designed to produce an image circle suitable for full-frame digital or 35mm film cameras, but can be used on APS-C cameras too, albeit with a reduced field of view.

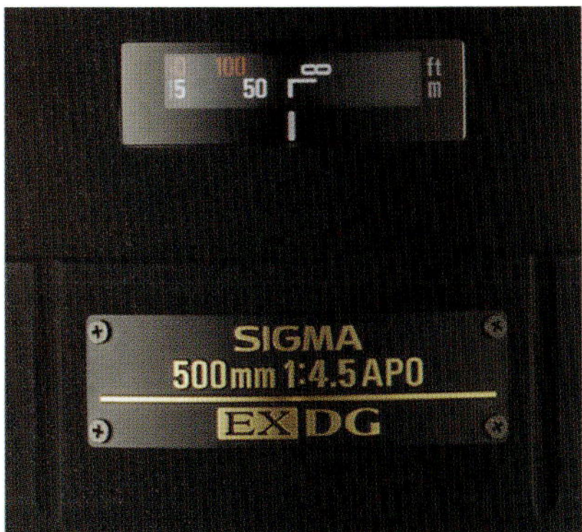

DG LENSES
Sigma's DG lenses are noted for their high contrast and wide tonal range.

DG lenses deliver superior image quality corrected for all types of aberration, especially distortion. High contrast and a wide tonal range are characteristics of all DG lenses, along with good peripheral brightness showing minimal, if any, tendency toward vignetting. The most recent lenses feature improved light distribution from image center to edge, resulting in even better contrast and apparent sharpness. Chromatic aberration, a common issue with digital cameras that produces color fringing usually only noticeable at higher magnifications, is significantly reduced. Furthermore, DG lenses benefit from Sigma's own Super Multi-Layer Coating technology, so they reduce flare and ghosting due to reflection between the image sensor and lens surfaces.

DC lenses

DC lenses are dedicated digital SLR camera lenses with an image circle designed to suit APS-C image sensors—technology developed during Sigma's own digital SLR program aided in the process of optimizing the optical performance of the DC range.

These high-performance lenses combine evolving technology such as optical design, improved lens coatings, and optical stabilization with the vast experience acquired by Sigma designers and technicians during four decades of developing interchangeable lenses for film users with SLR cameras. With a reduced image circle, Sigma have achieved a series of lenses that are extremely compact and light in weight. In addition, Sigma have far outstripped even the likes of Nikon and Canon in producing an extensive range of DC lenses that covers the wider focal lengths, including fisheye lenses.

If DC lenses are fitted to full-frame digital or 35mm cameras, significant vignetting will occur, as the projected image circle does not have sufficient diameter to cover the sensor or film area (see page 12).

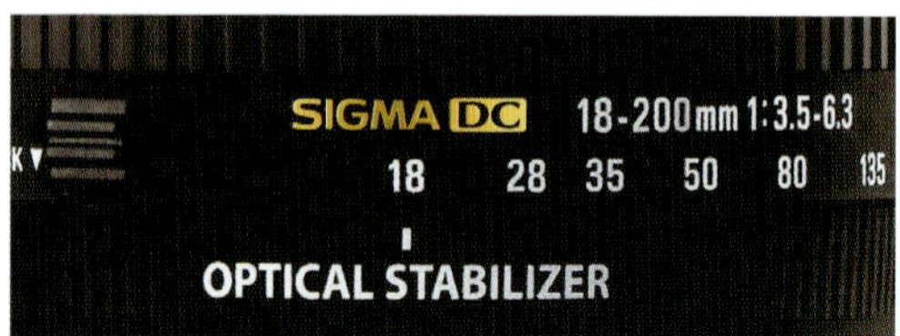

DC LENSES
Sigma's DC lenses are designed specifically for digital SLRs with APS-C image sensors.

Lens construction

All Sigma lenses are designed and manufactured by the company themselves at their original factory in Japan, right down to the last detail. Every metal component is cut and machined, every plastic (actually hard-wearing polycarbonate resin) part is injection-molded, and every integrated circuit chip is clean-room produced at the Aizu factory, though Research and Development has more recently been relocated to a new corporate headquarters in Tokyo. Arguably most important of all, every glass element is cut, ground, and polished by Sigma's highly trained craftsmen before each individual lens is hand-assembled.

Aspherical lenses

Sigma lenses incorporate various features in different combinations. Many make use of Aspherical lens elements (ASP). A single Aspherical element can perform the functions of two or more conventional spherical elements, allowing the

Note
See page 18 for more on RF and IF, page 19 for more on HSM, and page 20 for more on OS.

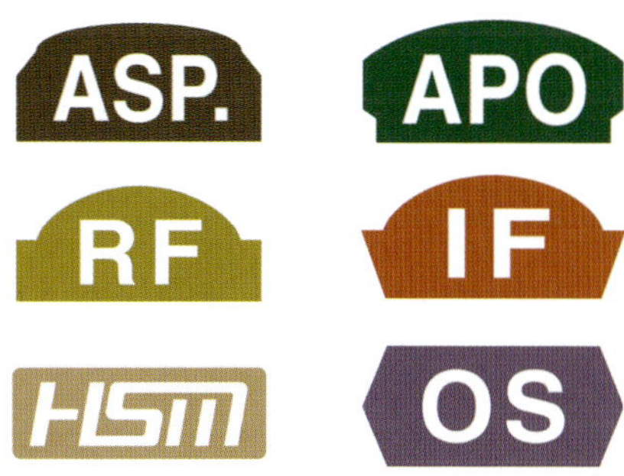

LENS FEATURES
Sigma use these symbols to denote the following features: Aspherical lens elements, APO technology, Rear Focus, Inner Focus, Hyper-Sonic Motor, and Optical Stabilizer.

lens to be made more compact and lightweight while retaining high levels of performance. They are effective in managing chromatic aberration (color fringing) as well as controlling potential distortion in wide-angle zoom lenses with an extensive focal length range. Less well publicized is their ability to eliminate the sagittal coma flare that accompanies large lens diameters at wide apertures when shooting high-contrast point light sources, such as when capturing townscapes at night.

In the optics diagrams that accompany each lens description in this book, Aspherical lens elements are colored pink.

Apochromatic lenses

Apochromatic lenses (APO) are prime telephoto and telephoto zoom lens designs that make use of Special Low Dispersion (SLD) or Extraordinary Low Dispersion (ELD) glass, pioneered by glass and filter manufacturers Hoya (owners of Pentax), to improve performance. Color aberration can occur in telephoto lenses because different colors form their images at different points due to differing wavelengths, a problem that SLD glass was designed to counteract.

The highly effective use of SLD glass has been proven over many years, but Sigma were the first to use the more recently developed and more efficient ELD glass, adopting it for use in the 300mm f/2.8, 500mm f/4.5, 800mm f/5.6, and 300–800mm f/5.6. All APO lenses give greater contrast, improved sharpness, and better color characteristics than a comparable non-APO lens. In some cases, Sigma manufacture a lens both with and without APO features—examples include the 70–300mm f/4–5.6 DG Macro and APO 70–300mm f/4–5.6 DG Macro.

One of Sigma's great successes has been to merge the characteristics of the APO telephoto lens with those of the close-focusing, high-contrast, high-resolution macro lens, producing a number of APO macro zoom lenses that offer magnifications as great as half life-size. All Sigma apochromatic lenses are identified by the APO designation in their names and descriptions.

In the optics diagrams that accompany each lens description in this book, Special Low Dispersion glass lens elements are colored blue, while Extraordinary Low Dispersion glass is shown in green.

ELD GLASS
The 300mm f/2.8 makes use of Extraordinary Low Dispersion glass in its construction.

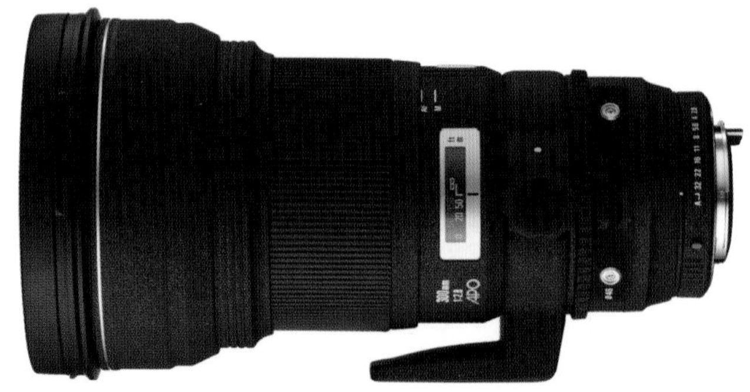

Chromatic aberration

Special Low Dispersion glass is used for lens elements that reduce chromatic aberration (color fringing) by bringing the focus points of different light waves—representing different colors—to a single point, as shown in the diagram on the right.

Available mounts

Every current Sigma lens is available with Sigma, Canon, and Nikon mounts. The vast majority are also available for Sony and Pentax cameras. Users of the Four Thirds system are catered for by approximately 25% of the range.

All Nikon versions are compatible with D type cameras, along with many Sony versions—the exceptions generally being the lenses with the longest focal lengths.

Autofocus on the Pentax and Sony versions will not function unless the camera supports HSM. The Pentax versions are not fully compatible with the SF-X and SF-7

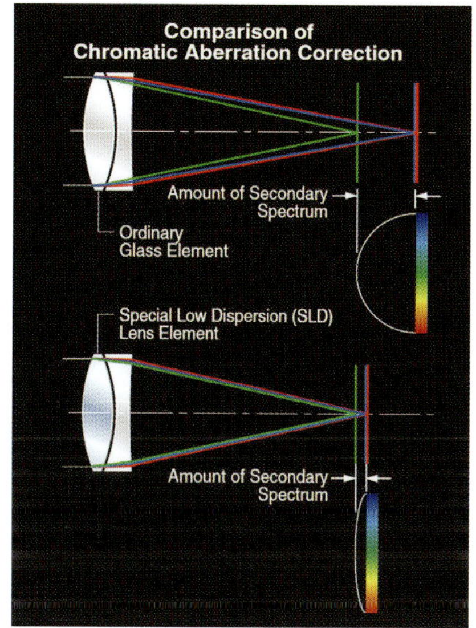

cameras. Neither Pentax nor Sony versions of lenses that normally feature Optical Stabilization will incorporate that feature.

Lenses normally accepting the 1.4× or 2× converters may not be used with selected Four Thirds cameras in that combination.

Rear Focus (RF)

Conventional focusing is normally achieved by moving either all the lens groups as a fixed unit, or just the first lens group. In contrast, the rear focus system moves the rear lens group for fast, silent focusing and is favored for very wide-angle lenses that have a large front element (see diagram below).

Inner Focus (IF)

The most significant advantage of internal-focus lenses is that they maintain a constant length, with no lens extension when focusing. Sigma have developed an inner focus system that moves two lens groups inside their telephoto and telephoto macro lenses. This system has floating elements that substantially improve the close-up capability of the lens.

Dual Focus (DF)

This system makes use of Sigma's trademark "clutch" mechanism to disengage the linkage between the internal focusing mechanism and the focusing ring when the focusing ring is moved to the AF position. The great advantage of this is that the focusing ring itself does not rotate when set to AF. This means you are free to adopt the most comfortable position for your supporting hand, while you retain the option to switch to manual focusing quickly and easily, thus reengaging the linkage to the internal focusing mechanism.

REAR FOCUS
The optics diagram for the 20mm f/1.8 EX DG lens, with the rear focus system indicated.

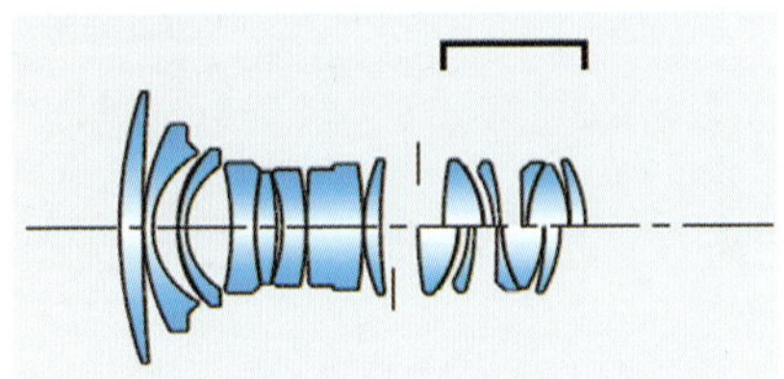

INNER FOCUS
The optics diagram for the APO 70–200mm f/2.8 II EX DG lens, with the inner focus system indicated.

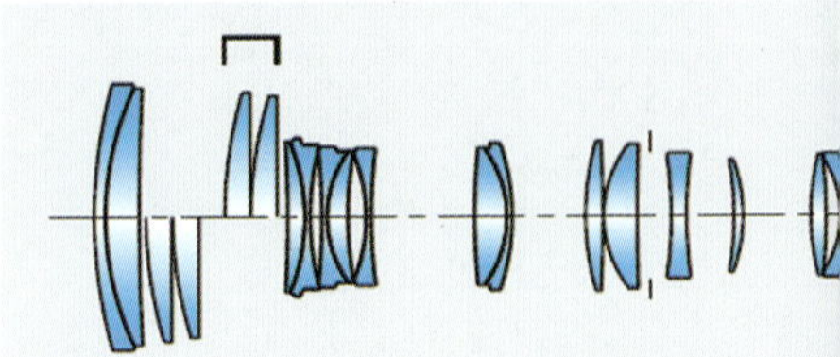

Hyper Sonic Motor

The abbreviation HSM stands for Hyper Sonic Motor. These motors, triggered by ultrasonic waves, drive the focusing mechanism and by necessity must be both fast and as quiet as possible. The technology employed is similar to that used by other camera manufacturers. At the time of writing, Sigma is the only independent lens manufacturer that supplies lenses with this technology, mirroring as closely as possible the products of camera manufacturers themselves in order to maximize the combined functionality of both camera and lens.

Sometimes a Sigma lens is available in both HSM and non-HSM versions. In addition, an HSM lens may be available for, say, Nikon, but not Canon. One feature common to most, but not quite all, HSM lenses is full-time manual focus, enabling the focus to be tweaked manually even when using AF.

Each and every lens in this book comes in various fittings and may or may not have HSM, but there are obvious constraints with regard to the space available for illustrations. Where there is a choice,

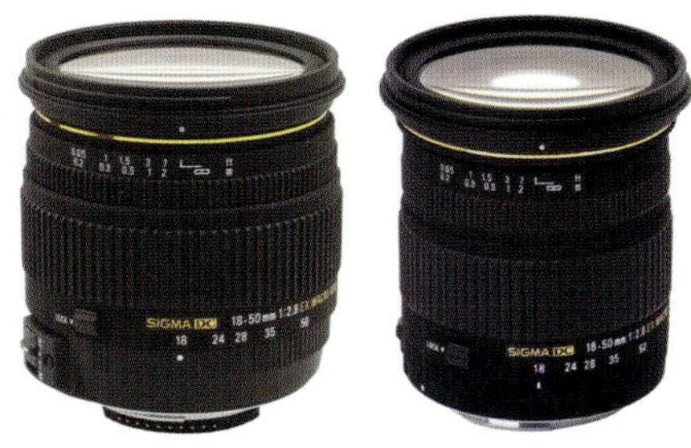

DIMENSIONS
The HSM version (left) and the non-HSM version (right) of the 18–50mm f/2.8 EX DC Macro. The girth of the HSM version is noticeably larger.

Note
Pentax and Sony camera bodies must be able to support HSM in order for autofocus to function.

the HSM version is usually the version illustrated and to which the specifications apply. However, there can be a significant difference in the dimensions of a non-HSM lens compared with its HSM equivalent. This can clearly be seen in the example shown above.

OPTICAL STABILIZER

Sigma's OS function makes use of a mechanism built into the lens that compensates for camera shake when shooting handheld. It uses two sensors to detect vertical and lateral movement, and works by moving an optical image-stabilizing lens group to compensate for camera movement. This involves a momentary delay during which, on some lenses, you will actually hear the OS process kick in. By maintaining partial pressure on the shutter release (or other button designated for achieving autofocus), you will see the image in the viewfinder settle. The advent of optical stabilization was originally accompanied by a degree of skepticism, a mood that didn't last for long as lens designers quickly raised their game. The earliest forms of optically stabilized lens could only safely boast two stops' advantage, perhaps two and a half. Sigma are now on their fourth generation of OS, and their latest lens provides four full stops of improvement over its non-stabilized equivalent.

Optical stabilization has been introduced by the major manufacturers into a variety of focal lengths, but they have tended to lag behind Sigma in providing this feature on wide-angle zooms, though with recent releases, both Canon and Nikon now match Sigma in this regard. Sigma has four stabilized lenses, all operating as wide as 18mm, which allows for considerably slower shutter speeds and thus narrower apertures with better depth of field as a result. This means that the drawback often associated with zoom lenses—slow maximum apertures—simply isn't that much of an issue any more.

True, slower stabilized lenses don't at first glance meet the need for the high shutter speeds necessary when shooting action, usually achieved by dialing in a fast maximum aperture. But don't forget that the noise created by higher ISO speeds has been significantly reduced in the last couple of years, so sports and action photographers can now work with, for example, f/5.6 at ISO 400 instead of f/2.8 at ISO 100, with little loss of quality at moderate enlargement. Combine this with an OS lens and you really can have the best of both worlds.

One final point that deserves mention is an answer to the obvious question: what happens when an optically stabilized lens is fitted to a body that has in-camera stabilization—Pentax, for example? Unfortunately, you will not benefit from both forms of vibration reduction, as the in-camera stabilization must be disabled in these circumstances.

Lens hoods

Sigma supply each lens complete with a dedicated lens hood, which is more than can be said for some mainstream camera manufacturers. Needless to say, they come in all shapes and sizes, but they are typified by the examples shown right. With virtually all lenses, the hood can be stored in reversed position on the front of the lens for convenience. Each hood is designed to provide the maximum shading for the focal length(s) concerned.

Two of the hoods shown here are petal-shaped. The very deep one is designed for the 70–200mm f/2.8 EX DG Macro. The very shallow lens hood is from a wide-angle zoom, namely the 10–20mm f/4-5.6 EX DC, though it also fits the 24mm f/1.8 and the 28mm f/1.8. The third hood shown is of conventional shape and belongs to the 70mm f/2.8 EX DG Macro. This style is also used for the longer telephoto lenses.

All the lens hoods pictured have a straightforward bayonet fit with a click stop at the end of the travel.

The deep conventional hoods of the longer telephoto lenses also have a small locking screw. The latter type of hood fits outside the front of the lens, adding around 2.5cm (1in) in width, which makes a noticeable difference when it comes to fitting these already large telephoto lenses into a camera bag.

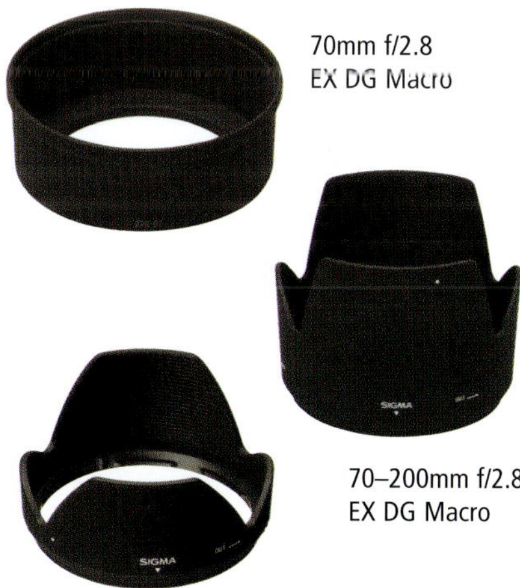

70mm f/2.8
EX DG Macro

70–200mm f/2.8
EX DG Macro

10–20mm f/4-5.6 EX DC

Choosing the right lens

Once a lens has been purchased, you will be married to it—so, as in any relationship, consider your choices carefully. Divorce, although feasible, will cost you money.

The factors that have the greatest priority vary from person to person, but the most likely ones are as follows: DG/DC, cost, focal length(s), weight, maximum aperture, macro capability, image quality, and possibly the ability to add a 1.4× or 2× converter. All except image quality are quantitative and therefore relatively easy to pin down in some sort of priority order that is appropriate to your circumstances and needs. When you are looking for a single lens which will satisfy a wide range of needs, the same logic applies—just clarify the two extremes within which you wish to work.

Image quality, however, is the most difficult factor to assess. Many lens reviews, both in magazines and on the internet, are not scientific and are necessarily subjective. Despite quality control by the manufacturer, unless strictly scientific tests are carried out on numerous random examples of the same lens, the

SPOILED FOR CHOICE
Sigma manufacture nearly 50 different lenses from which to choose.

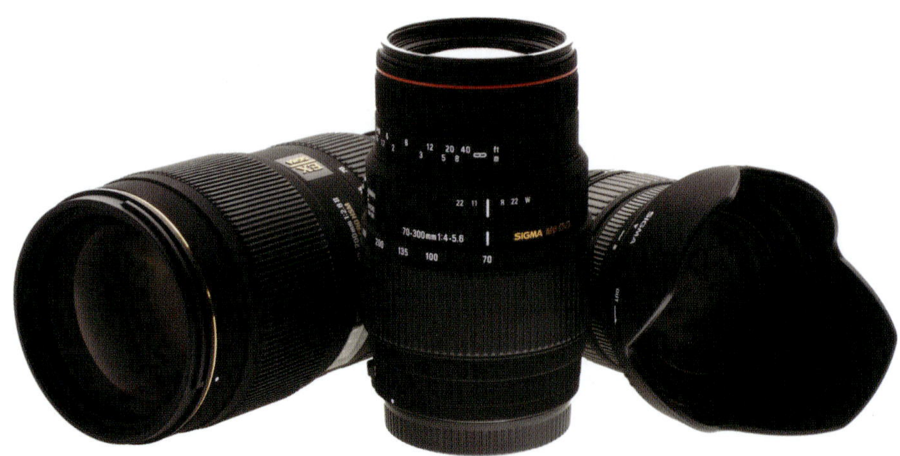

results may not be true for the one you actually buy. The worst kind of review is the personal comment on an internet forum, unless you have some idea of the pedigree of the so-called reviewer. (For the record, the author has had 16 books published along with thousands of images, regularly using Canon L-series lenses, and assesses every image at least full-screen on a 1920 × 1200 monitor.)

There are a number of choices you can make that will improve the odds of getting the best image quality. To start with, if you are an APS-C user, choose a full-frame DG lens. You will pay appreciably more, but, generally, you will get what you pay for.

Macro lenses usually give crisper images, especially "true macro" fixed focal length lenses, as do those using ELD and, to a lesser extent, SLD glass. In general, try to choose a lens with which you will mostly work in its mid-range, whether in terms of focal length or range of apertures. Finally, learn to interpret MTF charts and compare different lenses.

MTF charts

Charts showing MTF (Modular Transfer Function) illustrate contrast and resolution at specific apertures or, if not stated, at maximum aperture (the latter applies to the Sigma MTF charts used in this book). The ability of the lens to capture sets of fine parallel lines at differing densities on a test chart is assessed, with the red lines measuring lens contrast at 10 lines/mm, and the green lines measuring lens sharpness at 30 lines/mm.

The horizontal axis shows the distance (mm) from the center of the image to its border, exceeding 20mm for full-frame lenses, but stopping short of 15mm for crop-sensor lenses, which project a smaller image circle. The vertical axis shows the level of performance, with 1 being the maximum.

Ideally, on the vertical axis, all these lines would start as near to 1 as possible, and continue evenly across the chart. In reality, these lines will drop away as they measure the reduced performance that usually occurs nearer the edges of the image. (When assessing a full-frame lens for use on a crop-sensor body, any drop-off after 15mm is irrelevant.)

The test chart shows various groupings of parallel lines. When running parallel to a diagonal line that runs corner to corner, these are called Sagittal lines. The quality of their capture is represented by the two continuous lines on the MTF chart. Sets of lines at 90° to these are called Meridional lines; the quality of their capture is illustrated by the dotted lines on the MTF chart.

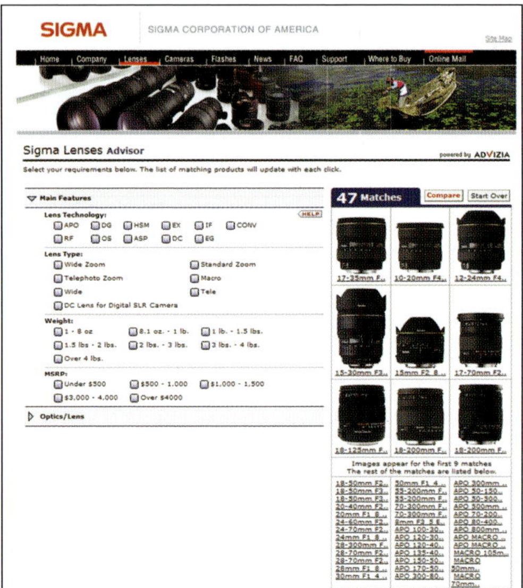

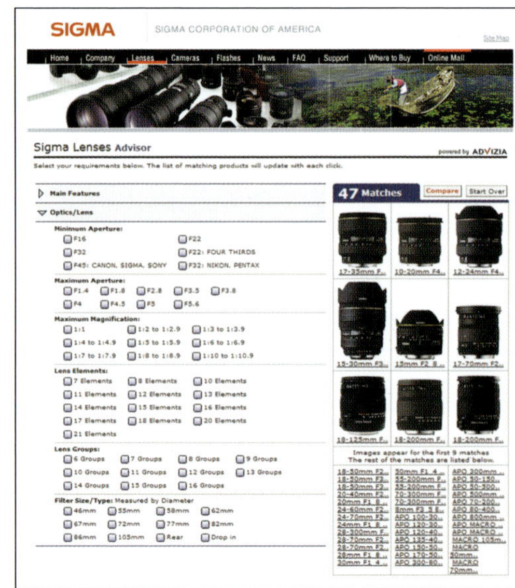

SIGMA LENS ADVISOR

The Sigma USA website at www.sigmaphoto.com offers a Lens Advisor Tool to help you find the lens you need. In the first screen (top), you check the boxes that match the lens features you require. In the second (below), you select the desired optical specifications. With each box you check, the list is updated to show only those lenses that match your requirements. In these illustrations, no boxes are ticked, so the full list of options is shown.

Focal length comparison

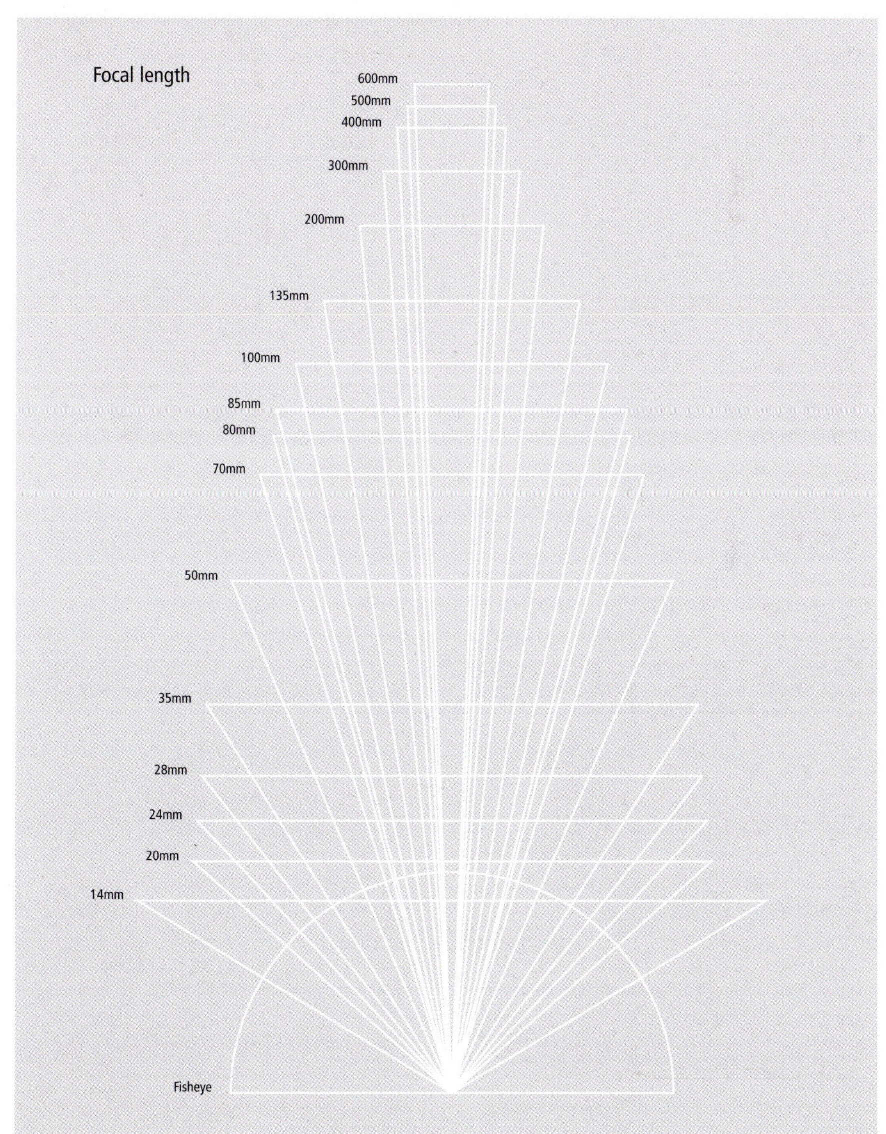

Depth of field

This image and the three images that follow were all captured on a day out to a seaside resort near my home. They have been included as a group to demonstrate the variety of images one might encounter on any given day. In the image shown here, I wanted great depth of field, but with so many straight lines in the subject I also had to prevent distortion, so I needed a lens no wider than 24mm. At that focal length, an aperture of f/8 provided more than enough depth of field for the task at hand.

SOUTHPORT THEATRE, UK

Settings
Focal length: 24mm
ISO: 100
Aperture: f/8
Shutter: 1/400

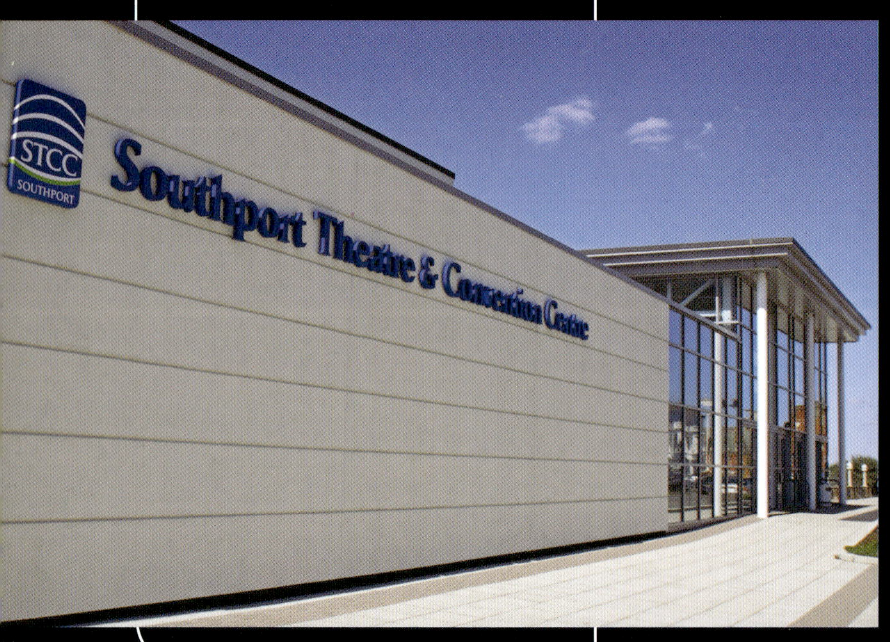

Sharpness

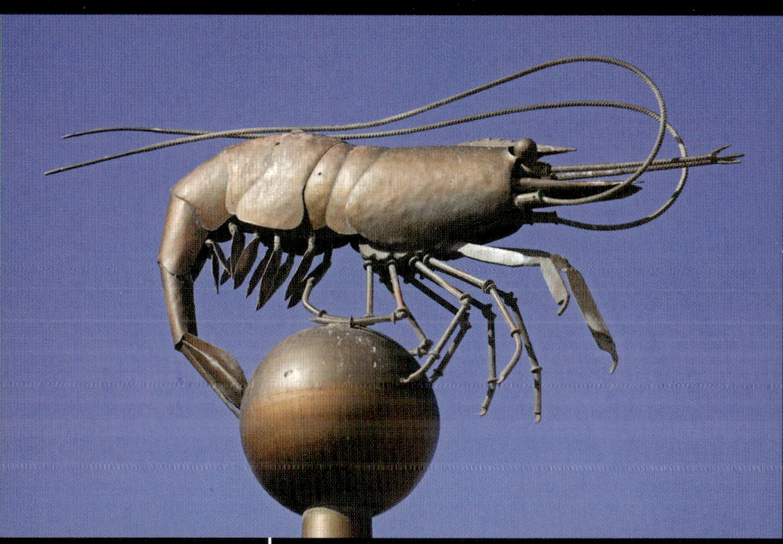

MORECAMBE BAY SHRIMP, UK

Settings
Focal length:150mm
ISO: 200
Aperture: f/4
Shutter: 1/2000

This striking copper creation celebrates one of the area's best known, though declining, sources of income for its fishermen. As part of a photo essay, the topic of shrimps simply had to be included and this image provided a completely different way of illustrating the subject. The Sigma 150mm f/2.8 EX DG Macro provided a bitingly (forgive the pun) sharp image in crisp lighting. For subjects that demand such sharpness, especially if a little distant, the clear dry air that follows the passage of a weather front can be a real bonus.

Shooting times

With early evening rain clouds gathering, the last rays of direct sunshine picked out these ornamental fish, providing a scene which just had to be recorded. The fact that one or two of the fish had rotated so as not to reflect the light, combined with the darker sky, added useful contrast to the subject. Both the beginning and the end of the day can be magical times for photography, with lighting that is more directional and significantly warmer in color.

FLYING FISH

Settings
Focal length: 105mm
ISO: 200
Aperture: f/8
Shutter: 1/500

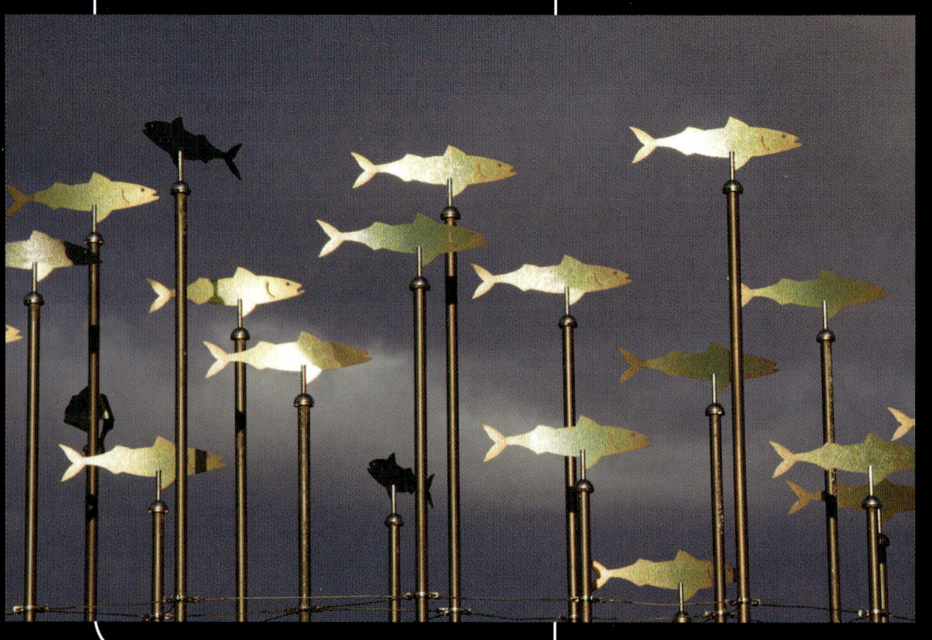

Seascape

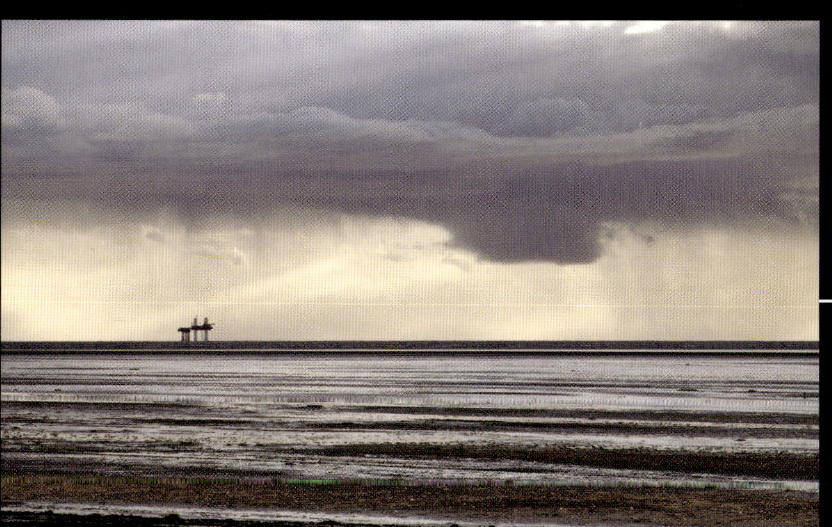

Quite by chance, both this image and the one on the facing page made use of the same focal length, yet the two treatments are very different. Moderate telephoto lenses, or their zoom equivalent, are often underestimated as tools for recording landscapes—or in this case, a seascape. More depth of field is available than many people realize, and a medium aperture, say f/8, is sufficient to render everything from around 45m (50 yards) to infinity in sharp focus. If you are fortunate enough to own an OS zoom, you can capitalize on even narrower apertures in the same lighting conditions.

GAS RIG AT LOW TIDE

Settings
Focal length: 105mm
ISO: 200
Aperture: f/8
Shutter: 1/400

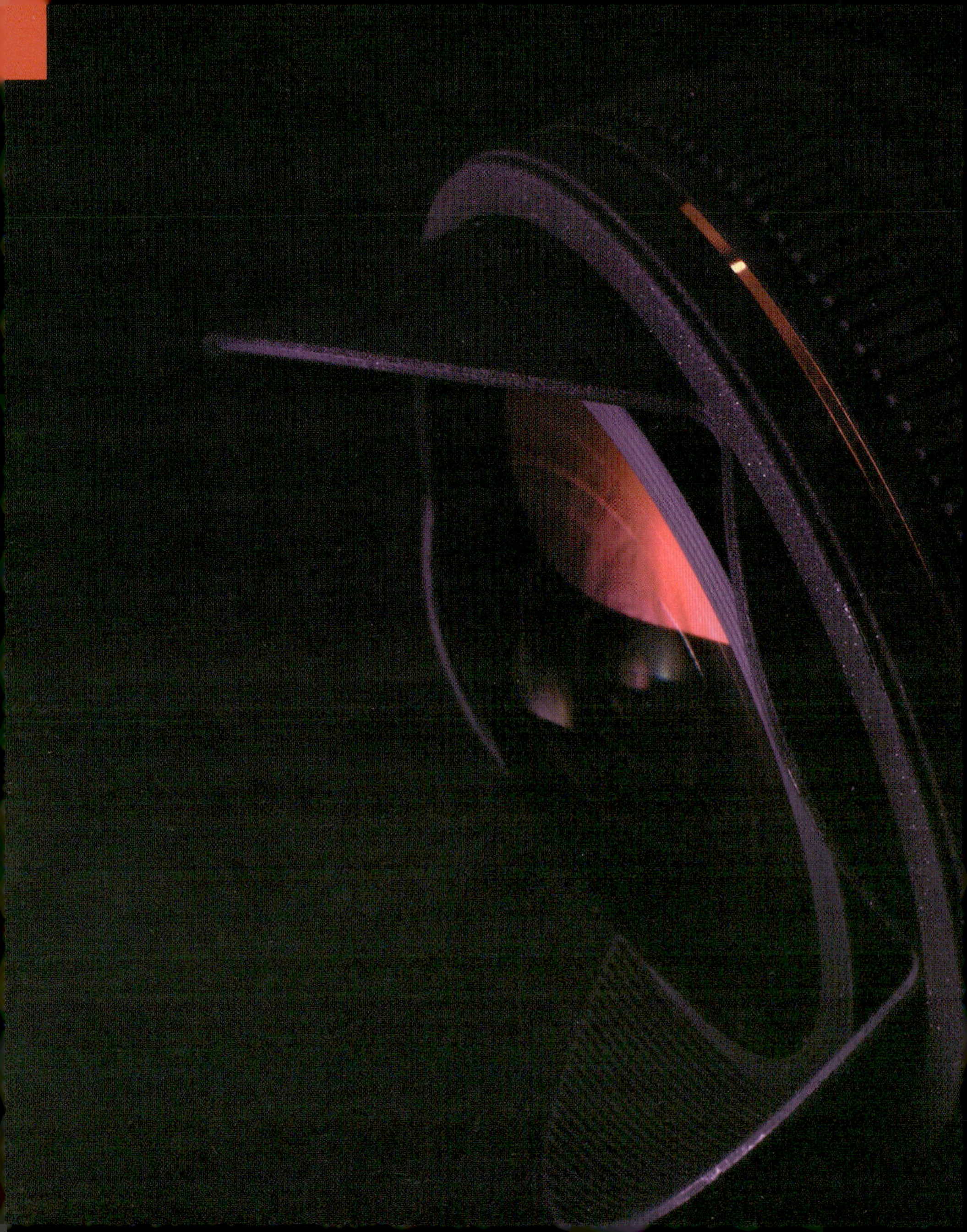

Chapter **2**

Fisheye lenses

The nearest most people get to a fisheye lens is either the peephole in a hotel room door or the fresh fish counter in the supermarket. Fisheye lenses are not huge sellers. They are, however, unique—at least in the case of circular fisheye lenses. When buying lenses, there is usually an argument for purchasing an alternative focal length to the one you've decided upon; with circular fisheye lenses, nothing else will suffice.

There are two types of fisheye lens: circular and diagonal. A circular fisheye lens, used on the format for which it was designed, whether full-frame or APS-C, will deliver an image that does indeed resemble the view through a hotel room peephole. The image itself consists of a full circle with the rest of the rectangular frame being black (see page 35). Obviously, distortion is very much a feature of such an image. A full-frame circular fisheye lens used with an APS-C sensor will render what clearly starts out as a circular image, but it will be cropped along each edge and the corners will vignette (see image opposite).

A diagonal fisheye lens will produce a rectangular image, but one that exhibits distinct distortion of straight lines. This distortion increases with proximity to the edge of the frame. A full-frame diagonal fisheye lens can be used quite successfully on an APS-C camera, and the distortion will be reduced because the outer parts of the projected image are not used (see comparison on page 41).

With a 180° angle of view, it is necessary to ensure that unwanted elements—the person next to you, for example—do not creep into the edges of the frame. With such extreme coverage, incidentally, the different APS-C sensor sizes and consequent crop factors associated with different makes (Nikon 1.5×, Canon 1.6×, and Sigma 1.7×) make a noticeable difference, with the 10mm DC diagonal fisheye having coverage of 180°, 167°, and 154° respectively.

One of the issues that may be encountered when using either diagonal or circular fisheye lenses, no matter which camera system is used, is that of metering. Systems which can normally be relied upon to perform well under most circumstances, such as Canon's evaluative metering, may not perform as well with these lenses, and it may be necessary to use exposure compensation, bracketing, or spot metering, if available.

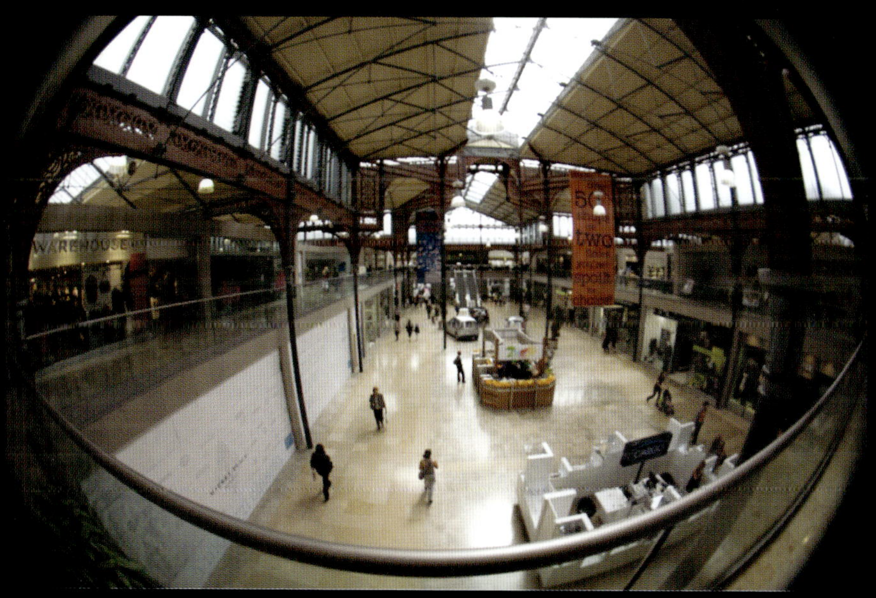

VIGNETTING

Using the 8mm f/3.5 EX DG lens with a crop-sensor camera will result in vignetting in the corners of your pictures.

Settings

Focal length:
8mm on APS-C
ISO: 200
Aperture: f/4
Shutter: 1/250

4.5mm f/2.8 EX DC IF HSM Circular fisheye

Specifications (based on Sigma mount)

Lens construction: 13 elements in 9 groups
Angle of view: 180°
Diaphragm blades: 6
Min. aperture: f/22
Min. focusing distance: 13.5cm (5.3in)
Max. magnification: 1:6
Filter: Rear (gelatin) type
Dimensions: 76.2mm (W) × 77.8mm (L)
(3in × 3.06in)
Weight: 470g (16.5oz)
Mounts: Sigma, Canon, Nikon (D)

Note: The appearance of lenses may differ depending on the camera mount.

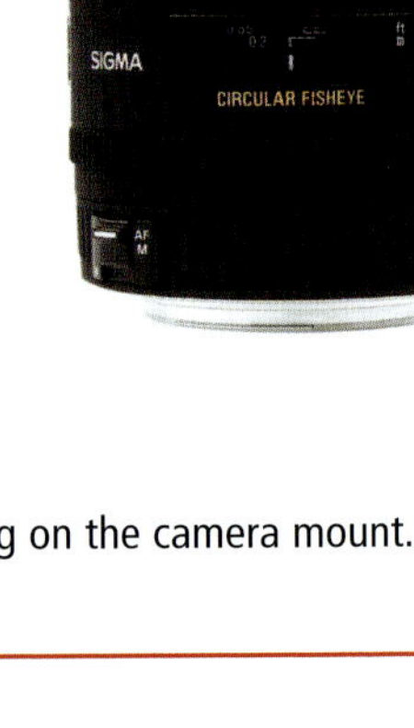

This is very much a special-purpose lens, capable of amazing 180° coverage that will actually take in the person standing next to you. The circular image projected by the lens obviously produces an immense amount of distortion and doesn't suit all subject matter. It is most effective when applied to large structures and is often used to depict sports stadiums and the like. Even lighting also works most effectively, and extensive areas of shadow are certainly best avoided.

Whatever their position in the image, straight lines will appear anything but straight, with those nearest the edge of the frame being bent the most. As with all wide-angle lenses, some thought is necessary regarding extensive foreground. Any graphic element using straight lines, such as in the image opposite, will add to the overall effect.

LENS CONSTRUCTION

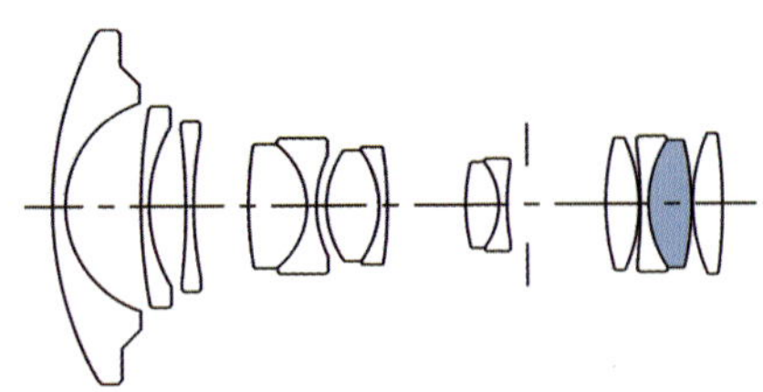

■ SLD lens

COLUMNS (1)
Straight lines and rectangles are the ideal subjects to accentuate the fisheye lens effect. See page 41 for the same subject photographed with the 15mm f/2.8 diagonal fisheye.

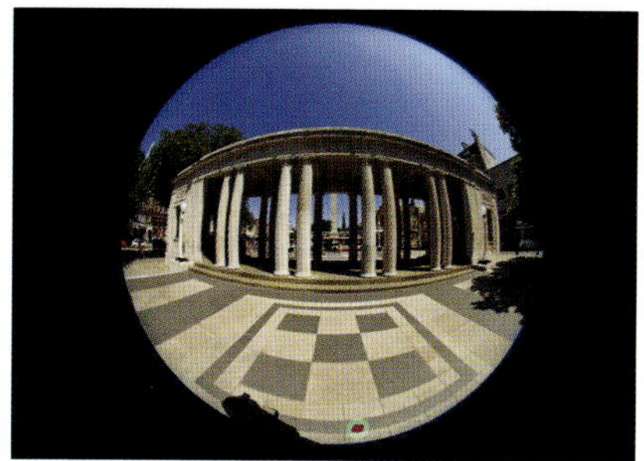

With 180° coverage it isn't possible to fit or incorporate any shape of lens hood. However, there is a protective cover that slides onto the front of the lens and to which the clip-on lens cap is fitted. To give some idea of the phenomenal depth of field provided, in the viewfinder you can clearly pick out the inside of this lens cover when it is fitted without the lens cap, even at maximum aperture.

Obviously, given the bulbous front lens element, front-mounted filters cannot be fitted directly onto the lens, but it is possible to insert gelatin filters into a slot incorporated into the back of the lens.

Chromatic aberration is quite well controlled by the use of SLD (Special Low Dispersion) glass, and flare is not an issue provided obvious precautions are taken to avoid point light sources within the frame. This is one lens where you will always need to place the sun at your back.

Sigma also claim that this is "an ideal lens for astro- and aurora-photography and that, due to the quantifiable relationship between angle and area, it can be used for scientific and arts applications such as solid angle measurements of cloud distribution over the sky or vegetation distribution of the forest."

MTF Chart 4.5mm

Verdict
For anyone regularly shooting sporting events or structures on a grand scale, this is a useful lens for adding eye-catching images to a portfolio.

8mm f/3.5 EX DG Circular fisheye

Lens construction: 11 elements in 6 groups
Angle of view: 180°
Diaphragm blades: 6
Min. aperture: f/22
Min. focusing distance: 13.5cm (5.3in)
Max. magnification: 1:4.6
Filter: Rear (gelatin) type
Dimensions: 73.5mm (W) × 68.6mm (L)
(2.9in × 2.7in)
Weight: 400g (14oz)
Mounts: Sigma, Canon, Nikon (D)

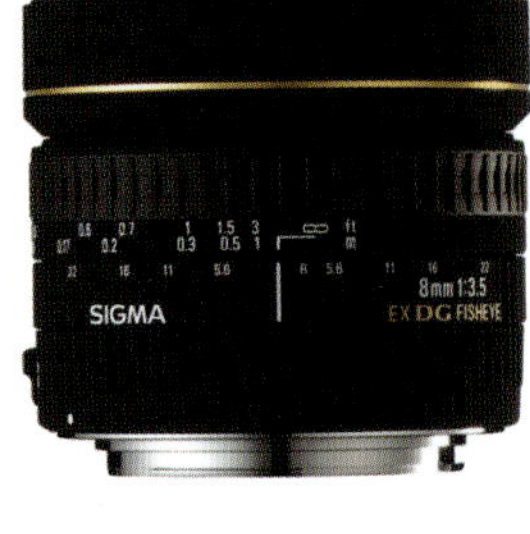

Note: The appearance of lenses may differ depending on the camera mount.

This is the full-frame equivalent of the lens on the previous page and will provide a similar circular image when used on full-frame bodies. Much of what is written there also applies here. This lens can be used on a crop-sensor camera body, but will vignette in the corners, at least, depending on the aperture used (see page 33). There is no built-in lens hood, as the lens provides a 180° view. Construction and finish are of the high standard normally associated with EX lenses. However, particular care needs to be taken when the protective slide-on cap (which the lens cap clips onto) is

LENS CONSTRUCTION

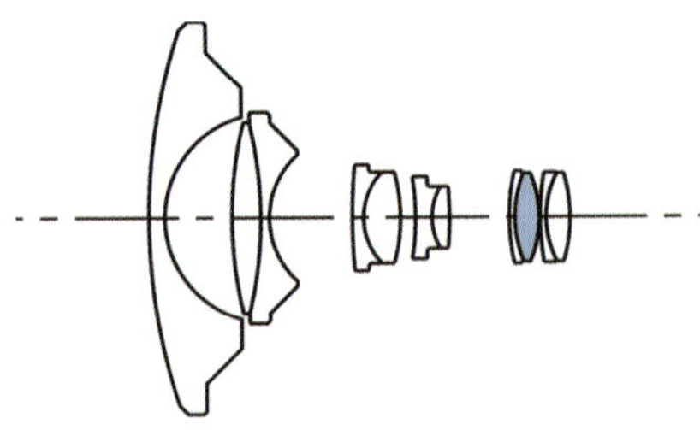

SLD glass

removed, as the front element protrudes slightly and is flush with the lens barrel, as shown here.

In use, this lens—as with all lenses providing 180° coverage—demands that you pay particular attention to the edges of the image, as they will include whatever or whomever you are standing next to. Most of us develop a sixth sense with regard to subject matter potentially encroaching into the image from the sides, people cutting across in front of us, and so on, but the awareness required here goes beyond that. In any case, it is always good practice to scan the edges of the frame through the viewfinder, no matter which lens you are using.

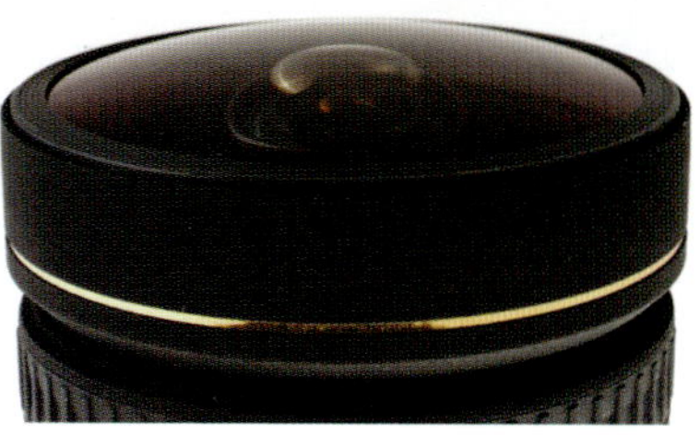

CAUTION
Take care to protect the protruding front element.

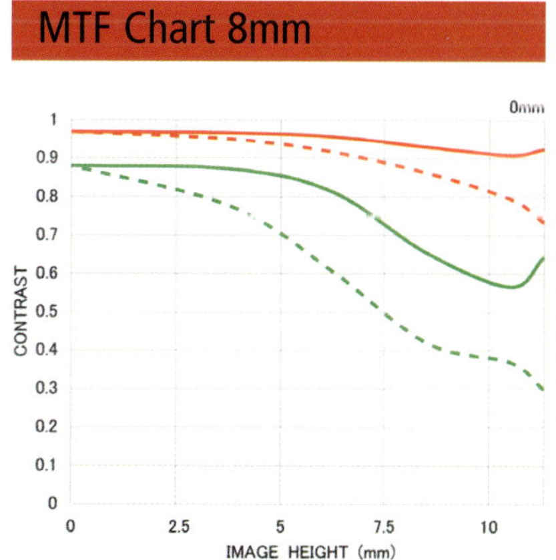

MTF Chart 8mm

Verdict

If you require spectacular images that encompass huge structures, and your budget can stand the expense for a lens that will not be used very often, this lens needs to be considered as a long-term investment. With circular fisheye lenses you are advised to buy the lens that is intended for the size of sensor you plan to use: a DG lens for full-frame or a DC lens for a crop-sensor camera.

10mm f/2.8 EX DC HSM Diagonal fisheye

Lens construction: 12 elements in 7 groups
Angle of view: 180° (Nikon), 167° (Canon), 154° (Sigma)
Diaphragm blades: 7
Min. aperture: f/22
Min. focusing distance: 13.5cm (5.3in)
Max. magnification: 1:3.3
Filter: Rear (gelatin) type
Dimensions: 75.8mm (W) × 83.1mm (L)
(3in × 3.3in)
Weight: 475g (16.8oz)
Mounts: Sigma, Canon, Nikon (D)

Note: The appearance of lenses may differ depending on the camera mount.

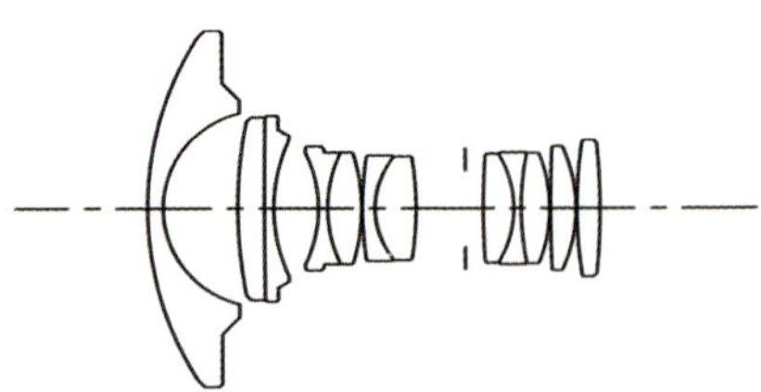

While the full impact of the curvature associated with the 15mm DG diagonal fisheye lens (see pages 40–1) is cushioned when that lens is fitted to a crop-sensor body, this DC lens will display the full range of distortion. Any straight line in the center of the frame will appear straight, though barrel distortion will still be present. Look at the central book in the image opposite: it appears thinner at the top and at the bottom, even though the spine is straight. The outermost books exhibit extreme curvature. However, the degree of curvature is determined by proximity to the edges of the

LENS CONSTRUCTION

image. The nearer the edge of the frame, the greater the distortion. It is possible to reduce this by including extraneous subject matter around the central subject and cropping the image later. With full 180° coverage, this means no more than taking a step backward, and often even less.

Shifting the focusing ring from its closest focusing distance of 13.5cm (5.3in) to infinity, the bulbous front element extends by 0.5cm (0.2in), but this is still well within the protection afforded by the built-in lens hood. For carrying purposes, a slip-on cover protects the front of the lens and it is to this cover that the lens cap is attached. Finish and manufacturing quality are to the normal EX standard. Gelatin filters can be used on the rear of the lens.

The close-focusing distance of 13.5cm (5.3in) allows a magnification ratio of one-third life-size, with the lens hood practically touching the subject—but you will have to deal with shadows cast by the camera and yourself. The books in the image on this page were only a few inches from the lens, and it was necessary to

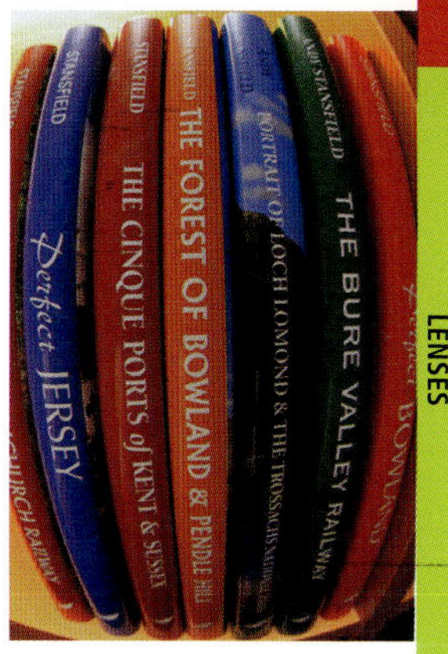

BOOKS
Distortion increases dramatically toward the edges of the frame.

bounce flash off the ceiling in order to get rid of shadow and provide relatively even lighting.

On the subject of light sources, any lens with a protruding curved front element like this will be subject to flare, no matter how diligently the manufacturer has worked to reduce it, so you will want to place the sun behind you. Point light sources, such as streetlamps, pose much less of a problem because they are so tiny within the frame.

MTF Chart 10mm

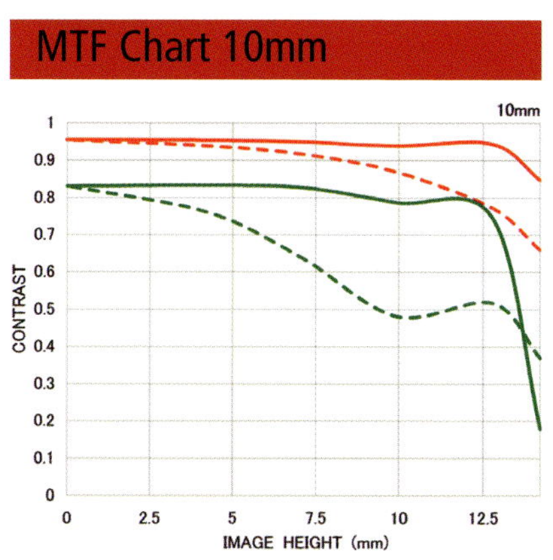

Verdict
A good choice for anyone who spends a lot of time shooting in cramped spaces, or in huge sports stadiums, and for whom distortion is not an issue.

15mm f/2.8 EX DG HSM Diagonal fisheye

Specifications (based on Sigma mount)

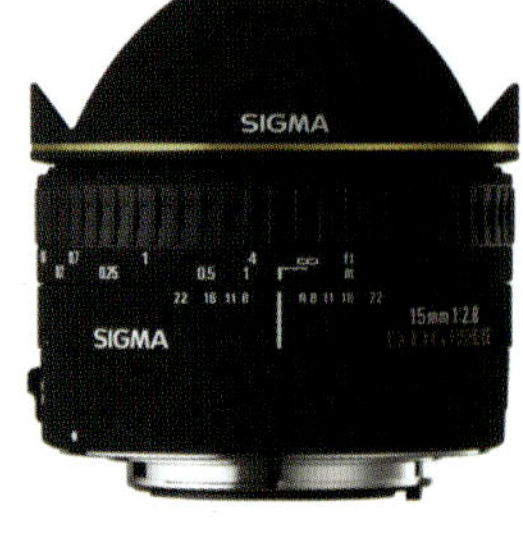

Lens construction: 7 elements in 6 groups
Angle of view: 180°
Diaphragm blades: 7
Min. aperture: f/22
Min. focusing distance: 15cm (5.9in)
Max. magnification: 1:3.8
Filter: Rear (gelatin) type
Dimensions: 73.5mm (W) × 65mm (L)
(2.9in × 2.6in)
Weight: 370g (13oz)
Mounts: Sigma, Canon, Nikon (D), Sony, Pentax

Note: The appearance of lenses may differ depending on the camera mount.

Although it offers 180° coverage across the diagonal, this fisheye lens produces a very different image from a 180° circular fisheye, as well as from that of a rectilinear lens (which won't produce the same distortion) of the same focal length. Sadly, Sigma no longer make their rectilinear 14mm lens, though used examples can occasionally still be found.

Furthermore, the effect of its coverage on a full-frame body is distinctly different to that obtained on an APS-C body (see images opposite). The extent to which straight lines are rendered as curves is the same in both images relative

LENS CONSTRUCTION

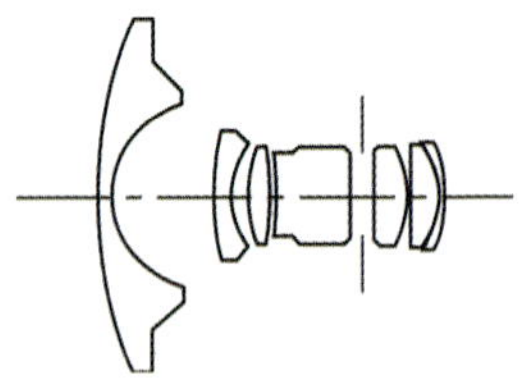

to the whole image circle, regardless of how near the linear feature is to the edge of the frame. What counts is how near the straight lines are to the edge of the image circle; it's just that the APS-C crop doesn't show as much of the projected image circle as the full-frame version does.

COLUMNS (2)
Coverage on a full-frame body (top) and an APS-C body (bottom) are distinctly different. See page 35 for the same subject shot with the 4.5mm f/2.8 circular fisheye.

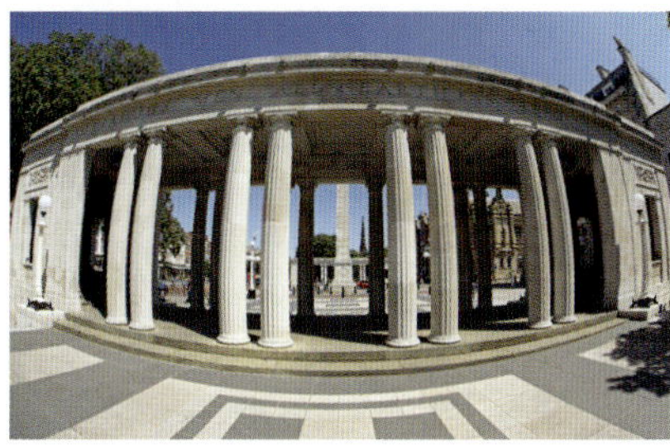

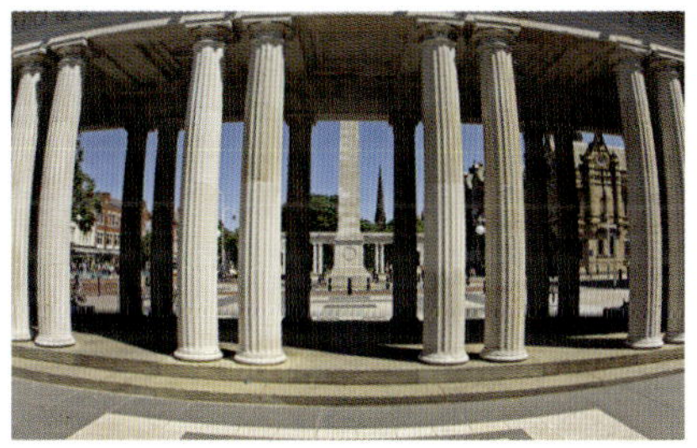

The lens finish is the standard matte black EX treatment, which has always denoted Sigma's premium lens range. Removing the protective cover, which the lens cap clips onto, reveals the petal-shaped built-in lens hood and a wide bulbous front element, which is considerably wider even than that of the 4.5mm DC circular fisheye. Front-mounted filters cannot be fitted directly onto the lens, but it is possible to insert gelatin filters into a slot incorporated into the back of the lens.

The focusing ring has to travel through approximately 135° from infinity to the minimum focusing distance of 15cm (5.9in). This task is performed without rotation and with barely 5mm (0.2in) of lens extension.

Center sharpness when used on the full-frame EOS 5D Mk II was simply staggering when viewed at 100%.

MTF Chart 15mm

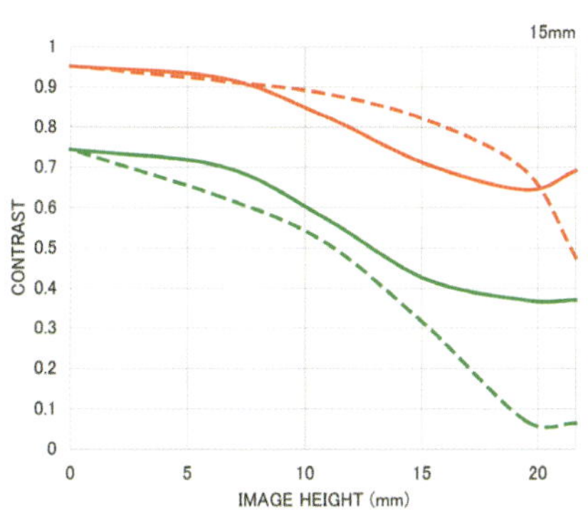

Verdict
A very useful tool for either full-frame or crop-sensor bodies, depending on just how wide you want to go. If you own both types of body, this lens should definitely find a home in your camera bag.

DG on APS-C (1)

When a full-frame circular fisheye lens like the 8mm f/3.5 EX DG is used on an APS-C body, the usual circular image effect (see page 35) is lost, due to the narrower field of view. Instead, the image appears as a rectangle with serious vignetting in the corners at wider apertures. The image would require extensive cropping to remove this completely.

Alternatively, as in the example shown here, the vignetting can be made to look as if it is part of the composition. However, at narrower apertures the vignetting extends down the shorter sides of the image, making it even more difficult to compose an image.

In this photograph, taken from a balcony, distortion is reduced because the lens wasn't tilted at all. The trick with all wide-angle lenses is to find a viewpoint that gives you extra height relative to the subject.

With circular fisheye lenses, you should always buy the lens that is intended for the size of sensor you plan to use: a DG lens for full-frame, or a DC lens for a crop-sensor camera.

SHOPPING MALL

Settings
Focal length: 8mm (APS-C)
ISO: 200
Aperture: f/4
Shutter: 1/250

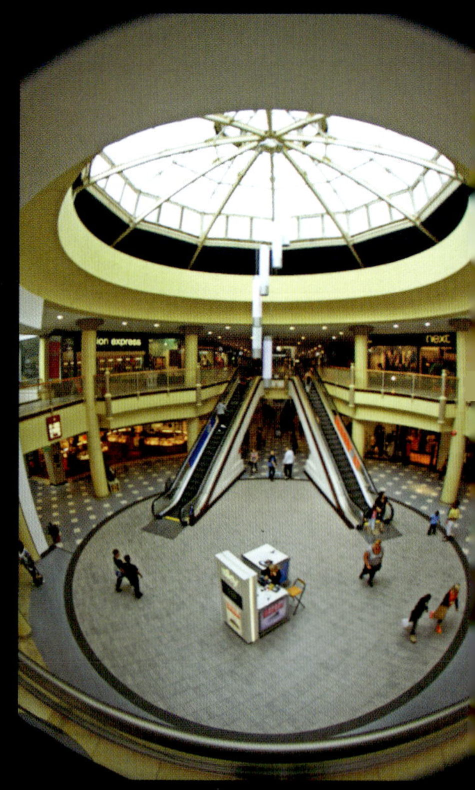

DG on APS-C (2)

OPEN AIR JAZZ

Settings
Focal length: 15mm
(APS-C)
ISO: 100
Aperture: f/8
Shutter: 1/250
Exp. comp: -2/3

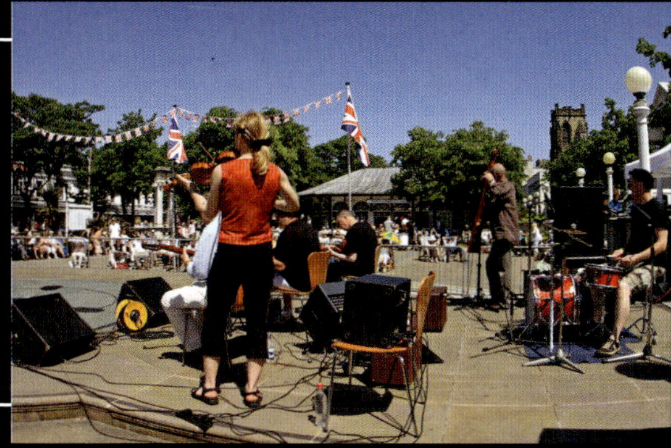

An outdoor music event was the subject for this slightly cropped image, which was captured with the full-frame 15mm f/2.8 EX DG diagonal fisheye lens mounted on an APS-C body.

Vignetting is not a problem as the image circle produced by the lens is far wider than is required for the sensor (see page 12). As a result, distortion near the edges of the frame, in which straight lines appear curved, is also reduced, as the most affected part of the projected image is "cropped" by the smaller sensor. A little judicious cropping during post-processing can minimize this distortion to a point where it is barely evident, if at all, in the final image. Whenever possible, keeping the lens straight (that is, not tilting the camera) and finding some extra height in your viewpoint certainly helps with perspective.

When composing a shot, avoid prominent straight lines near the edges of your image, vertical lines near the side, and horizontal lines near the top and bottom. Sometimes, changing position by just a couple of steps means you can use elements of the subject to mask these lines—in this image, the drummer masks part of the prominent white lamp post.

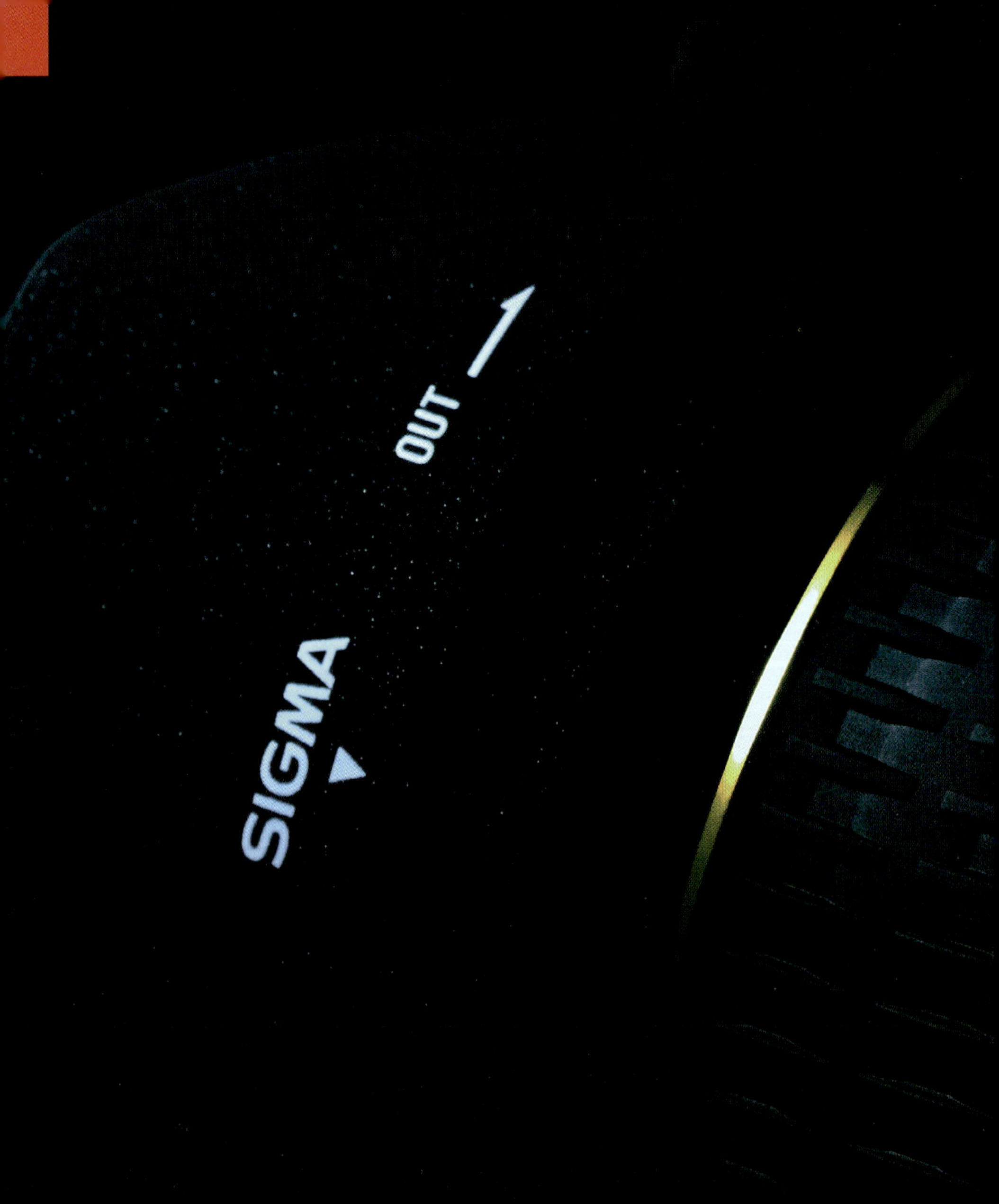

OUT
SIGMA

Chapter **3**

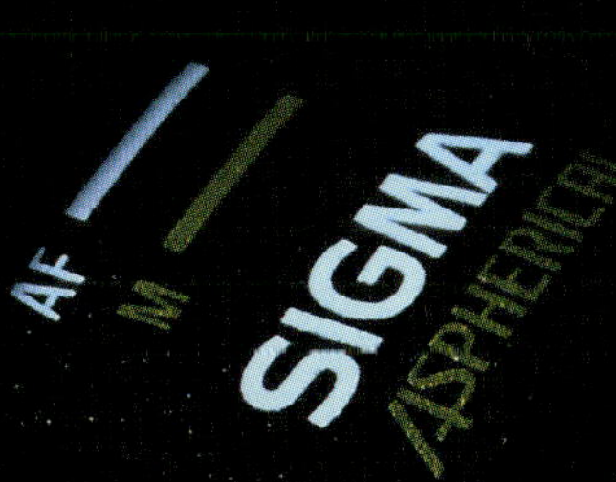

Wide-angle zooms

The increasing availability of wide-angle zoom lenses is one aspect of photography that has been very welcome in recent years, particularly for users of APS-C digital cameras. Of the five lenses included in this chapter, only two are for the full-frame user, and one of those has now been discontinued. The other, though, set the world alight when it was launched, receiving a string of awards, and to this day the 12–24mm EX DG remains a popular and flexible choice. How did we manage without such exotic fare?

Many photographers remember, not always fondly, when a 28mm lens on full-frame was thought of as wide, 24mm as extremely wide, and 21mm as downright outrageous. That was in the days when a fast moderate wide-angle such as a 35mm f/1.4 was the photojournalist's mainstay, supported by the ubiquitous 50mm standard lens and a moderate telephoto of 105mm or 135mm.

Zoom lenses didn't arrive on the scene at all until 1959. They were first introduced by Voigtlander for use on their Bessamatic, and in a separate Exacta mount. Although this lens looks a clumsy, if not clunky, beast by today's standards, its specification is worth thinking about—as is its name.

This inaugural zoom lens was the 36–82mm f/2.8 Voigtlander Zoomar, designed by Dr. Frank Back. To start with, this lens gave rise to the very term "zoom"—and a maximum aperture of f/2.8 in such a lens would not be sniffed at today. The zoom range might be considered short, but Sigma still find it worthwhile to manufacture two versions of a 24–70mm f/2.8—covering a 46mm range, just like the Zoomar. In addition, Dr. Back employed "new rare-earth glass elements" in its construction, the forerunners of the Special Low Dispersion and Extraordinary Low Dispersion lens elements used today.

But back to the present. Full-frame users are quite well catered for with fixed focal length "prime" lenses (see Chapter 5), but the greatest variety of wide-angle zoom lenses is reserved for the APS-C user: in Chapter 4 you will find no fewer than seven DC zoom lenses that start at 18mm, at which focal length the field of view is the same as 28mm on full-frame.

In this chapter, each of the five lenses included is of inner focus design, so there is no lens extension when focusing. All five also make use of aspherical lens elements to ensure optical performance within a compact design.

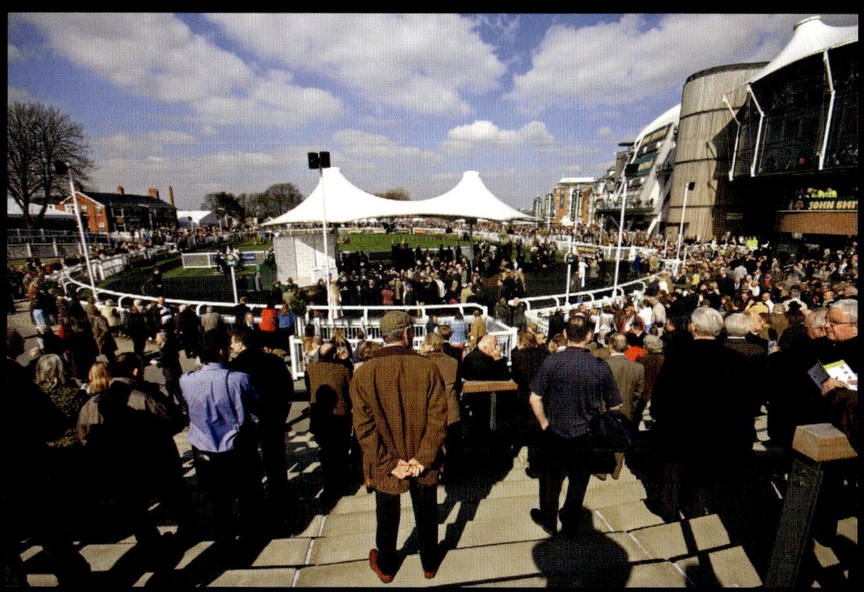

COVERAGE

Extreme wide-angle lenses are useful for busy
scenes like this, but expect some distortion,
especially around the edges of the frame.

Settings

10–20mm at 10mm
ISO: 200
Aperture Priority
Shutter: 1/500 at f/8

10–20mm f/4–5.6 EX DC HSM IF ASP

Specifications (based on Sigma mount)

Lens construction: 14 elements in 10 groups
Angle of view: 63.8°–102.4°
Diaphragm blades: 6
Min. aperture: f/22
Min. focusing distance: 24cm (9.4in)
Max. magnification: 1:6.7
Filter: 77mm
Dimensions: 83.5mm (W) × 81mm (L)
(3.3in × 3.2in)
Weight: 470g (16.6oz)
Mounts (HSM): Sigma, Canon, Nikon (D), Four Thirds
Mounts (non-HSM): Sony, Pentax

Technical Image Press Association Best Consumer Lens 2006

Note: The appearance of lenses may differ depending on the camera mount.

This lens has now been superseded by a faster version with a constant maximum aperture. However, it will continue to be produced side by side with the newer version for the foreseeable future, as it has proved to be one of Sigma's bestsellers.

LENS CONSTRUCTION

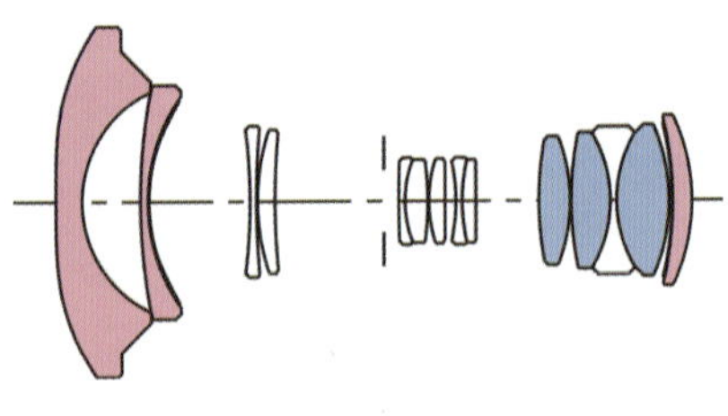

SIGMA LENSES

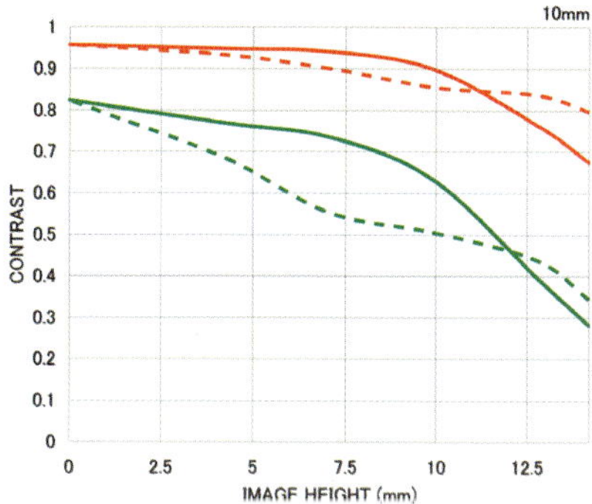

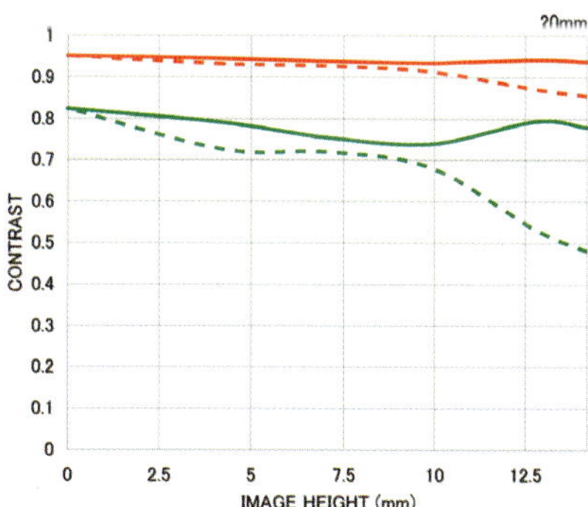

Verdict

A delight to handle, the lens only extends a few millimeters when zoomed—and not at all during focusing, as it uses IF technology. The shallow, petal-shaped lens hood can be reverse-mounted for compact storage, but it is essential in use because—as with all very wide-angle lenses—flare is easily encountered. That said, the front element on this lens is nowhere near the diameter of Sigma's earlier and sadly discontinued prime 14mm f/2.8, so flare is kept to a reasonable minimum given the maximum focal length. As this is a DC lens, the full image area is always used. Therefore, with regard to edge sharpness, the lens functions best of all at medium apertures and when extended a little beyond its widest focal length.

10–20mm f/3.5 EX DC HSM ASP IF (NEW)

Specifications (based on Sigma mount)

Lens construction: 13 elements in 10 groups
Angle of view: 63.8°–102.4°
Diaphragm blades: 7
Min. aperture: f/22
Min. focusing distance: 24cm (9.4in)
Max. magnification: 1:6.6
Filter: 82mm
Dimensions: 87.3mm (W) × 88.2mm (L)
(3.43in × 3.47in)
Weight: 520g (18.3oz)
Mounts: Sigma, Canon, Nikon (D), Sony (D), Pentax*

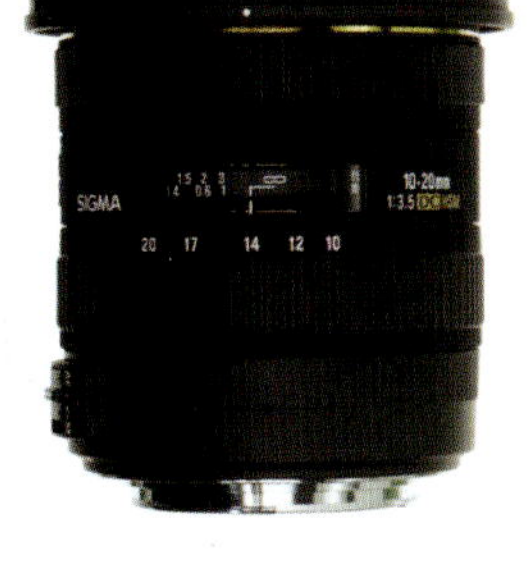

*If Pentax body does not support HSM, autofocus will not function.

Note: The appearance of lenses may differ depending on the camera mount.

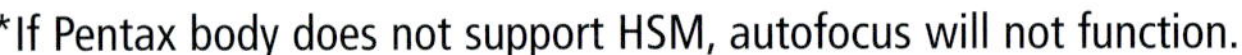

Verdict

The new version of this lens boasts a consistent maximum aperture throughout the zoom range and one that is faster, too, at the expense of slightly larger glass filters. If you regularly use glass filters, such points are worth considering, as quality 82mm filters are expensive items. The apertures and focal lengths that give better image quality also apply with the updated version. For reference, the life-size bust opposite was shot with the front of the lens only 23cm (9in) from its face.

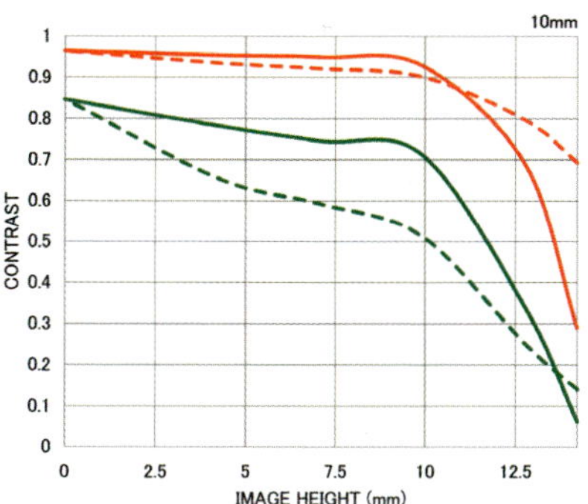

LENS CONSTRUCTION

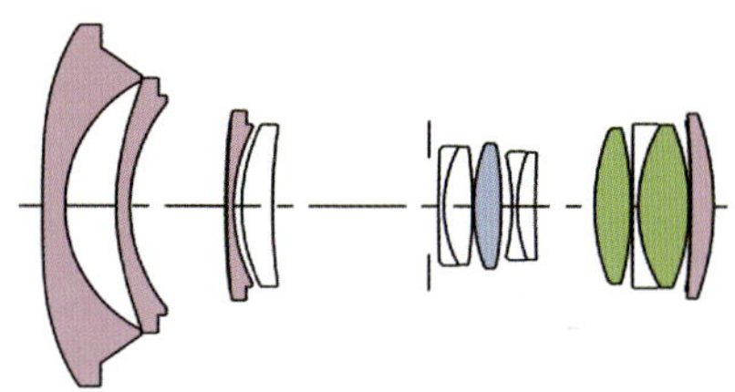

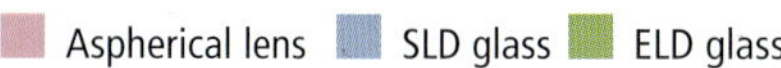

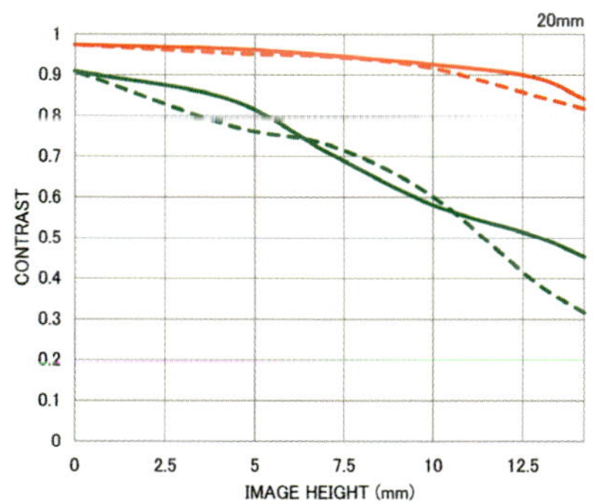

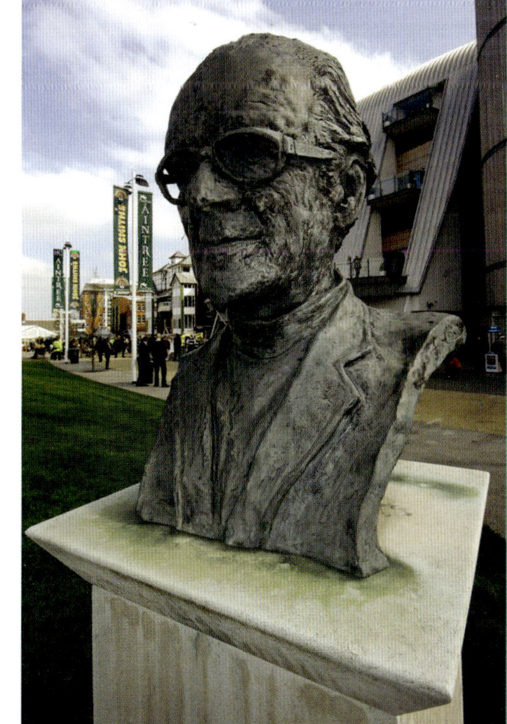

BUST

This image was captured with the lens only a few inches away from this life-size bust. Had it been a real person, such close proximity would have felt very intrusive.

12–24mm f/4.5–5.6 EX DG HSM IF ASP

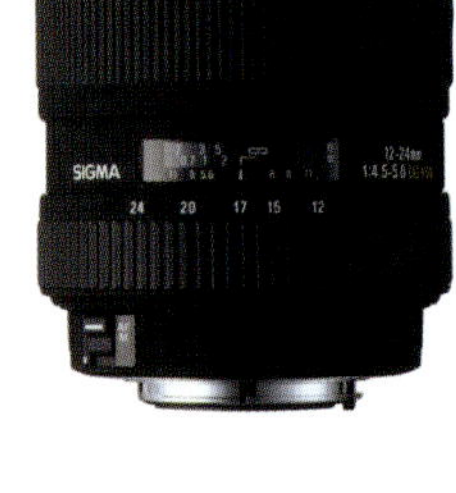

Specifications (based on Sigma mount)

Lens construction: 16 elements in 12 groups
Angle of view: 84.1°–122°
Diaphragm blades: 6
Min. aperture: f/22
Min. focusing distance: 28cm (11in)
Max. magnification: 1:7.1
Filter: Rear (gelatin) type
Dimensions: 87mm (W) × 102.5mm (L)
(3.4in × 4in)
Weight: 600g (21.2oz)
Mounts (HSM): Sigma, Canon, Nikon (D)
Mounts (non-HSM): Sony (D), Pentax

EISA Lens of the Year 2004–2005
Amateur Photographer Lens of the Year 2005
BIPP Photo Industry Award 2005

Note: The appearance of lenses may differ depending on the camera mount.

A smooth operator in more ways than one, this full-frame lens sets new standards for wide zooms. It has all the hallmarks of EX finish and construction, with silky zoom and focus rings smooth enough for easy adjustment, yet firm enough to retain their settings. Removing the protective cover, to which the lens cap clips, reveals the petal-shaped built-in lens hood and a bulbous

LENS CONSTRUCTION

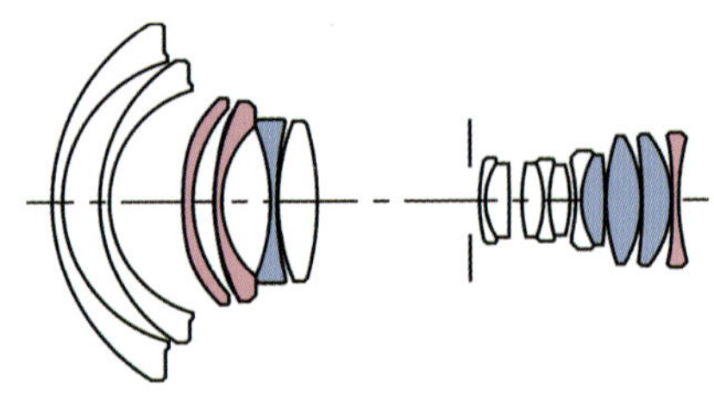

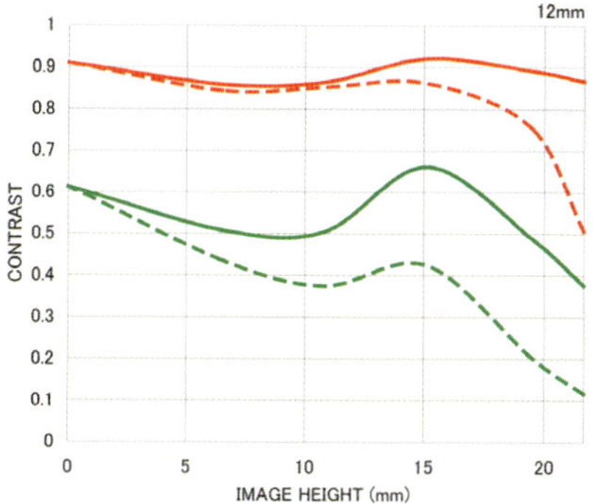

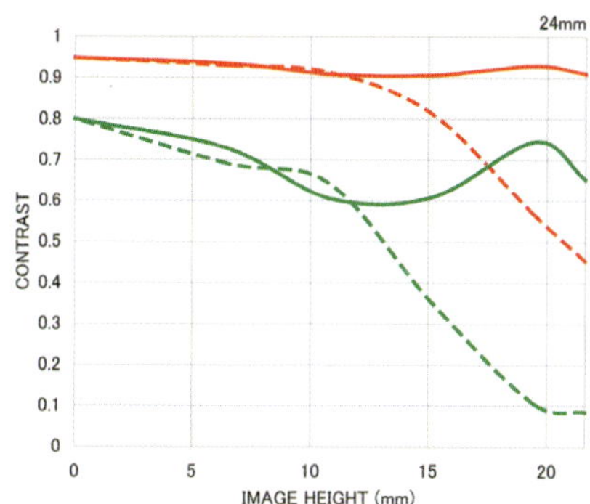

front element, the combination of which means that front-mounted filters cannot be fitted directly onto the lens, though gelatin filters can be mounted on the rear. The front element moves in and out very slightly when zooming, but there is no extension during focusing. The focusing scale has sufficient markings, both metric and imperial, to easily dispense with autofocus and to rely on using the hyperfocal focusing technique instead. For example, simply set the focusing ring to 0.7m, and at 12mm everything from 40cm (15.7in) to infinity will be in focus at f/8. See the depth of field table on page 54 for other options.

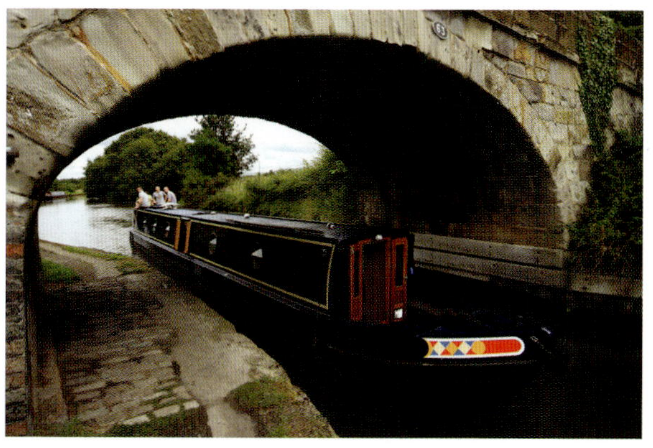

PERSPECTIVE
Even at 12mm, it is possible to achieve a fairly natural perspective with some subjects. Depth of field at f/8 is immense—the brickwork on the left is only about 60cm (2ft) away.

Depth of field (m): 12–24mm f/4.5–5.6 EX DG HSM IF ASP at 12mm

Circle of confusion: 0.3333mm

Focused at	Aperture	4.5	5.6	8	11	16	22
0.28m	Near	0.26	0.25	0.24	0.23	0.22	0.20
	Far	0.31	0.32	0.35	0.40	0.51	1.02
0.4m	Near	0.34	0.32	0.30	0.28	0.25	0.23
	Far	0.52	0.56	0.69	1.08	21.76	inf
0.7m	Near	0.48	0.45	0.40	0.35	0.30	0.26
	Far	1.54	2.19	inf	inf	inf	inf
1m	Near	0.58	0.54	0.46	0.39	0.33	0.27
	Far	7.73	inf	inf	inf	inf	inf
2m	Near	0.76	0.68	0.55	0.44	0.36	0.29
	Far	inf	inf	inf	inf	inf	inf
infinity	Near	1.11	0.93	0.69	0.52	0.40	0.31
	Far	inf	inf	inf	inf	inf	inf

Verdict

For full-frame or crop-sensor use, this lens will deliver great image quality across the frame on a sunny day. For low-contrast subjects, some post-processing can be expected. In practical terms, although it has a focal length range of only 12mm, the sheer variety of options provided in terms of framing is surprising. There are wider and faster zooms in the same price range, but these are usually for APS-C bodies only, making this arguably the best option for full-frame use, or for crop-sensor bodies when you demand corner-to-corner punch in images with strong foregrounds. Your results will be particularly pleasing if you can work some blocks of strong color into the immediate foreground. Some distortion is inevitable at such focal lengths, but it is very well controlled—the image on page 53 was taken at 12mm with the part of the bridge nearest the camera only 60cm (2ft) from the lens, yielding a perspective that also looks fairly natural.

15–30mm f/3.5–4.5 EX DG ASP IF

Specifications (based on Sigma mount)

Lens construction: 17 elements in 13 groups
Angle of view: 71.6°–110.5°
Diaphragm blades: 8
Min. aperture: f/22
Min. focusing distance: 30cm (11.8in)
Max. magnification: 1:6
Filter: Rear (gelatin) type
Dimensions: 87mm (W) × 132.5mm (L)
(3.4in × 5.2in)
Weight: 615g (21.7oz)
Mounts: Sigma, Canon, Nikon (D), Pentax, Sony/Minolta

DISCONTINUED

Note: The appearance of lenses may differ depending on the camera mount.

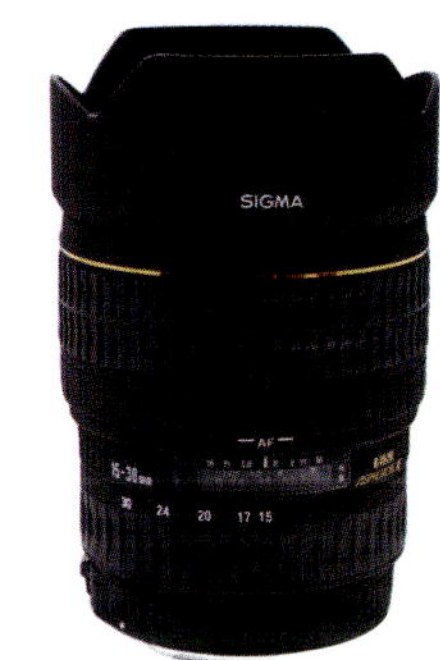

Although it has been discontinued, this lens is still available (at the time of writing) from certain dealers as a new item, and it certainly merits inclusion in this book. It is a fairly large, but surprisingly light lens, which handles extremely well and is easy to carry. It has a built-in petal-shaped lens hood, and an open-fronted cover to which the clip-on lens cap can be attached.

The cover also has an 82mm thread, making it possible to use a filter or other attachment in certain

LENS CONSTRUCTION

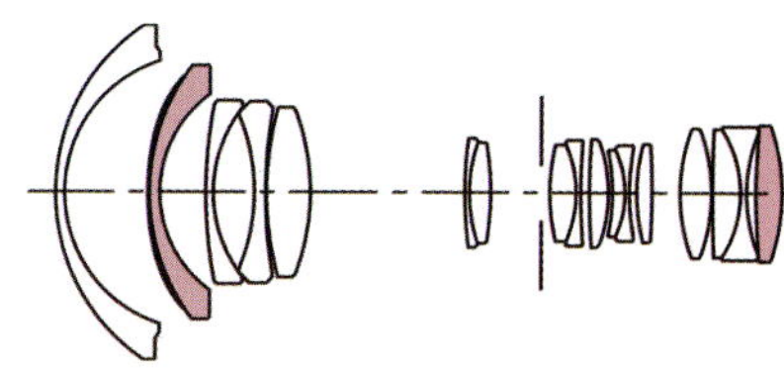

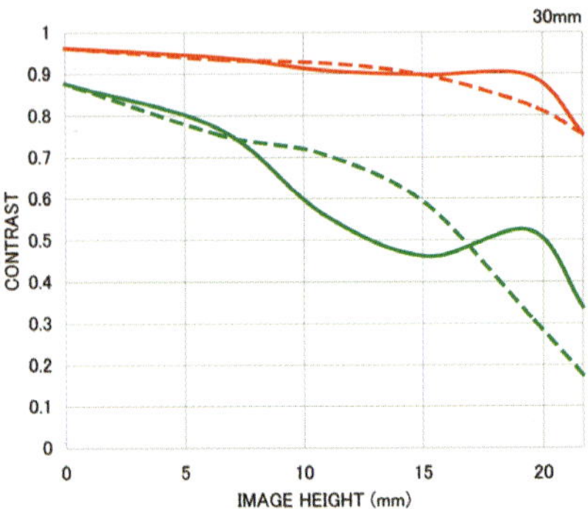

circumstances. Mounted on a full-frame camera body (such as the Canon EOS 5D Mk II), with just the cover on the lens, and set at 30mm, the viewfinder shows no vignetting. With a polarizing filter attached, the vignetting just starts to be visible.

No setting wider than 30mm is possible on a full-frame camera without cropping. However, on a 1.6× crop body (such as the Canon EOS 40D), the viewfinder showed no vignetting with a polarizer attached throughout the zoom range until just reaching the 15mm mark. Single filters, thinner than a polarizer, should pose no problem.

With its internal focusing and exceptionally close focusing ability—just 30cm (1ft) from subject to focal plane—this lens is also an excellent tool for close-ups outdoors as well as for photojournalism and sweeping views. In fact, it tends to favor subject matter closer to the lens when it comes to resolving power.

It is possible to switch to manual focusing by gripping the focusing ring and pulling it toward you, operating the "clutch" mechanism that Sigma use on a number of lenses, plus sliding the AF/MF switch to the manual focus setting (according to camera manufacturer).

Two other points worth noting are that the lens does not rotate, and the minimum aperture of f/22 at 15mm increases to f/29 at 30mm.

Verdict

This is a very flexible lens, covering a useful range, whether it is used on a full-frame or a crop-sensor body. Performance across all apertures is sustained better at 30mm than at 15mm, but it is still no slouch at the wide end. At the time of writing, the last few are available new at half the original price, which will also help to artificially lower its used value. An excellent bargain if you hunt around.

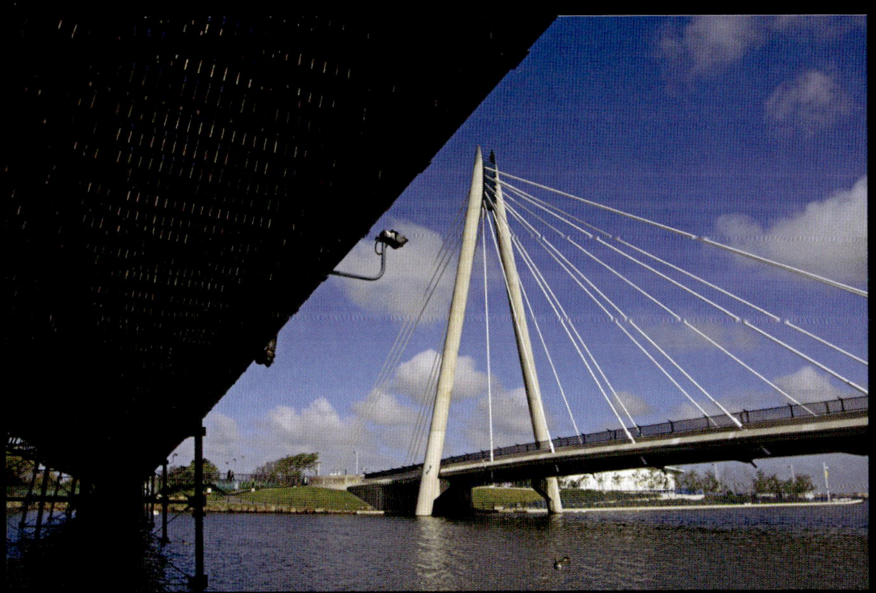

EXPERIMENT

At its widest focal length, this lens will have you trying different approaches to deal with large expanses of sky.

Settings

Focal length: 15mm
ISO: 100
Aperture: f/5.6
Shutter: 1/1000

17–70mm f/2.8–4.5 DC Macro IF ASP HSM

Lens construction: 15 elements in 12 groups
Angle of view: 20.2°–72.4°
Diaphragm blades: 7
Min. aperture: f/22
Min. focusing distance: 20cm (7.9in)
Max. magnification: 1:2.3
Filter: 72mm
Dimensions: 79mm (W) × 82.5mm (L)
(3.1in × 3.2in)
Weight: 455g (16oz)
Mounts (HSM): Nikon (D)
Mounts (non-HSM): Sigma, Canon, Sony, Pentax

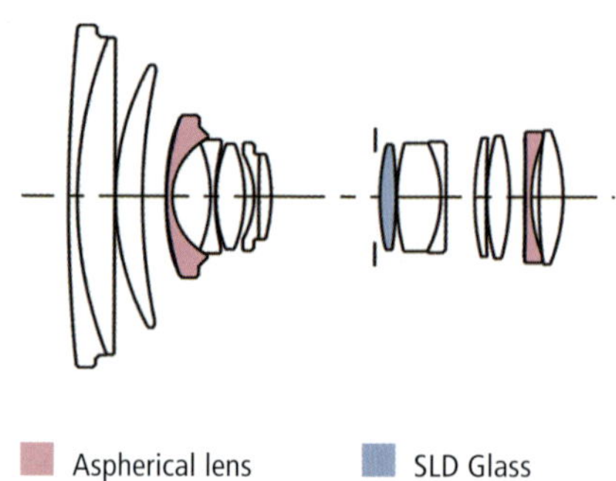

Note: The appearance of lenses may differ depending on the camera mount.

Some lenses perform outstandingly well in one particular respect—and if this feature suits your style of photography, you can often obtain striking results by limiting your style (and often your budget) to suit the optimum settings of the lens concerned. Sigma's 17–70mm f/2.8–4.5 DC lens falls into that category.

It is relatively inexpensive, but its construction, operation, and finish are of the same high quality that you would expect from an EX series lens. Its most desirable quality, however, is its performance at the longer end

LENS CONSTRUCTION

of the zoom range when it is used at medium apertures. This is, quite simply, stunning.

At 17mm, better performance is achieved by avoiding both the widest and the narrowest apertures, but at 17mm and f/11, both center sharpness and edge sharpness are very good. Some barrel distortion is evident, almost inevitably, at the widest focal lengths.

At 70mm, even when shooting at f/4.5 (the maximum aperture at this focal length), center sharpness was excellent and edge sharpness very good. At the longest focal length and f/36—an unusually narrow maximum aperture—lens performance falls away a little, being very good at the center, but only fair at the edges. Most experienced photographers will know that lenses perform better as you narrow the aperture from the maximum, but fewer realize that there comes another point when performance starts to tail off again. This often becomes an issue with macro lenses, when people automatically opt for the narrowest possible aperture only to find less image sharpness than they had expected. Sometimes it is better to sacrifice depth of field in order to achieve maximum sharpness in the area of the subject that will be in focus.

Now for the highlights: at 70mm and f/11, center sharpness was simply stunning and it was hard to see any reduction in quality at the edges, but there was just enough difference for the edges to be rated as "merely" excellent.

MTF Charts 17–70mm

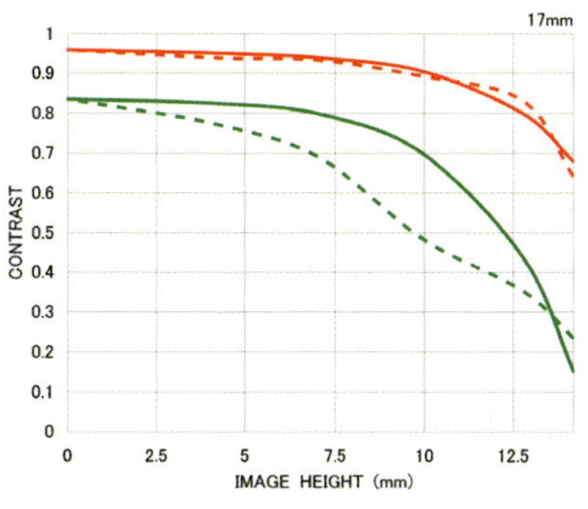

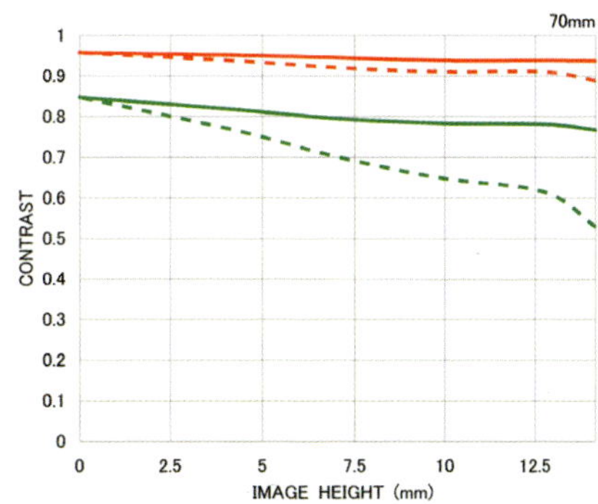

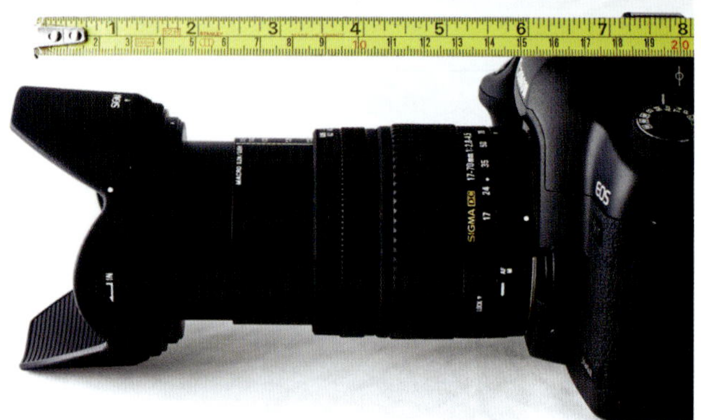

The other praiseworthy qualities of this lens are its close-focusing and macro facilities. True, this lens does not provide "true macro," as it will only magnify up to 1:2.3, but this brings the subject so close that it is almost touching the front element. The stated minimum focusing distance of 20cm (7.9in) makes it sound as if there is room to play with, but that is the distance to the focal plane (see image above). In fact, you have to remove the lens hood when using maximum magnification—that's how close you will get!

The locking catch secures the zoom ring at 17mm. It is located where you might expect to find the AF/MF switch (which is found farther around the lens barrel). When the lens is set to 70mm, both switches are virtually in line, which is a little confusing at first.

Stop Press

As this book went to press, Sigma announced an updated version of the 17–70mm f/2.8–4.0 DC Macro OS HSM. The lens has a slightly reduced magnification ratio at 1:2.7, but now includes Optical Stabilization and is slightly faster at its longest focal length.

Verdict

Used to its strengths, this lens will deliver very crisp images. If possible, keep to midrange apertures at the wider end of the zoom range. At 70mm and a medium aperture—f/11, for example—this lens will match almost any competition when it comes to real-world photography.

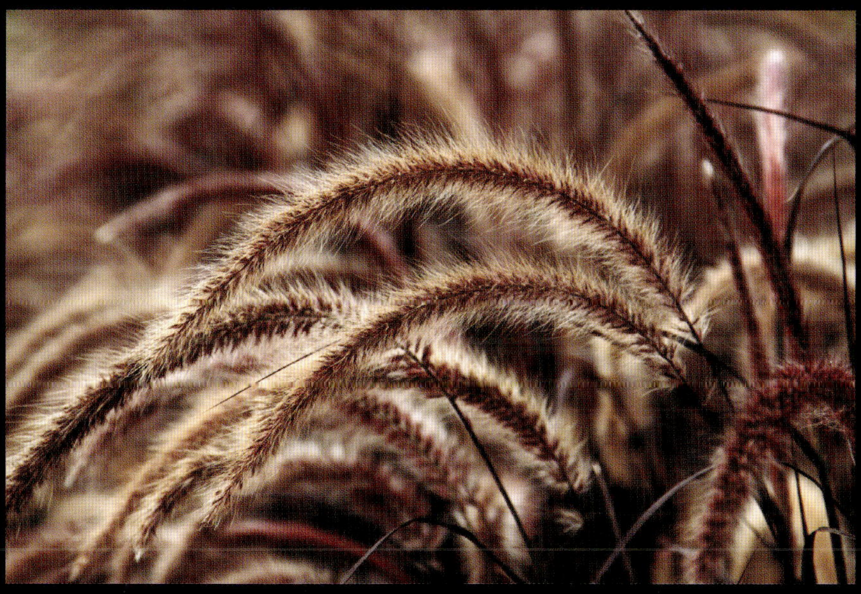

DIFFERENTIAL FOCUS

Sometimes a shot demands a very shallow depth of field, such as with these colorful grasses. The relatively wide aperture also enabled me to use a slow ISO setting to maintain better color and detail, with a shutter speed fast enough to freeze any slight movement. Differential focus is an excellent way to isolate a subject from its background, but the background also needs to be assessed by using the depth-of-field preview button.

Settings

Focal length: 105mm
ISO: 100
Aperture: f/4
Shutter: 1/400

Foreground

One feature of wide-angle lenses that cannot be avoided, and which causes compositional problems for beginners, is their expansive foreground. The equally typical expansive skies don't seem to pose the same problem.

By stopping down to a fairly narrow aperture and using your camera's depth-of-field preview button to check the zone of sharpest focus, it is fairly easy to include interesting features in the immediate foreground. Choose features that will complement rather than dominate the main subject. With wider lenses, you can use moderate apertures such as f/8 and still capture everything in focus from a few feet away to infinity, though you may need to switch to manual focus and use the hyperfocal focusing technique.

This technique dispenses with the usual focusing methods altogether, and involves rotating the focusing ring so that the infinity mark on the depth-of-field scale is just inside the mark for the aperture you have chosen. Depth-of-field

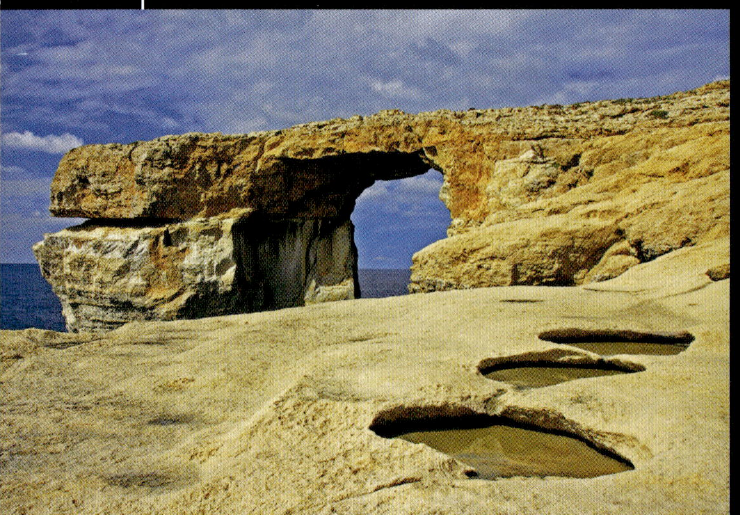

ROCK FORMATIONS

Settings
Focal length: 24mm
ISO: 100
Aperture: f/8
Shutter: 1/125

Settings
Focal length: 24mm
ISO: 100
Aperture: f/8
Shutter: 1/125

scales are often omitted on modern lenses, but a depth-of-field table such as those included throughout this guide will inform you of the distance at which to manually set your focus for any given aperture in order to maximize the depth of field.

To accentuate the foreground, it is often better to lower the camera position by squatting down on one knee, rather than tilting the camera and lens downward. An alternative to lowering the camera position, one that is also useful when using slightly longer lenses, is to rotate the camera to the vertical or "portrait" position—a technique used to good effect in the image on this page.

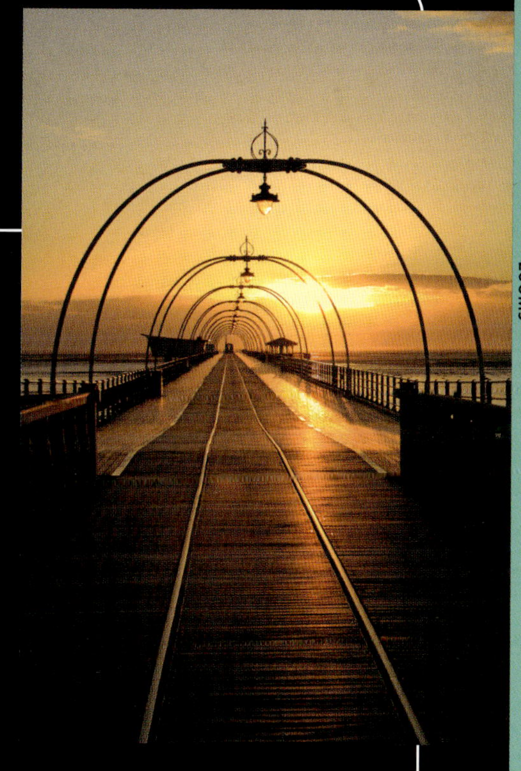

PIER AT SUNSET

Graphic composition

Sometimes the foreground of an image provides us with an excuse to take a bold approach to composition. Most beginners concentrate solely on the main subject and, in effect, the center of the frame, while professional photographers try to consider every part of the image and pay close attention to the edges and corners. This is where unwanted elements can detract from the main subject by distracting the viewer. With this in mind, don't be afraid of deliberately using the bottom corners of the frame for elements of the subject that will lead the viewer's eye into the picture. This approach is particularly useful with wide-angle lenses. The image below, of Blickling Hall in Norfolk, UK, is a case in point.

Settings
Focal length: 32mm
ISO: 100
Aperture: f/5.6
Shutter: 1/640

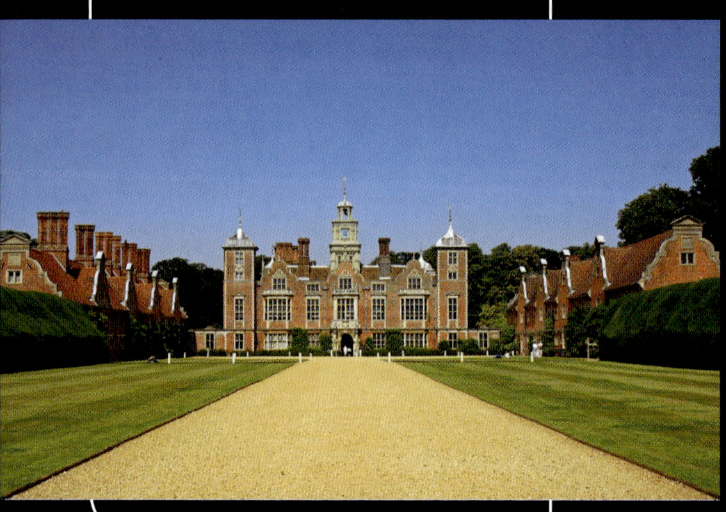

BLICKLING HALL, NORFOLK, UK

Context

One thing wide-angle lenses in particular are good at is placing the subject in context. It isn't always advisable to get in close to the subject—the usual approach with wide-angles in photojournalism. Sometimes it helps to give the viewer the opportunity to see the subject in relation to its surroundings. The image below of La Corbière lighthouse on the island of Jersey shows it with expansive skies and with plenty of sea surrounding it, suggesting the way the lighthouse is at the mercy of the elements.

LA CORBIÈRE LIGHTHOUSE, JERSEY

Settings
Focal length: 28mm
ISO: 200
Aperture: f/4
Shutter: 1/400

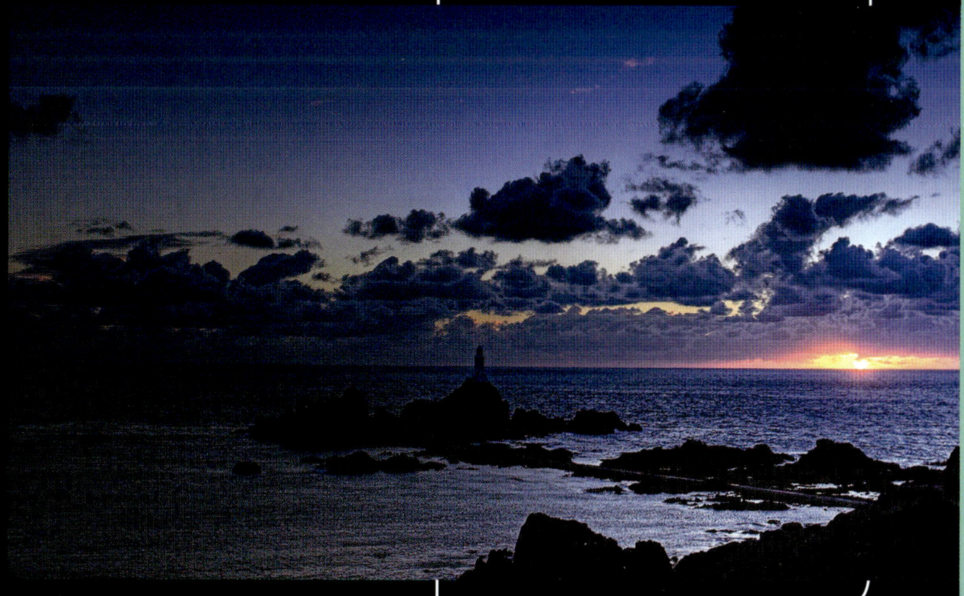

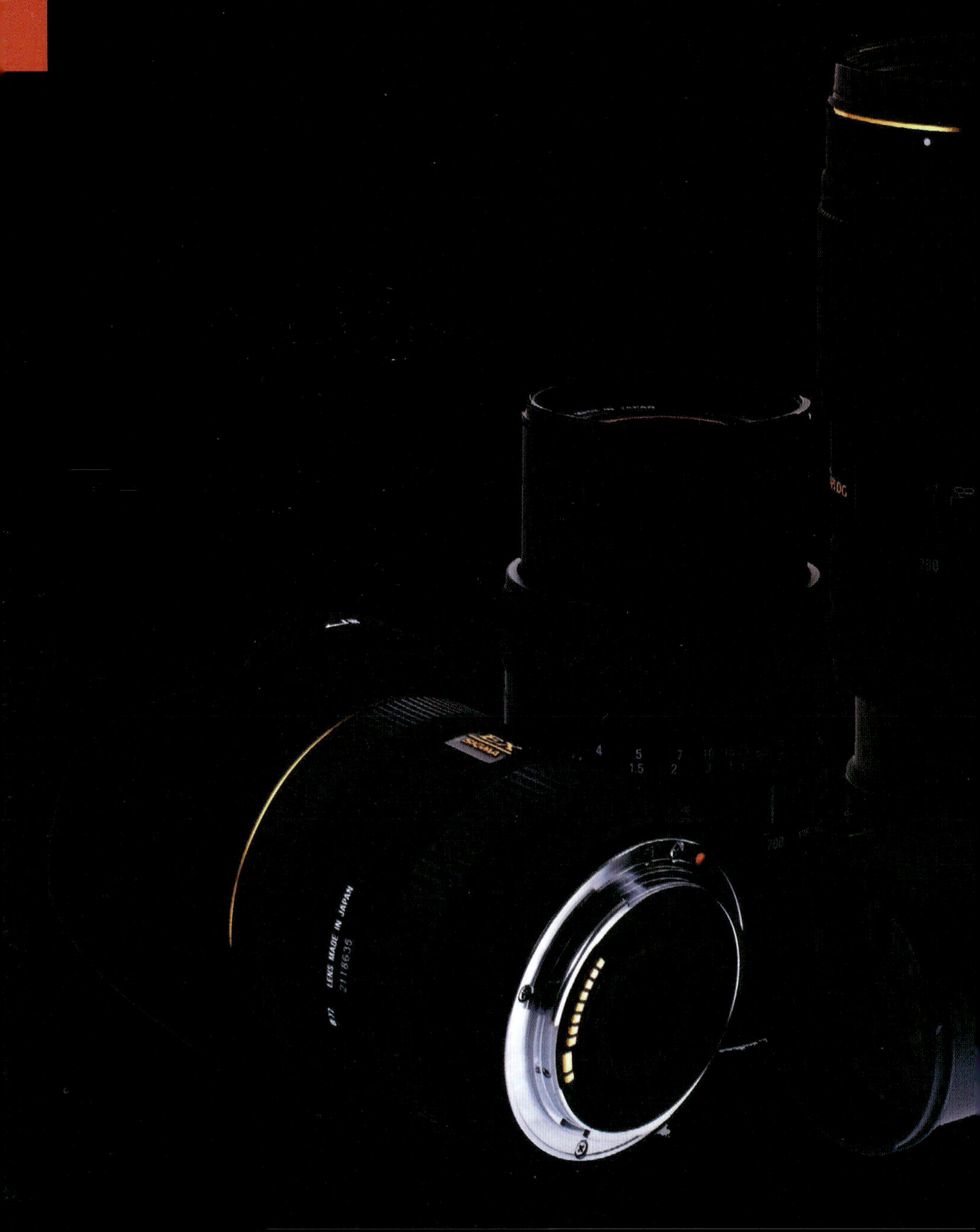

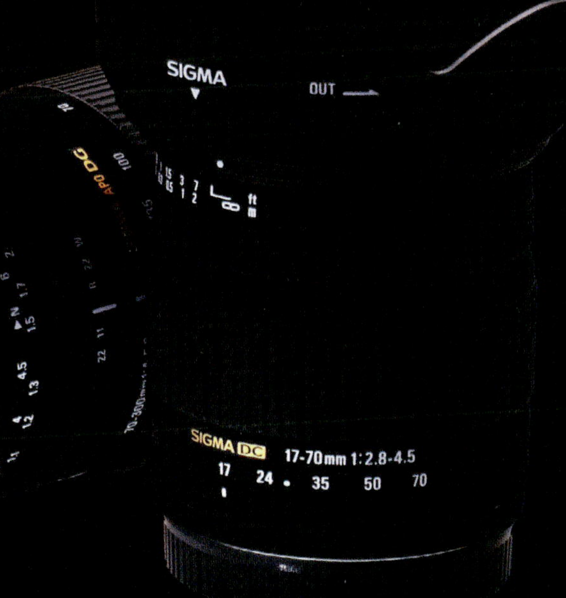

Chapter **4**

Zooms starting at 18mm

18–50mm f/2.8–4.5 DC OS HSM IF ASP

Specifications (based on Sigma mount)

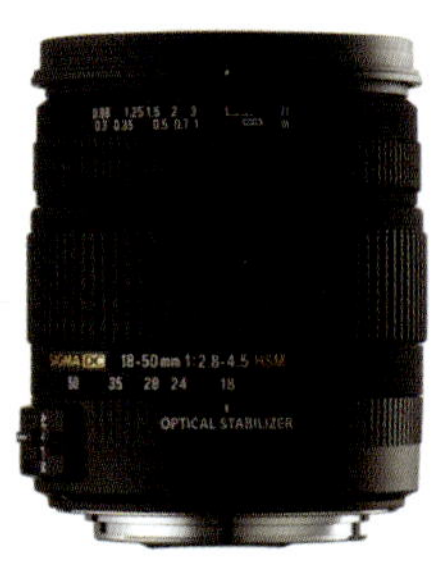

Lens construction: 16 elements in 12 groups
Angle of view: 27.9°–69.3°
Diaphragm blades: 7
Min. aperture: f/22
Min. focusing distance: 30cm (11.8in)
Max. magnification: 1:4.1
Filter: 67mm
Dimensions: 74mm (W) × 88.6mm (L)
(2.9in × 3.5in)
Weight: 395g (13.9oz)
Mounts: Sigma, Canon, Nikon (D), Sony (D), Pentax*

*If Pentax body does not support HSM, autofocus will not function.

Note: The appearance of lenses may differ depending on the camera mount.

One of Sigma's newest offerings, this lens is very light considering its high number of lens elements. It is also good to see Sigma adding optical stabilization to a wide optic, as this opens up new opportunities for shooting handheld images of subjects such as waterfalls, when shutter speeds of 1/4 sec or longer are required to achieve attractive blurring of the water.

LENS CONSTRUCTION

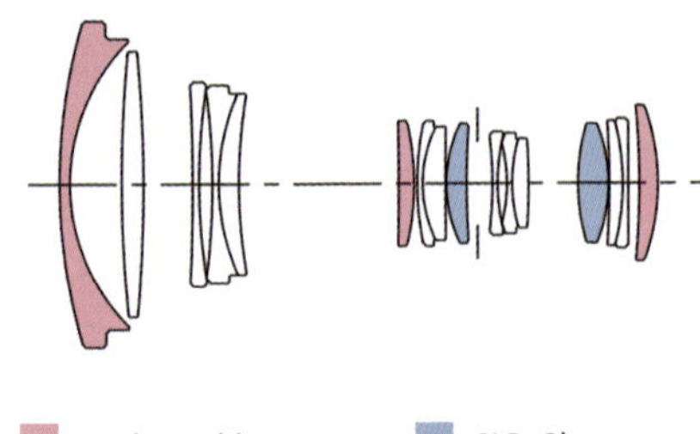

PRODUCT SHOT
The 18–50mm f/2.8–4.5 DC lens rose to the challenge under difficult lighting conditions.

Extreme depth of field can also be accomplished handheld at very slow shutter speeds. The shot on the right, for example, set several challenges: poor light, a low ISO for maximum detail without noise in the blue stripe, and huge depth of field. The graphic nearest the

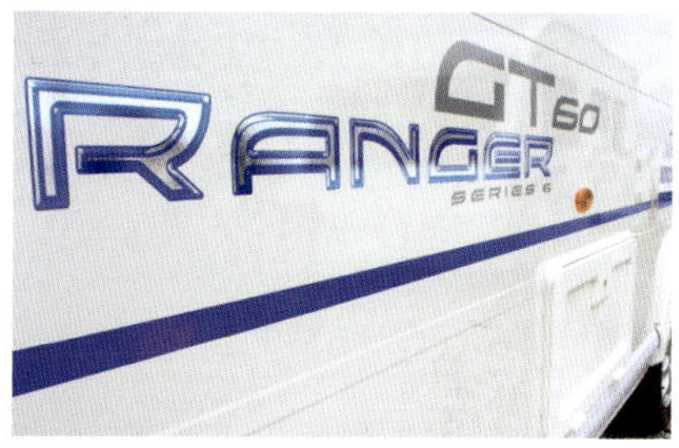

camera was just inches away from the lens, but f/22 and 1/4 sec handheld proved sufficient.

No extension is caused by either the zoom or focusing rings, both of which are very smooth and positive. Two SLD glass elements and three Aspherical lenses do a good job of correcting aberrations, while the HSM (Hyper Sonic Motor) and the short travel of the focusing ring (approx. 45°) ensure quick, quiet, and accurate autofocus. With a minimum focusing distance of just 30cm (11.8in) throughout the entire zoom range, and a maximum magnification ratio of 1:4.1, this makes an excellent walkaround lens.

MTF Charts 18–50mm

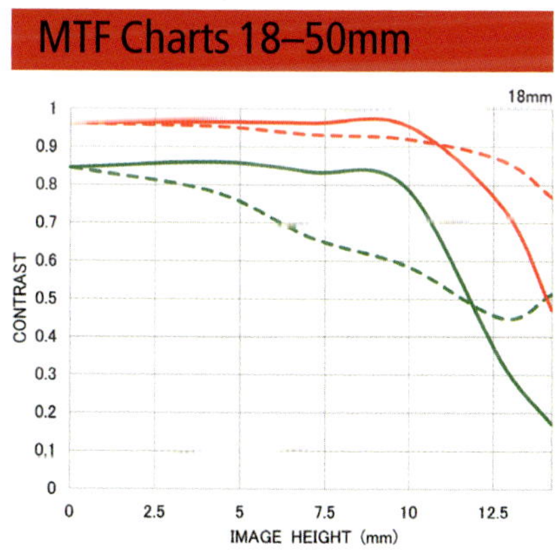

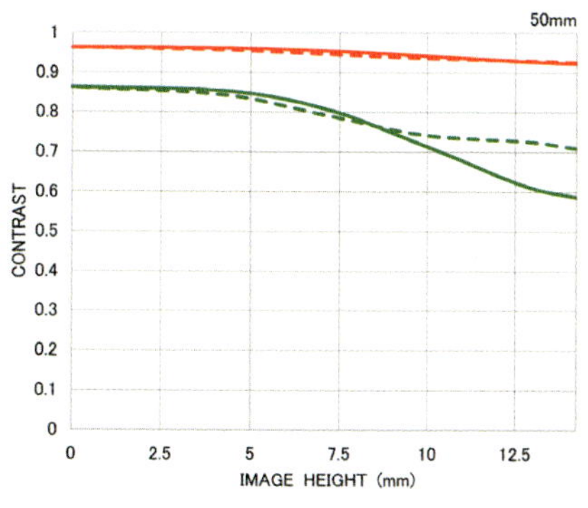

Verdict
If you are happiest with a fairly narrow range of focal lengths, need a lightweight lens, and will benefit from optical stabilization (no need to carry a tripod!), this lens is worth a close look.

18–50mm f/3.5–5.6 DC

Specifications (based on Sigma mount)

Lens construction: 8 elements in 8 groups
Angle of view: 27.9°–69.3°
Diaphragm blades: 7
Min. aperture: f/22
Min. focusing distance: 25cm (9.8in)
Max. magnification: 1:3.5
Filter: 58mm
Dimensions: 67.5mm (W) × 62mm (L)
(2.7in × 2.4in)
Weight: 250g (8.8oz)
Mounts (non-HSM): Sigma, Canon, Sony, Pentax, Four Thirds
Mounts HSM: Nikon (D)

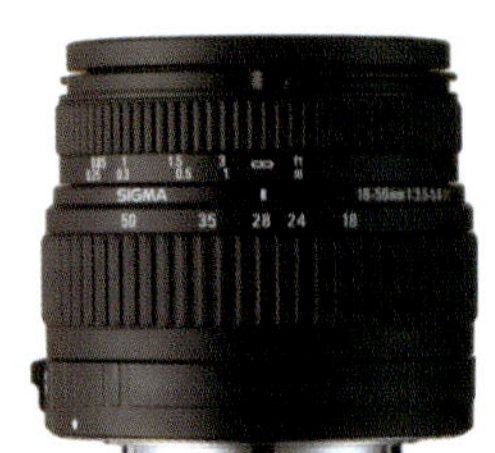

Note: The appearance of lenses may differ depending on the camera mount.

This lens is the lightest and least expensive model in Sigma's line-up, weighing just 250g (8.8oz) due to its use of plastics, though it does sport a metal mount. Lens extension is at its minimum when focused at infinity and when zoomed to 28mm. As you zoom to either more than 28mm or less than 28mm, the lens extends by 14mm or 13mm respectively.

Verdict
For those on a tight budget, this lens represents excellent value for money.

18–50mm f/2.8 EX DC Macro IF ASP

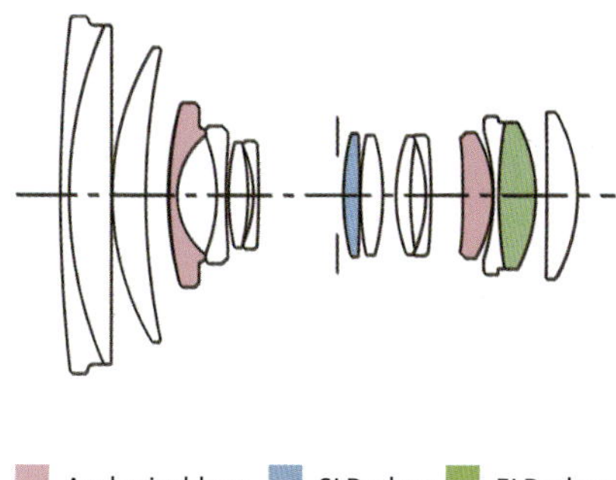

Specifications (based on Sigma mount)

Lens construction: 15 elements in 13 groups
Angle of view: 27.9°–69.3°
Diaphragm blades: 7
Min. aperture: f/22
Min. focusing distance: 20cm (7.9in)
Max. magnification: 1:3
Filter: 72mm
Dimensions: 79mm (W) × 85.8mm (L) (3.1in × 3.4in)
Weight: 450g (15.9oz)
Mounts (HSM): Nikon (D)
Mounts (non-HSM): Sigma, Canon, Sony, Pentax, Four Thirds

Note: The appearance of lenses may differ depending on the camera mount.

The last of the trio of 18–50mm lenses is another DC model for crop-sensor bodies. It is badged as a macro lens, but, in truth, it achieves only slightly higher magnification than the other two 18–50mm lenses (see pages 68–70). Its main advantages are that it is an EX lens, and that it has a constant f/2.8 maximum aperture across the full zoom range.

Although very compact, this lens is surprisingly heavy. This adds to its impression of solidity and sturdy, but refined construction. The rubberized zoom and focus grips work well

LENS CONSTRUCTION

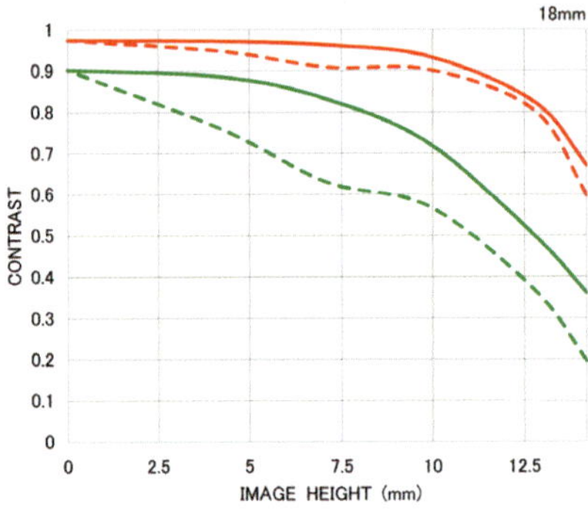

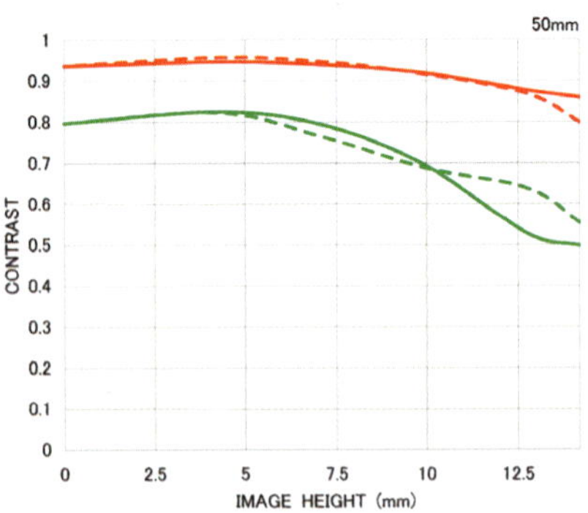

with the matte EX finish, both in appearance and fingertip sensitivity. The zoom ring can be locked at 18mm, though the model tested displayed enough torque for there to be no zoom creep at all. In any case, the lens extension when zoomed from 18mm to 50mm is only 26mm, so the locking switch seems rather superfluous. When extended, the lens barrel displays markings for two magnification ratios, 1:3.6 and 1:3.

One of the most pleasing aspects of using the lens is the very short arc through which the focusing ring travels, ensuring rapid autofocus acquisition. Although the focusing ring rotates beneath your fingers if you hold the lens too far forward, the front element does not rotate, so any filters and filter holders can be used.

At 18mm (with a field of view equivalent to 28mm on full-frame), this lens permits a usefully wide perspective without the distortion associated with the more extreme wide-angle zooms.

Verdict

An excellent general-purpose lens, fast enough to use in low light, and with moderate close-up ability and good contrast across the range, as long as you don't need true macro or want to shoot lots of tightly framed candid shots of people. This is an excellent lens for landscapes.

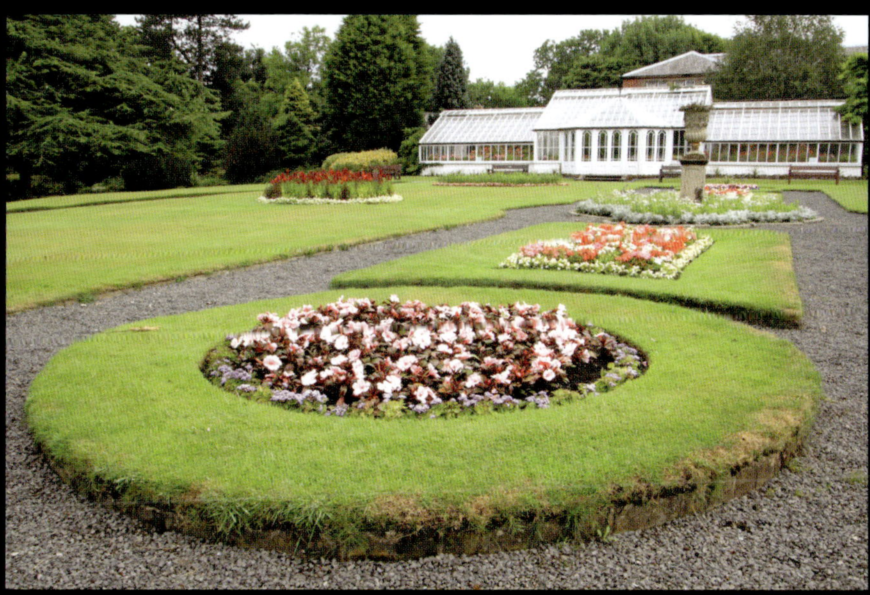

ANGLES

With wide focal lengths and strong lines
running into the image, such as the paths
in this shot, it is sometimes better to have
these lines run at an angle away from you,
rather than straight into the distance.

Settings

Focal length: 18mm
ISO: 400
Aperture: f/22
Shutter: 1/50

18–125mm f/3.8–5.6 DC OS HSM IF ASP

Specifications (based on Sigma mount)

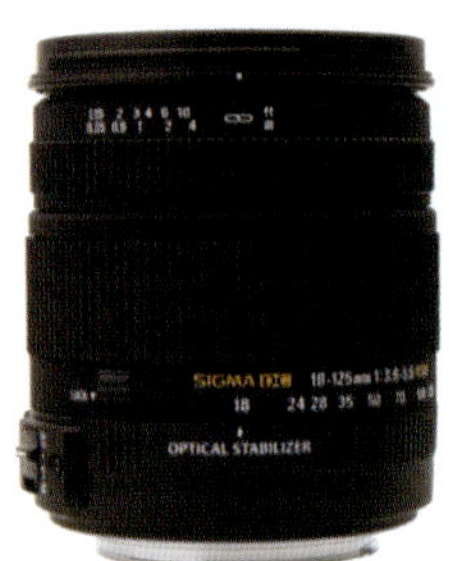

Lens construction: 16 elements in 12 groups
Angle of view: 11.4°–69.3°
Diaphragm blades: 7
Min. aperture: f/22
Min. focusing distance: 35cm (13.8in)
Max. magnification: 1:3.8
Filter: 67mm
Dimensions: 74mm (W) × 88.5mm (L) (2.9in × 3.5in)
Weight: 490g (17.3oz)
Mounts (OS): Sigma, Canon, Nikon (D)
Mounts (non-OS): Sony (D), Pentax

Note: The appearance of lenses may differ depending on the camera mount.

Designed solely for use on a crop-sensor body, this lens has an excellent range as well as ASP and SLD optics and Optical Stabilization, the latter being good for up to four stops. It is sufficiently lightweight to be easily portable all day long, yet heavy enough to sit comfortably in the hand without camera shake. This makes the Optical Stabilizer the icing on the cake, not only guaranteeing pin-sharp images, but doing so at slow shutter speeds when the light is poor. In addition, the OS system works across the full zoom range,

LENS CONSTRUCTION

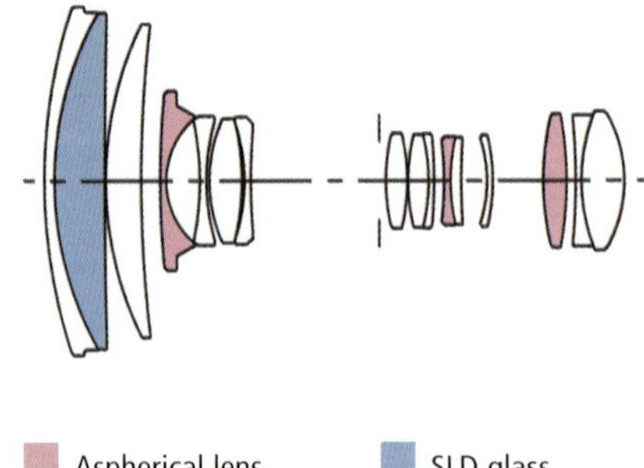

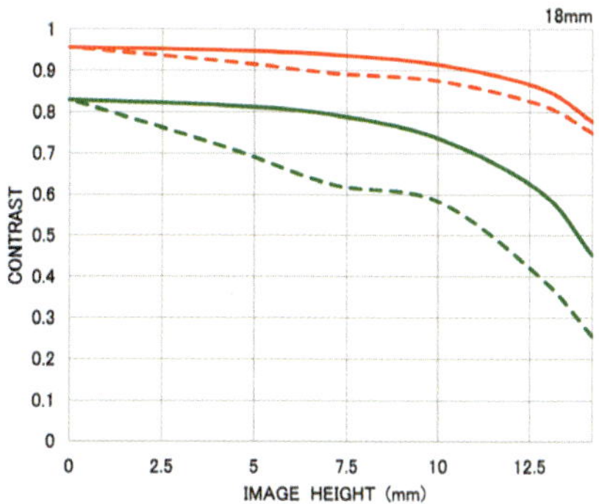

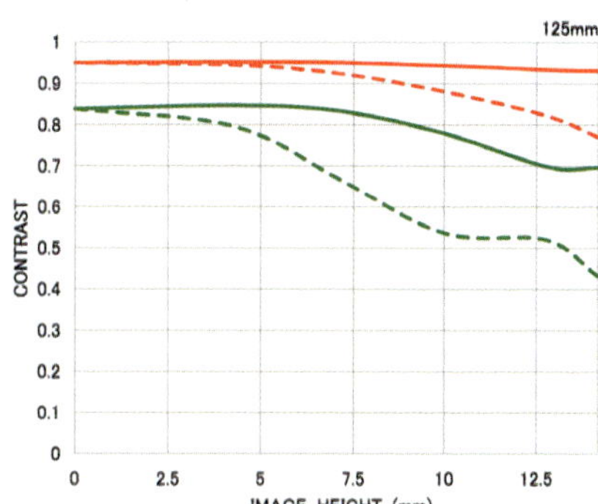

providing extra sharpness when working with narrower apertures for maximum depth of field at the wide end of the focal range. In this regard, the lens scores heavily when weighed against the competition, which has largely failed to recognize the market for image stabilization on wide-angle lenses.

Another useful feature is the zoom lock, which can be applied when the lens is set to 18mm. This ensures that there is no zoom creep when carrying the lens fitted to a camera, though the zoom ring has enough torque for creep to be fairly unlikely anyway.

The internal-focus construction means there is no lens extension when racking the lens out to infinity, though it does extend by 50mm when zoomed out to its longest focal length, revealing magnification

markings of 1: 3.8 to 1:8 on the lens barrel. When I tested it on Canon's lightweight EOS 500D/Rebel T1i, the lens remained perfectly balanced even when zoomed out to 125mm, and no adjustment of the supporting hand was necessary—a small but significant factor when you become engrossed in an image-rich environment. On the same note, both the AF/MF and OS switches fall easily beneath the thumb of the supporting left hand, too.

Autofocus on the HSM lens tested was very positive, quiet, and extremely quick even in very low light and with low-contrast subjects, regardless of the focal length used. Optical performance holds up better at longer focal lengths, producing very crisp images at medium apertures.

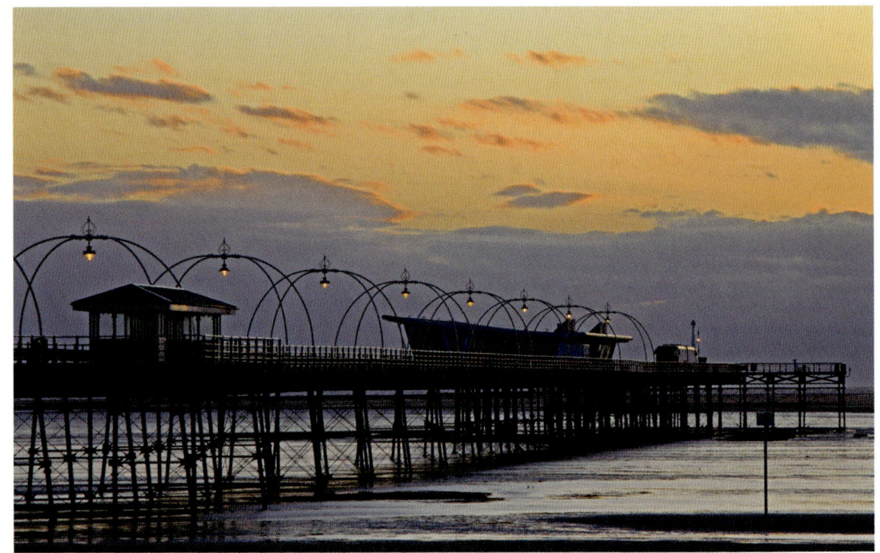

One other praiseworthy point: the petal-shaped lens hood, reversed for storage, is as smooth a fit as you could imagine, but locks into place with a comforting click.

RECIPROCAL
Conventional wisdom is that a shutter speed should be at least the reciprocal of the focal length—for example, 1/125 sec at 110mm, as seen here—but Optical Stabilization ensures an even sharper image.

Verdict

Although it is not badged as an EX lens, because this designation is now reserved for fixed aperture lenses, this model has EX finish and build quality. At its current price, it represents excellent value for money. If most of your images are captured at medium or longer focal lengths, but you sometimes require an extra-wide field of view, this is a strong candidate. If your images are rarely used larger than 7 × 5in (17.8 × 12.7cm), you'll probably be perfectly happy with the results throughout the zoom range and in any lighting situation. And you'll be pleasantly surprised at the price.

18–200mm f/3.5–6.3 DC IF ASP

Specifications (based on Sigma mount)

Lens construction: 15 elements in 13 groups
Angle of view: 7.1°–69.3°
Diaphragm blades: 7
Min. aperture: f/22
Min. focusing distance: 45cm (17.7in)
Max. magnification: 1:4.4
Filter: 62mm
Dimensions: 70mm (W) × 78.1mm (L)
(2.75in × 3.1in)
Weight: 405g (14.3oz)
Mounts (OS): Sigma, Canon, Nikon (D), Sony (D), Pentax

Note: The appearance of lenses may differ depending on the camera mount.

This lens is the non-stabilized version of the model on pages 80–81, though there are slight differences in configuration. In fact, this version has an additional Special Low Dispersion lens element compared with the OS version. Performance, however, is not quite as good as the OS version, with both contrast and resolution falling away very slightly near the edges of the frame. The MTF charts on the following page, though, appear to do this lens a disservice when it comes to the wide end of the zoom range, with the lens performing noticeably

LENS CONSTRUCTION

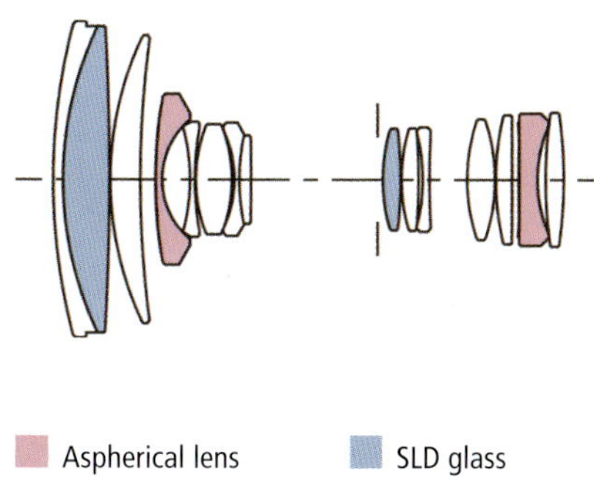

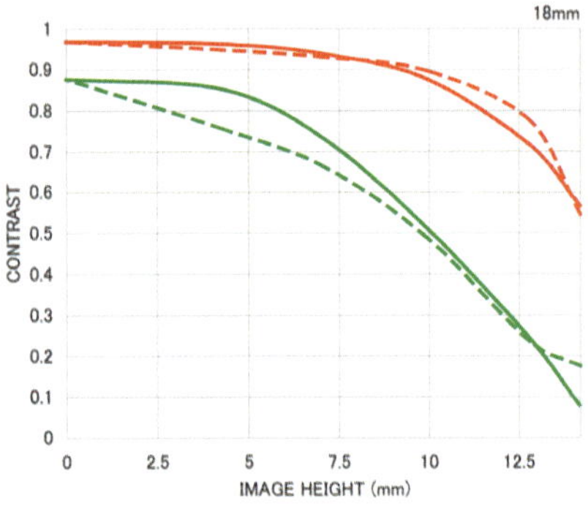

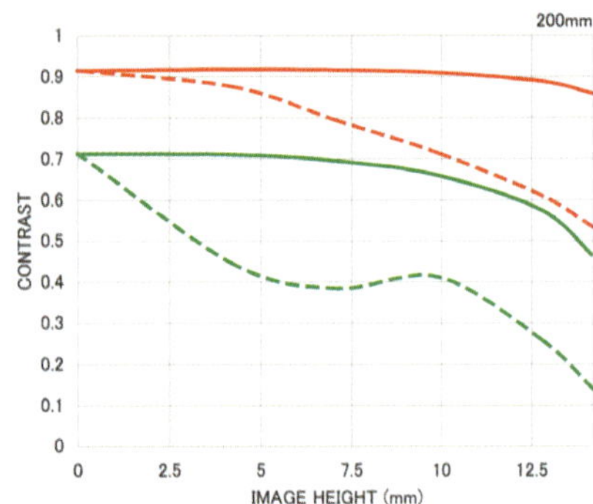

better than is suggested by the MTF chart at 18mm—but remember that these MTF charts only illustrate the performance of the lens at the maximum aperture.

The lens is extremely compact with a wide, ribbed zoom ring, but a very narrow focusing ring at the front of the lens. The lens doesn't extend far when zoomed fully, but nevertheless there is a zoom-lock switch to prevent any "zoom creep" when carrying the lens pointed downward on the camera.

When the lens is fully extended, 50mm is added to its length, but it still remains quite unobtrusive for candid street photography. Once racked out so the lens barrel is fully in view, magnification ratio markings are displayed from 1:15.4 to 1:4.4. At such magnifications, the markings are almost superfluous, but they do add a touch of class, as does the red stripe at the end of the lens.

Focusing is a touch noisy, it has to be said, but compensates for this by being so fast that it barely matters. This is due in part to the very short travel needed by the focusing ring—approximately 30° from close focus to infinity—and partly to an excellent design that acquires focus on dark, low-contrast subjects with ease, even in poor light. The lens comes with a bayonet-mount, petal-shaped lens hood, which fits smoothly and clicks firmly into place. The hood can also be carried reversed on the front of the lens.

78

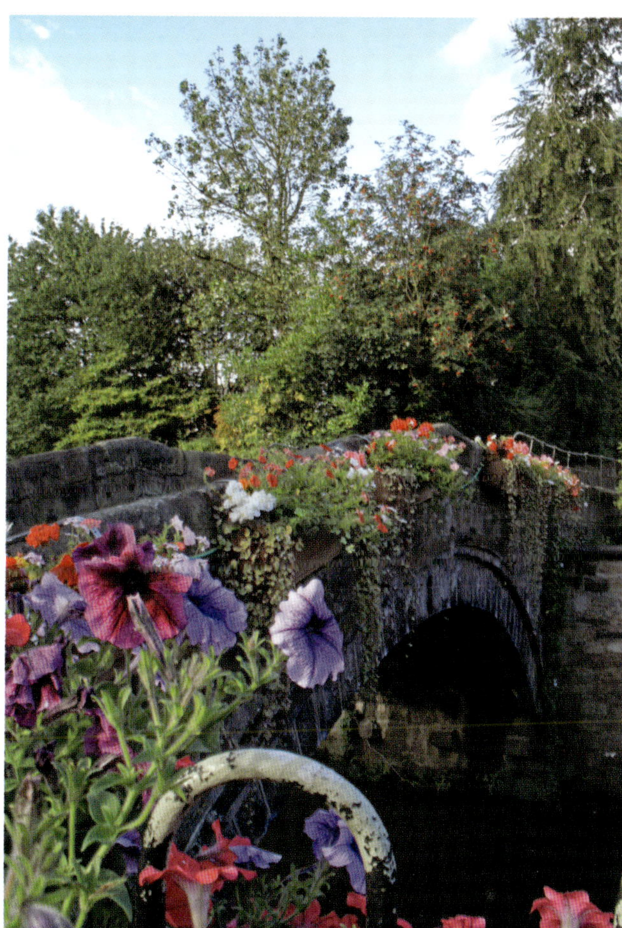

STRETCH
Even without Optical Stabilization, you can usually shoot at a shutter speed as slow as the reciprocal of the focal length (see also page 76). In this image, 1/13 sec handheld was used at 18mm, which is stretching things a little.

Verdict

For sheer value for money, this lens is hard to beat if you want to carry just one lens on your travels and can live with its slower maximum apertures.

Its main competition comes in the form of its stabilized sibling (see page 80), which, at the time of writing, doesn't cost very much more.

18–200mm f/3.5–6.3 DC OS IF ASP

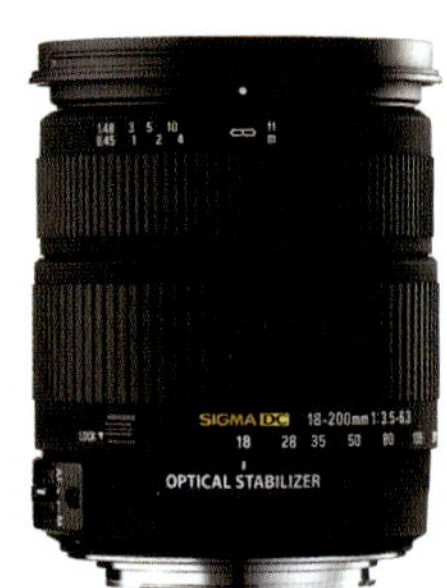

Specifications (based on Sigma mount)

Lens construction: 18 elements in 13 groups
Angle of view: 7.1°–69.3°
Diaphragm blades: 7
Min. aperture: f/22
Min. focusing distance: 45cm (17.7in)
Max. magnification: 1:3.9
Filter: 72mm
Dimensions: 79mm (W) × 100mm (L)
(3.1in × 3.9in)
Weight: 610g (21.5oz)
Mounts (HSM): Nikon (D)
Mounts (non-HSM): Sigma, Canon

Note: The appearance of lenses may differ depending on the camera mount.

This lens comes in an HSM version for Nikon and a non-HSM version for Sigma and Canon. Sony and Pentax users should consider the 18–250mm f/3.5-6.3 DC OS IF ASP instead (see page 83).

Being a Canon user, I used the non-HSM model. It was paired with the 300–800mm (see page 180) for a visit to a village cricket match, making for an interesting combination: the 18–200mm attached to the rather diminutive Canon EOS 500D for handheld shots, and the huge 300–800 mounted on a Canon EOS 40D

LENS CONSTRUCTION

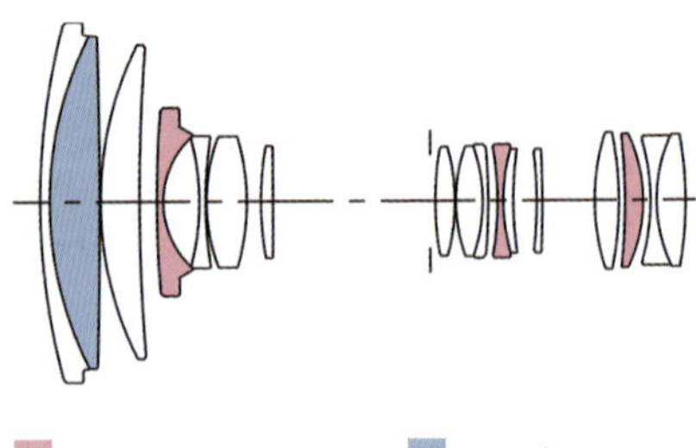

with battery grip on a substantial Manfrotto monopod. Switching from one to the other proved to be far easier than I had anticipated.

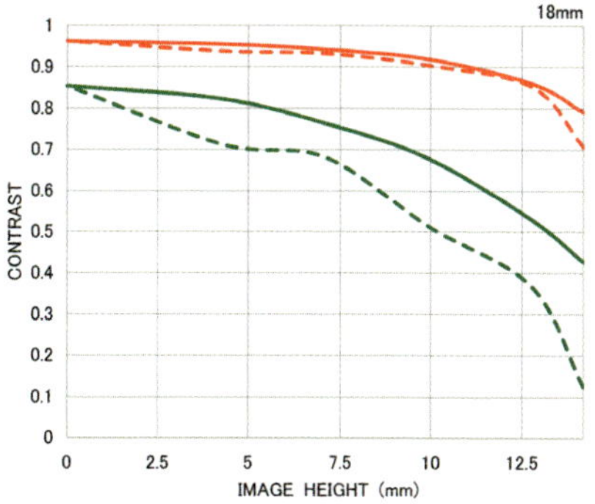

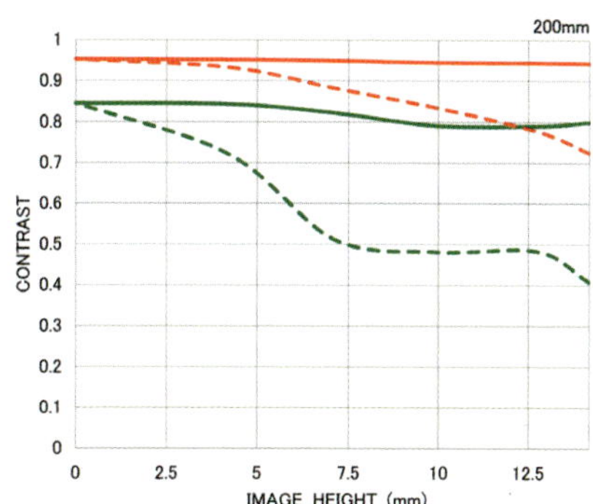

Like a number of other recent Sigma lenses, this is not an EX lens, but it looks and feels like one, with positive switches and a smooth-fitting petal-shaped hood that clicks firmly into place. It sits comfortably in the hand, heavy enough to have the inertia to reduce camera shake even without using the Optical Stabilizer.

There is a zoom lock that can be employed when the zoom ring is set to 18mm; an AF/MF switch; and an off/on OS switch. (There is no OS setting for panning as can be found on some other lenses.) Due to the internal focus design, there is no lens extension when focusing, but zooming out to 200mm brings a lens extension of about 63mm, revealing magnification markings from 1:12.8 down to 1:3.9, according to the zoom setting at the minimum focusing distance of 45cm (17.7in).

Verdict

It would be unfair to make a direct comparison between the non-HSM Canon version of this lens and the HSM 18–250mm DC OS (see page 83). Nevertheless, as a Canon user, these were the two versions I was able to play with, and the 18–250mm model won easily, even though it costs a good deal more at the time of writing. Nikon users who can access the HSM version of this lens may well find it just as good as I found the 18–250mm, thus saving themselves some money, too.

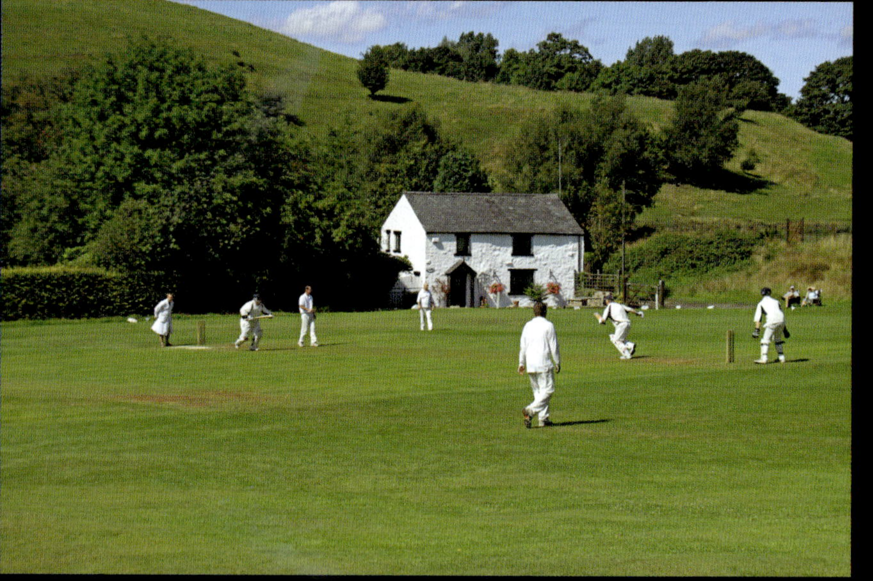

ZOOM RATIO

For sporting events, carrying a single lens with
an extensive zoom ratio—such as that provided
by the 18–250mm lens shown opposite—is ideal
on a sunny day. However, the slower maximum
apertures will demand higher ISO speeds when
the weather isn't so kind.

Settings

Focal length: 50mm

ISO: 200

Aperture: f/8

Shutter: 1/640

18–250mm f/3.5–6.3 DC OS HSM IF ASP

Specifications (based on Sigma mount)

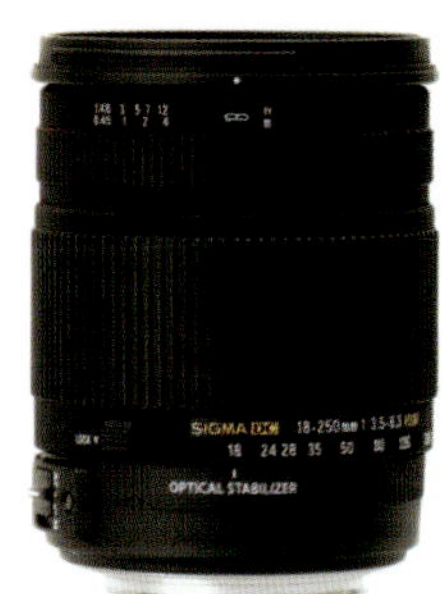

Lens construction: 18 elements in 14 groups
Angle of view: 5.7°–69.3°
Diaphragm blades: 7
Min. aperture: f/22
Min. focusing distance: 45cm (17.7in)
Max. magnification: 1:3.4
Filter: 72mm
Dimensions: 79mm (W) × 101mm (L)
(3.1in × 4in)
Weight: 630g (22.2oz)
Mounts: Sigma, Canon, Nikon (D), Sony, Pentax

Note: The appearance of lenses may differ depending on the camera mount.

Compact, a pleasant weight, a huge zoom range, fast autofocus, and a superb four-stop Optical Stabilizer, all at a very competitive price: what more could you want?

This lens acquires autofocus in astonishingly low light levels, provided there is a bit of contrast to be found. In addition, autofocus is quiet and extremely fast with the focusing ring traveling through a small arc considering the focal lengths it covers. It is necessary to support the lens slightly farther back than the weight distribution calls for in order for your foremost finger

LENS CONSTRUCTION

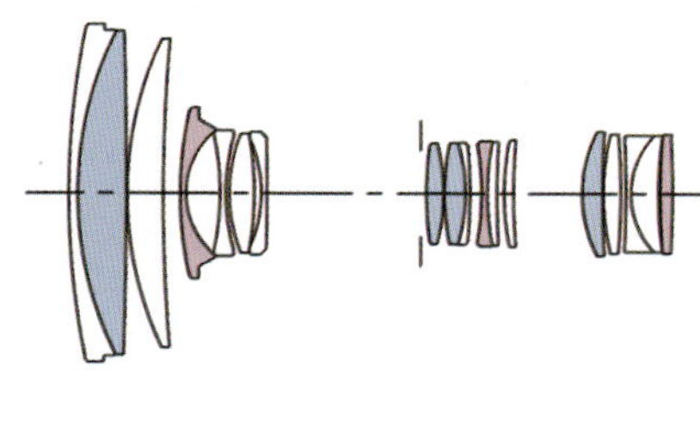

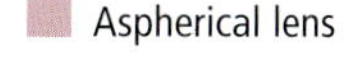
Aspherical lens

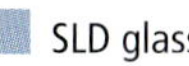
SLD glass

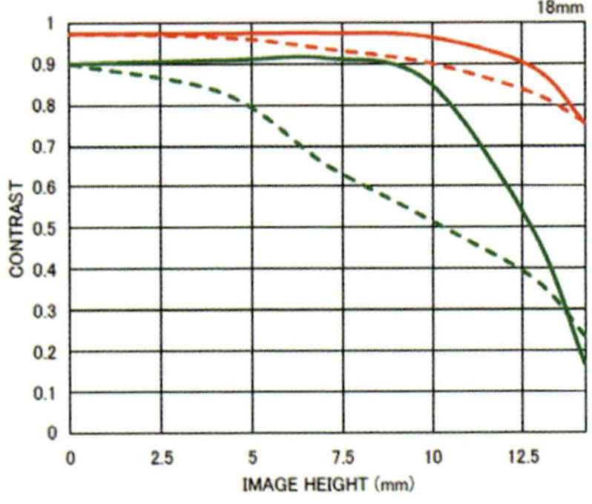

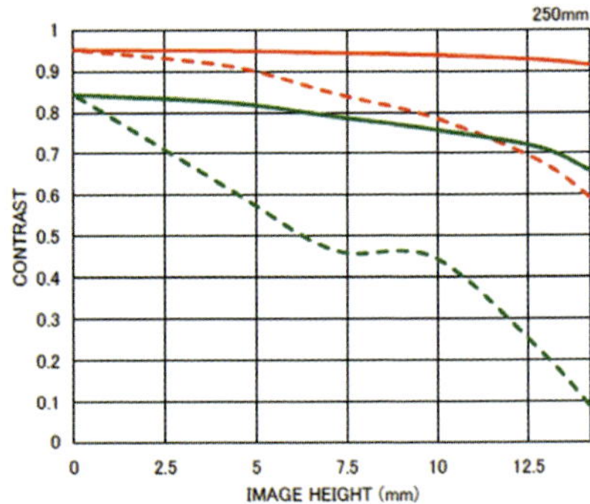

not to foul the rotating focusing ring (though the front element itself does not rotate). When zoomed out to 250mm, the lens barrel extends by 78mm (3in), which encourages you to hold the lens even farther forward on a lightweight camera body, again fouling the focusing ring. However, on a heavier body such as a Canon EOS 50D with battery grip, the lens remains well balanced when it is supported under the zoom ring. It's not a problem when you are accustomed to it. Likewise, with practice the lens can be held comfortably with the petal-shaped lens hood reversed in its carrying position.

Verdict

If you are looking for a single lens that will cater for all your needs without breaking the bank, this could very well be the one—provided you don't mind sacrificing a wider maximum aperture in favor of a higher ISO speed. With some of the most recent camera models, noise is well controlled at anything up to 3200 ISO as long as you don't need huge enlargements, so give this lens some serious thought. Its excellent four-stop image stabilizer could prove to be the deciding factor when making your decision.

The extended barrel carries six markings for magnifications ranging from 1:12.8 down to 1:3.4. When set to 18mm, using the locking switch makes sure there is no zoom creep. The distance scale markings only go up to 4m/12ft; after this, there is a blank section until the infinity mark.

The single most impressive feature of this lens is its four-stop Optical Stabilization system—which, incidentally, should be switched off before changing lenses, when the camera is mounted on a tripod, and when you need to conserve the camera battery.

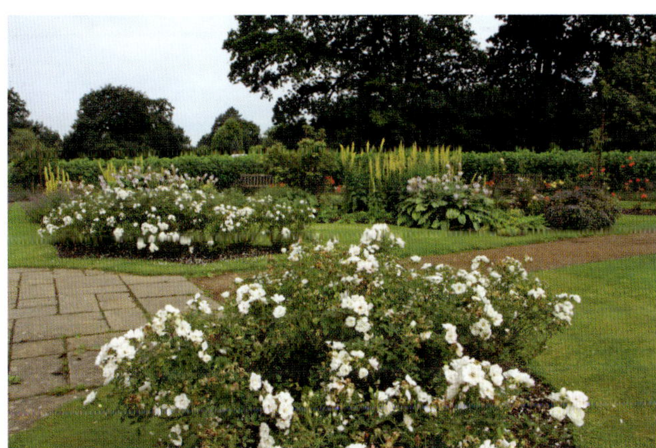

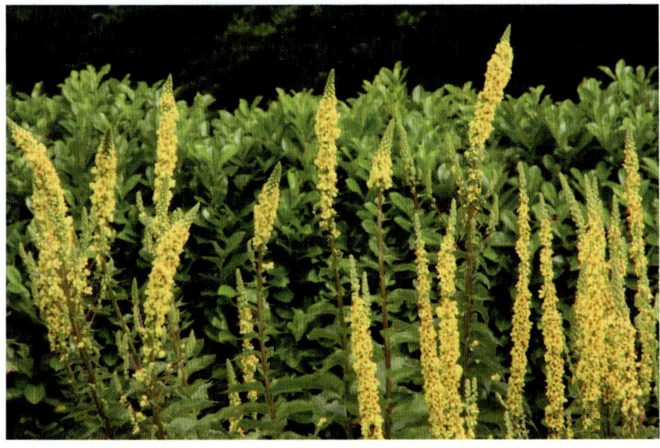

ZOOM SETTINGS
The same scene photographed from the same position at the 18mm setting (top) and the 250mm setting, without any cropping.

Sunsets

They are one of the most popular subjects, yet sunsets are also a frequent source of disappointment. It's easy to get tunnel vision when viewing sunsets and not consider the full image area, placing too much emphasis on the sky and not enough on the foreground, even if it is only a silhouette.

First, it's necessary to anticipate the likelihood of a good sunset, so a bit of amateur weather forecasting is required, and to find the shooting location with plenty of time to spare. You will also need to work out with reasonable accuracy where the sun will sink, below either the horizon or any bank of cloud on the horizon, and have a good idea of what time that will occur. Scouting the shooting location with a compass can be done days in advance and at any time of day, if you know the direction in which the sun will set.

By taking a meter reading from the sky—but not including the sun itself—you will obtain a reading that will give the sky some body, leaving the foreground in near-silhouette. To avoid disappointment later, don't include the setting sun in every shot, as highlight clipping is almost inevitable and the sun will be bleached out in the final image.

In the image shown below, the combination of ambient light at sunset and the color reflected by the water made for a stunning result.

Settings
Focal length: 55mm
ISO: 200
Aperture: f/8
Shutter: 1/50

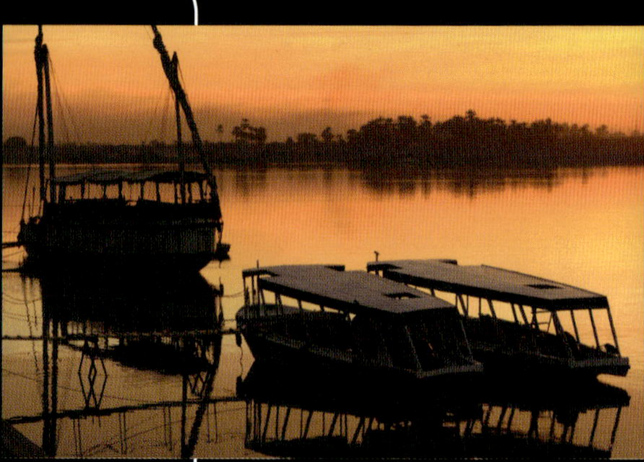

NILE SUNSET

Reflections

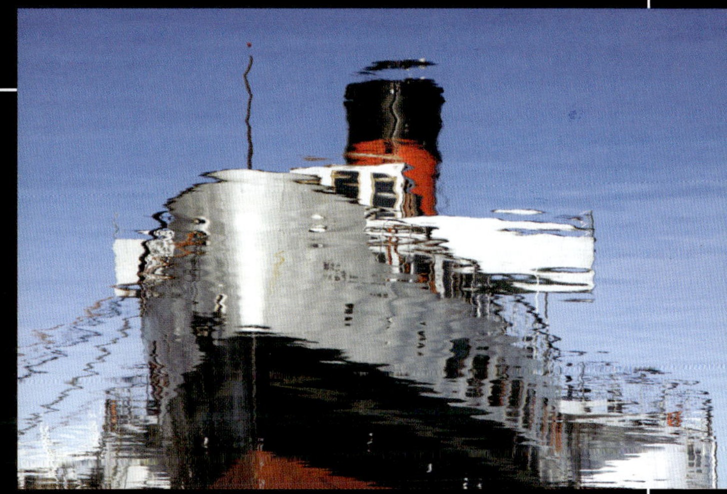

RIPPLES

Settings
Focal length: 105mm
ISO: 100
Aperture: f/5.6
Shutter: 1/400

All manner of reflective surfaces surround us in our everyday lives and can provide excellent opportunities for interesting images, even when other factors, like the weather, seem to be working against us. Curved reflective surfaces can give a "fisheye" effect, but demand good control of depth of field when working at close distances. Water is probably the most frequently used reflective surface, but take care to introduce strong reflected colors whenever possible.

The image above has been inverted so the subject appears the right way up. In this instance the strong colors and blue sky are essential components in conjunction with the reflection.

Posed

Participants in any event expect to be photographed. Most of the time they are happy to pose for the camera; indeed, some will invariably approach you and beg to be photographed. Strangely, the latter are actually harder to capture because they often find it hard to look natural and relaxed. Take your time—but not too much of theirs—and chat briefly before you start to place the subject where you want them. Continue to chat or ask questions about their involvement with the event—this usually draws their enthusiasm and a smile—while taking a short series of images. They will usually understand the need to simulate activity, controlled by you according to your choice of camera position, as opposed to them carrying blindly on with what they were doing while you struggle to get a better angle, better lighting, or to exclude unwanted background. In short, take control, but gently and at a relaxed pace, and don't squander the opportunity to take a variety of images while you have the chance.

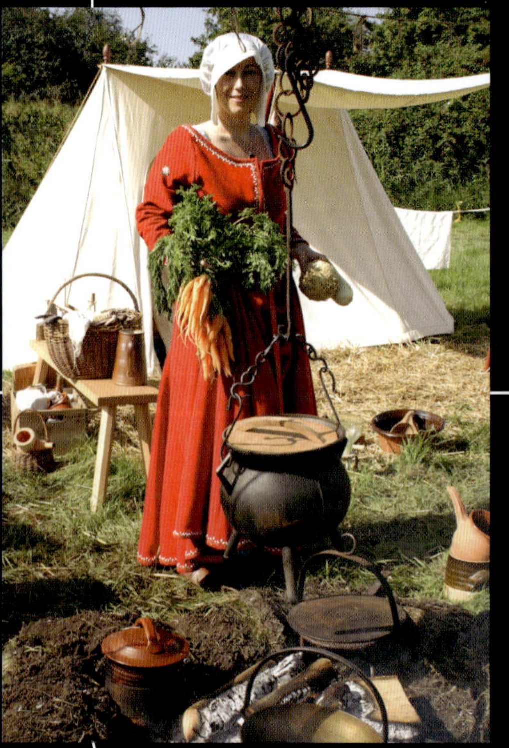

MEDIEVAL FARE

Settings
Focal length: 28mm
ISO: 200
Aperture: f/8
Shutter: 1/500

Settings

Focal length: 85mm
ISO: 400
Aperture: f/8
Shutter: 1/2500

BLUES SINGER

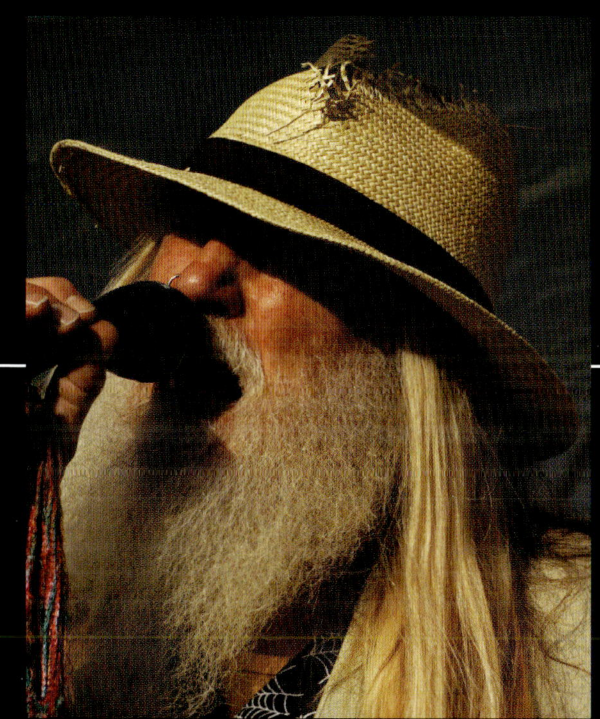

There will always be circumstances in which it simply isn't possible to get your subject to pose or simulate whatever it is they do—such as when capturing musicians live on stage, as shown above. In these situations it is important to be highly observant and to react quickly. Most people, and indeed many animals, have a tendency to repeat small sequences of movement and it is these that you need to watch out for. When you've noted a specific sequence, knowing what follows allows you to be ready to capture the subject with a reasonable degree of certainty about the end result.

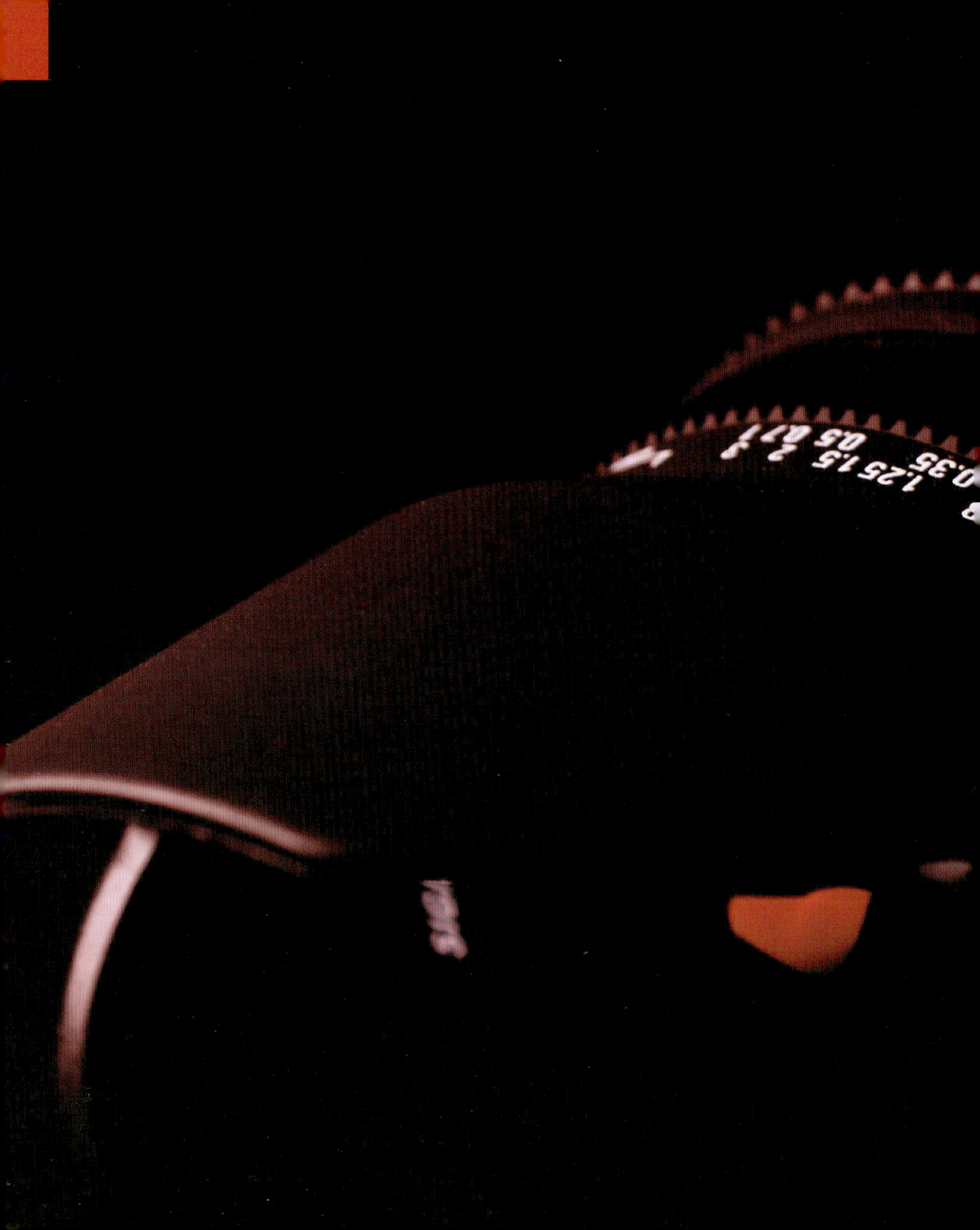

Chapter **5**

Wide & standard prime lenses

With four of the five lenses in this category being suitable for both full-frame and crop-sensor cameras, the dividing line between what is a wide-angle lens and what is a standard lens is inevitably blurred.

The only lens for which the definition is clear-cut is the 30mm f/1.4 EX DC, because it cannot be used on a full-frame camera. When multiplied by the appropriate crop factor, this lens has approximately the same field of view as a so-called standard lens (50mm on full-frame) when it is fitted to a Canon APS-C body. However, Nikon's APS-C sensor is marginally larger—23.6 × 15.8mm as opposed to Canon's 22.3mm × 14.9mm—and its crop factor of 1.5× gives this lens the same field of view as a 45mm. On a Sigma DSLR with a sensor of 20.7 × 13.8mm, the crop factor is different again at 1.7×.

Panoramic images

One way to deal with the large expanses of foreground and sky that often appear in images taken with wide-angle lenses when there is little choice in viewpoint, is to shoot what you know will later be cropped into a panoramic format. There is no precise definition of the ratio of this format, so you can define your own, bearing in mind the availability of suitable printer paper, photo frames, and so on. One of the most popular ratios is 6×17, which mirrors the ratio used by some medium format cameras.

When adopting this approach, you can give free rein to your artistic imagination, and it may also provide an opportunity to "rescue" an image that might otherwise be selected for deletion—perhaps because of something that intrudes into the image area, which, once cropped into panoramic format, would be removed. Or it might be that the image is a little fuzzy—in which

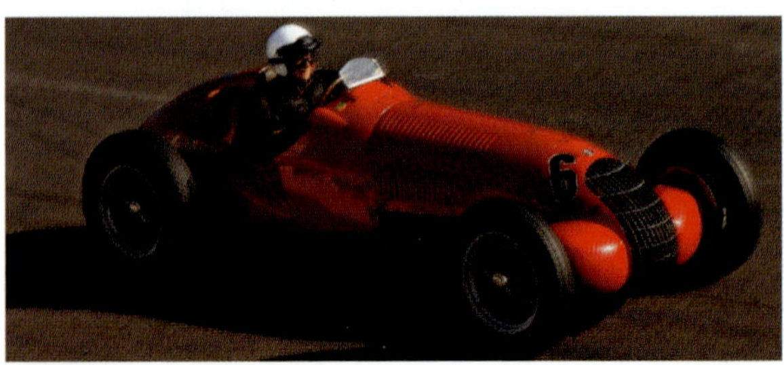

VINTAGE CAR
This image was a little soft, so I "rescued" it by cropping it to a panoramic format and applying an oil painting effect in Photoshop.

CREATING A PANORAMA

Stitching programs merge your photos automatically, but you can make manual adjustments if necessary, and crop and retouch the resulting image in the normal way. The process works in a broadly similar way in most stitching applications.

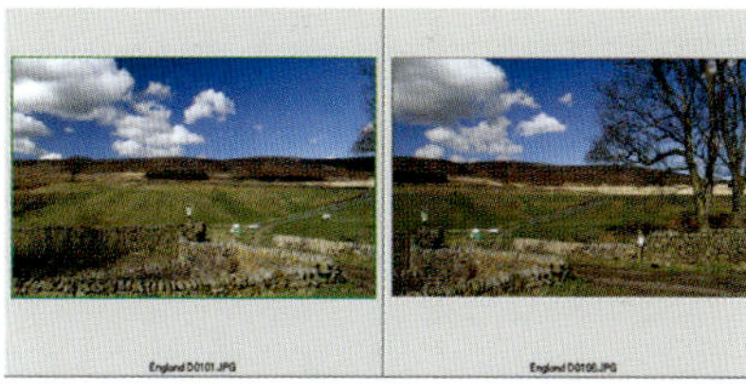

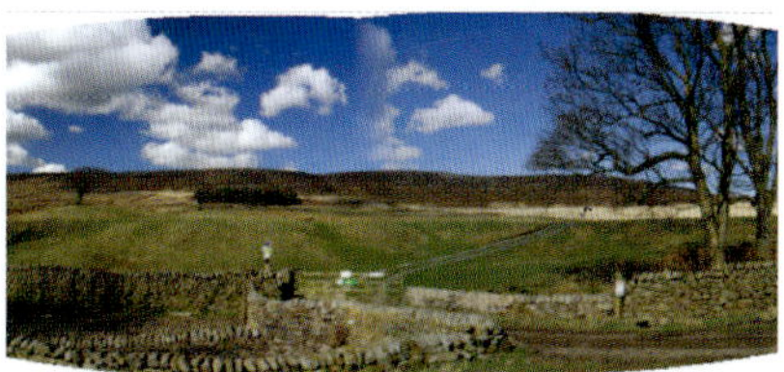

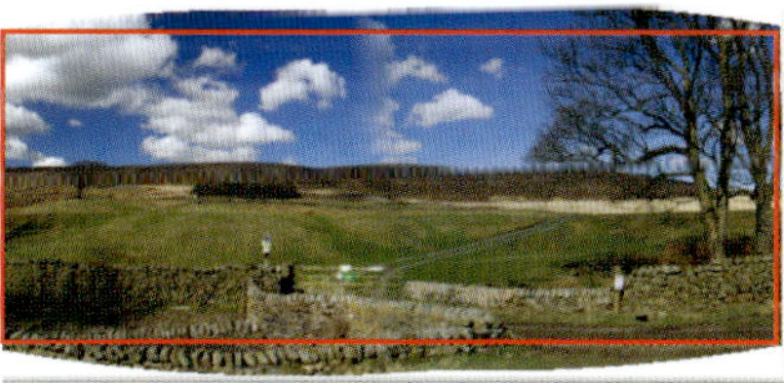

case, why not crop it to a panoramic format and use some of the art filters in Photoshop to create something a little different (see image opposite).

Stitching images

Another popular form of image manipulation is to merge a number of photos to form a single panoramic image. The usual way to do this is to use software designed specifically for the purpose, such as Canon's PhotoStitch, though it can be done manually if you are determined to make life laborious! As an example, PhotoStitch can stitch up to four images (JPEG only) into a single image. The process is fast and simple, and doesn't require your base images to be precisely aligned. The result is remarkably seamless.

If you're not happy with the arrangement of the images to be merged, you can simply drag them to adjust the composition. The merged image will automatically be cropped to the maximum possible area, and you can make adjustments to the final overall image size just as if you were cropping an image normally.

One problem that can arise during this process is that of exposure. When you're shooting a wide sweep of the landscape, at some point you may start shooting into the light, and this will affect one side or the other of the stitched image. If your software only permits the use of JPEGs, you are limited in what you can correct, compared with shooting RAW. Either way, the base images need to be corrected in relation to one another before stitching so that they are as consistent as possible in terms of contrast, brightness, and color rendition.

20mm f/1.8 EX DG ASP RF

Specifications (based on Sigma mount)

Lens construction: 13 elements in 11 groups
Angle of view: 94.5°
Diaphragm blades: 9
Min. aperture: f/22
Min. focusing distance: 20cm (7.9in)
Max. magnification: 1:4
Filter: 82mm
Dimensions: 88.6mm (W) × 89.5mm (L)
(3.49in × 3.52in)
Weight: 520g (18.3oz)
Mounts: Sigma, Canon, Nikon (D), Sony, Pentax (not SFX or SF7)

Note: The appearance of lenses may differ depending on the camera mount.

With the exception of the fisheye lenses (see Chapter 2), this is Sigma's widest focal length prime lens (at the time of writing) and is a design that has been around for several years. On a full-frame camera, it provides an exceptionally wide field of view with minimal distortion when it's not tilted, making it extremely useful for townscapes and landscapes. Its exceptional close-focusing ability, just 20cm (7.9in), also makes it a great choice in the field and as a travel lens.

The rear focus design means that the front element does not rotate, so the use of graduated filters or

LENS CONSTRUCTION

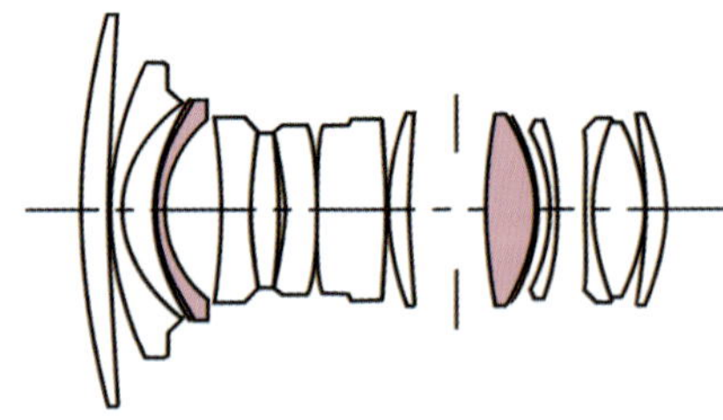

Aspherical lens

This is a versatile lens for use in the field as its close-focus capability makes it useful for capturing detail as well as wide shots. Note the delicately veined flowers on this wood sorrel.

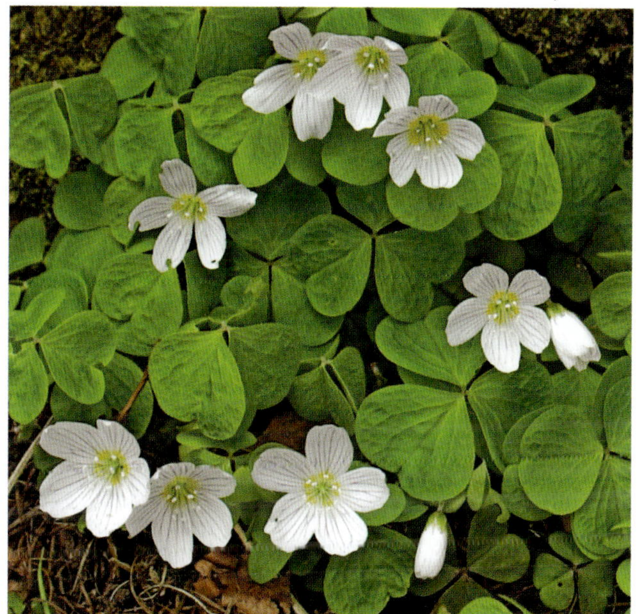

MTF Chart 20mm

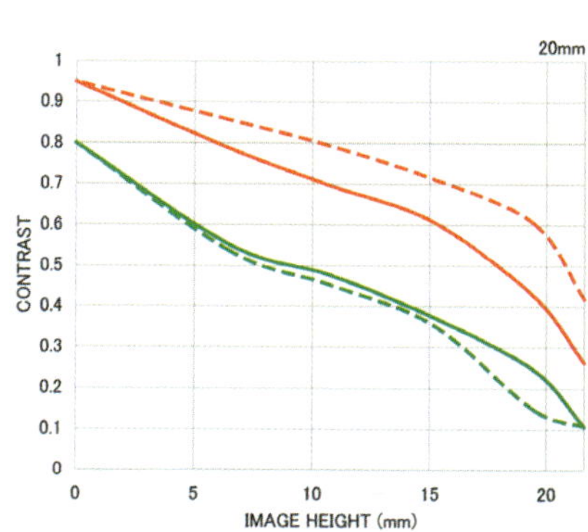

a polarizing filter is no problem. The focusing ring itself also does not rotate, making the wide, ribbed-rubber focusing ring easy to use when supporting the lens.

Although this lens may be used primarily to take advantage of its extensive depth of field (see table on page 96), it can also provide attractive out-of-focus backgrounds ("bokeh") at narrow aperture settings, due to its nine diaphragm blades and circular aperture.

Depth of field (m): 20mm f/1.8 EX DG ASP

Circle of confusion: 0.3333mm

Focused at Aperture		1.8	2.8	4	5.6	8	11	16	22
0.3m	Near	0.29	0.29	0.29	0.28	0.28	0.27	0.26	0.25
	Far	0.31	0.31	0.31	0.32	0.33	0.34	0.37	0.41
0.5m	Near	0.48	0.47	0.46	0.44	0.42	0.40	0.37	0.33
	Far	0.53	0.54	0.56	0.59	0.63	0.72	0.90	1.46
1m	Near	0.90	0.85	0.80	0.74	0.67	0.60	0.52	0.44
	Far	1.14	1.22	1.35	1.60	2.16	4.50	inf	inf
infinity	Near	6.94	4.59	3.28	2.34	1.69	1.22	0.89	0.66
	Far	inf	inf	inf	inf	inf	inf	inf	inf

Verdict

For use on either full-frame or APS-C cameras, the 20mm f/1.8 is a useful addition even if you already have a slow zoom covering this focal length, as its fast maximum aperture permits low-light photography that otherwise wouldn't be possible. It is especially good at dealing with close-ups.

If your preference is to make greatly enlarged landscapes with no significant foreground interest, you may prefer the wide end of the 24–70mm f/2.8 EX DG Macro (see page 117), and it is worth comparing the MTF charts of these two lenses before making your final decision.

24mm f/1.8 EX DG ASP

Lens construction: 10 elements in 9 groups
Angle of view: 84.1°
Diaphragm blades: 9
Min. aperture: f/22
Min. focusing distance: 18cm (7in)
Max. magnification: 1:2.7
Filter: 77mm
Dimensions: 83.6mm (W) × 82.5mm (L)
(3.3in × 3.2in)
Weight: 485g (17.1oz)
Mounts: Sigma, Canon, Nikon (D), Sony, Pentax (not SFX or SF7), Four Thirds

Note: The appearance of lenses may differ depending on the camera mount.

This is a compact, chunky lens with enough weight to give a feeling of solidity, yet light enough to carry comfortably all day when mounted on the camera. It has proved good enough not to need updating since its launch almost a decade ago. It has the traditional matte-black EX finish with a wide-ribbed rubber focusing ring. The complete focusing arc causes a mere 7mm (0.3in) lens extension, non-rotating, when shifted from infinity to the minimum focusing distance of 18cm (7in), owing to the floating focus system. This system moves different lens groups to different positions to

LENS CONSTRUCTION

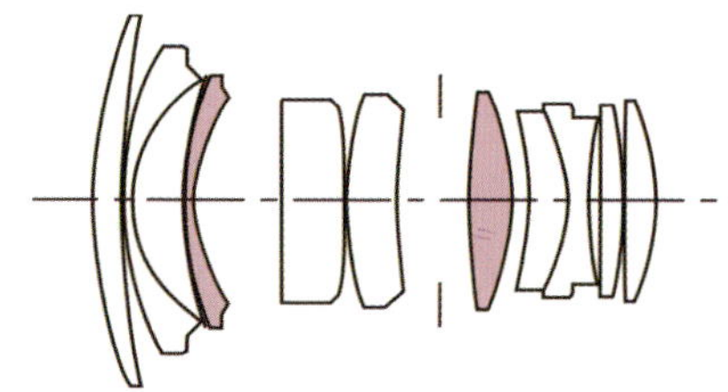

Aspherical lens

reduce the "telescope" effect when changing the focused distance.

The lens barrel is marked twice with magnification ratios of 1:5 and 1:2.7, one set of markings in white for autofocus and another in gold for manual focus. The latter is only fully visible when you pull the focusing ring toward you to operate Sigma's trademark Dual Focus "clutch" system for engaging manual focus.

In use, the lens handles superbly and the petal-shaped lens hood does a good job of shielding the lens to prevent flare. The contrast and resolution of test images proved to be excellent in the center even at wide apertures; in fact, by the time the lens was opened up to f/4, they were really quite outstanding.

Edge sharpness was also worthy of praise. Used handheld on a full-frame body, contrast and detail were extremely good right to the corners, giving the impression of uniform results across the frame unless an unusually high level of

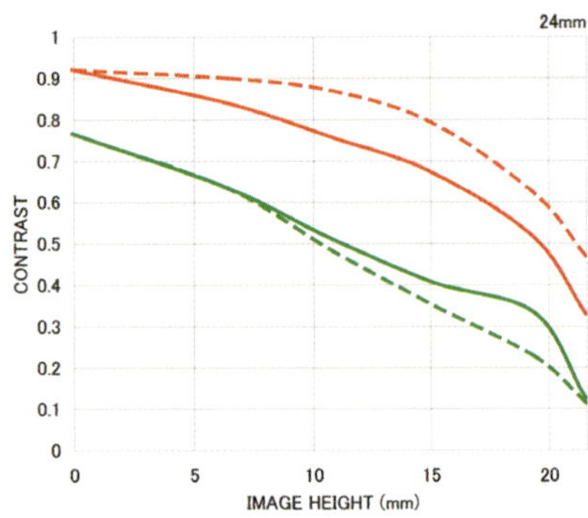

magnification was applied, and even then close examination was necessary to pick out any differences between the center and the edges. The nine diaphragm blades provide attractive background blur when the lens is used wide open at closer camera-to-subject distances.

Verdict

This lens is worthy of a place in anyone's bag and, in practical terms, performs much better than the MTF chart seems to imply. It is noticeably better than the full-frame 28mm f/1.8, which has a more complicated construction. Both of these lenses are especially good at rendering fine detail with subjects closer to the lens.

This, combined with very short minimum focusing distances, makes them useful general-purpose lenses, especially on crop-sensor bodies. My money, however, would be on the 24mm because of its extra coverage, its uniform performance across the frame, and its greater ability to render detail in more-distant subjects.

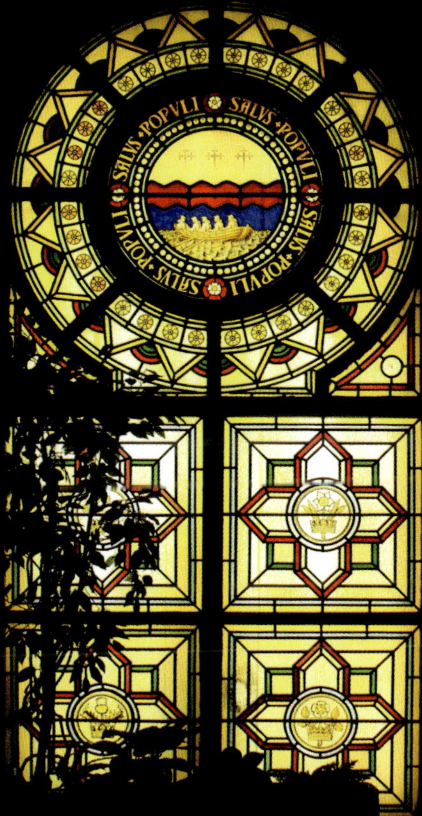

TEMPTATION
It was tempting to shoot this stained glass window at f/1.8 and a higher shutter speed, but 1/60 sec was fast enough and f/4 rendered the high-contrast subject just a little more crisply.

Settings
Focal length: 24mm
ISO: 100
Aperture: f/4
Shutter: 1/60

28mm f/1.8 EX DG ASP

> ## Specifications (based on Sigma mount)
>
> **Lens construction:** 10 elements in 9 groups
> **Angle of view:** 75.4°
> **Diaphragm blades:** 9
> **Min. aperture:** f/22
> **Min. focusing distance:** 20cm (7.9in)
> **Max. magnification:** 1:2.9
> **Filter:** 77mm
> **Dimensions:** 83.6mm (W) × 82.5mm (L)
> (3.3in × 3.2in)
> **Weight:** 500g (17.6oz)
> **Mounts (HSM):** Sigma, Canon, Nikon (D), Sony (D), Pentax
>
> **Note**: The appearance of lenses may differ depending on the camera mount.

Compact, relatively light, and with a lens extension of just 7mm (0.3in) at its closest focusing distance, this lens is certainly easy to carry, whether mounted on a camera or in a bag. It features Sigma's "clutch" mechanism for disengaging the AF by pulling the focusing ring toward the camera slightly. The AF/MF switch also needs to be adjusted, either on the lens or on the camera, depending on the manufacturer.

The image opposite shows the type of situation where the fast maximum aperture of f/1.8 comes into its own. Although taken on a tripod at settings of 1/3 sec at f/8 with an ISO of 100, on

LENS CONSTRUCTION

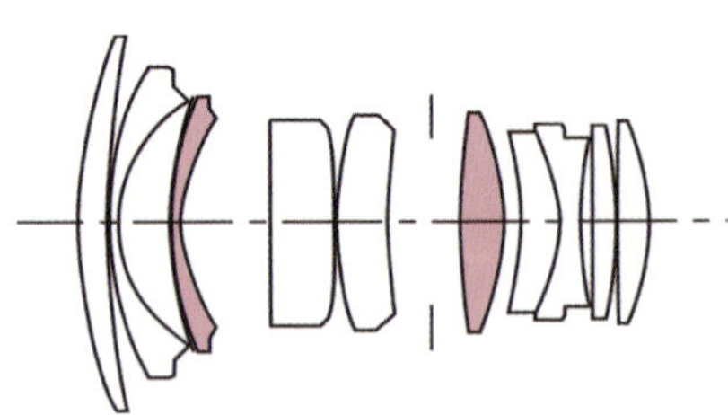

Aspherical lens

a different day, this image could have been captured handheld at 1/125 sec at f/1.8 and ISO 200. At those settings, the worst-case scenario would have

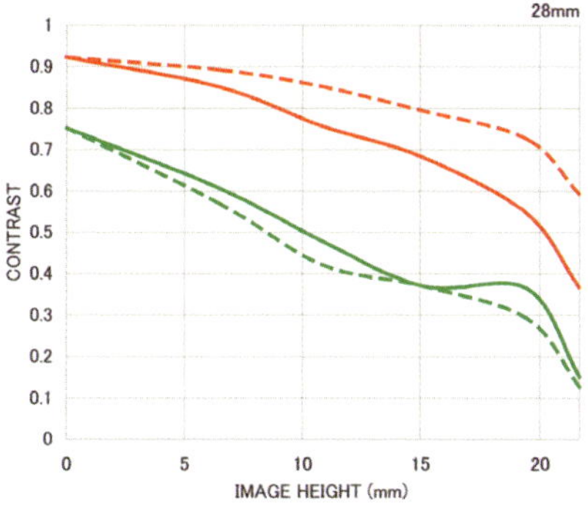

stretched the depth of field from 12m (39ft) into the far distance by focusing at infinity, losing depth of field only in the rather unimportant and badly lit foreground. Using the hyperfocal focusing technique, depth of field would actually have been much better than that.

Verdict

Not the widest of fixed focal length wide-angles for full-frame, perhaps, but this lens could easily serve as a standard lens on a crop-sensor body. Its maximum aperture of f/1.8 is especially useful in low light, when a higher shutter speed than normal might be needed, or when foreground can be dispensed with due to a higher viewpoint. If you can't exclude the foreground, make sure its lack of sharpness is obviously deliberate and that the main subject matter is more than 10–12m (33–39ft) away, as shown in the image on page 99.

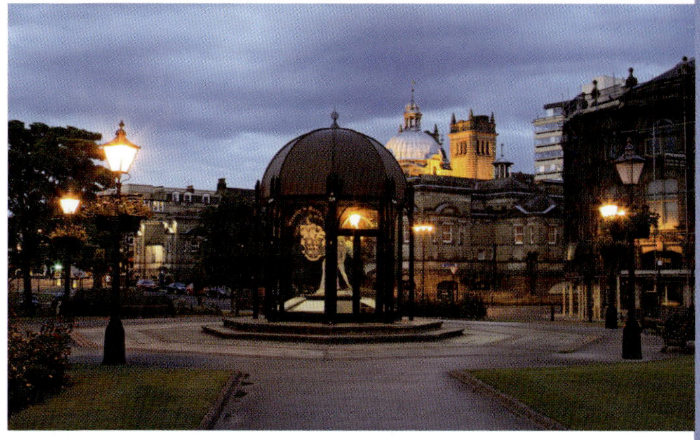

LOW LIGHT
With a maximum aperture of f/1.8, this lens is particularly useful in low-light situations, though depth of field in the foreground may suffer.

Depth of field (m): 28mm f/1.8 EX DG ASP at 12mm

Circle of confusion: 0.3333mm

Focused at	Aperture	1.8	2.8	4	5.6	8	11	16	22
0.2m	Near	0.20	0.20	0.20	0.20	0.20	0.19	0.19	0.19
	Far	0.20	0.20	0.20	0.20	0.20	0.21	0.21	0.21
0.3m	Near	0.30	0.30	0.30	0.29	0.29	0.28	0.27	0.26
	Far	0.30	0.30	0.31	0.31	0.32	0.32	0.34	0.35
0.5m	Near	0.49	0.48	0.47	0.46	0.45	0.43	0.41	0.38
	Far	0.51	0.52	0.53	0.55	0.57	0.61	0.67	0.78
1m	Near	0.94	0.91	0.87	0.83	0.78	0.71	0.64	0.56
	Far	1.08	1.12	1.18	1.27	1.44	1.78	2.68	10.89
infinity	Near	11.92	7.87	5.59	3.98	2.84	2.03	1.46	1.06
	Far	inf	inf	inf	inf	inf	inf	inf	inf

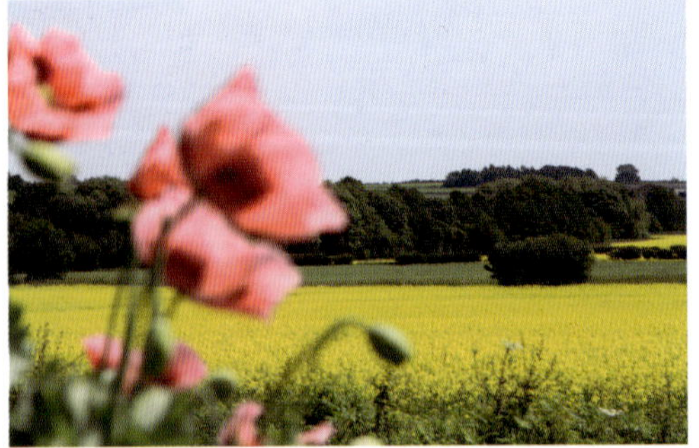

FOREGROUND BLUR
In this image, I compensated for the loss of depth of field in the foreground by creating an attractive blur with the flowers.

Note
Identical figures above indicate that incremental differences are smaller than the units shown. For example, identical figures of 0.20m for near and far at f/8 indicate that the difference is less than 1/100 meter, or 1cm (0.4in), when rounded up or down to two decimal places.

30mm f/1.4 EX DC HSM ASP

Lens construction: 7 elements in 7 groups
Angle of view: 45°
Diaphragm blades: 8
Min. aperture: f/16
Min. focusing distance: 40cm (15.7in)
Max. magnification: 1:10.4
Filter: 62mm
Dimensions: 76.6mm (W) × 59mm (L)
(3in × 2.3in)
Weight: 430g (15.1oz)
Mounts (HSM): Sigma, Canon, Nikon (D), Four Thirds
Mounts (non-HSM): Sony, Pentax

Note: The appearance of lenses may differ depending on the camera mount.

If there is one lens in the Sigma range that is suited to street photography, this is it. Compact and discreet, it won't attract attention, and its HSM-powered autofocus is as fast and quiet as you could wish for. In addition, this lens excels when used at its maximum aperture in poor light.

Its combination of aspherical lens elements and Extraordinary Low Dispersion and Special Low Dispersion glass delivers sharp images with excellent contrast and well-controlled chromatic aberration.

LENS CONSTRUCTION

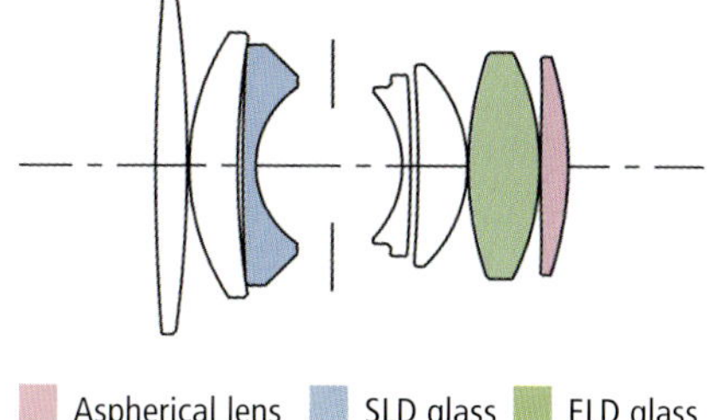

The HSM version also features full-time manual override of the focusing when in AF mode.

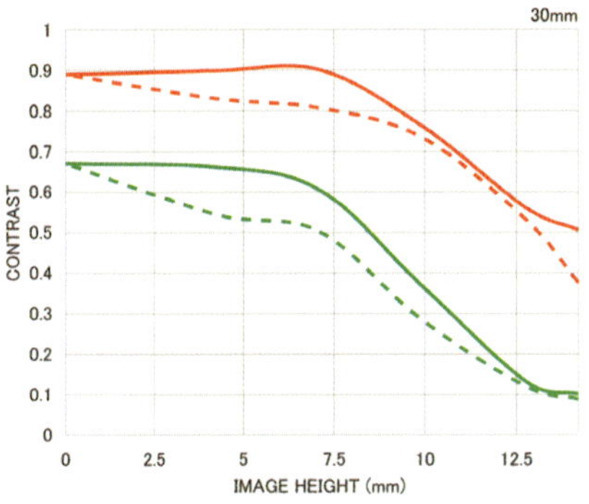

Verdict

Although the MTF chart suggests a steady fall-off in performance toward the edges of the frame, this is one of those lenses that performs noticeably better in "real life" than in tests. If your interest is in huge enlargements of landscapes, townscapes, or seascapes, you might well consider the alternatives, but if you want to get out on the streets shooting reportage images at all times of the day or night, you need look no farther.

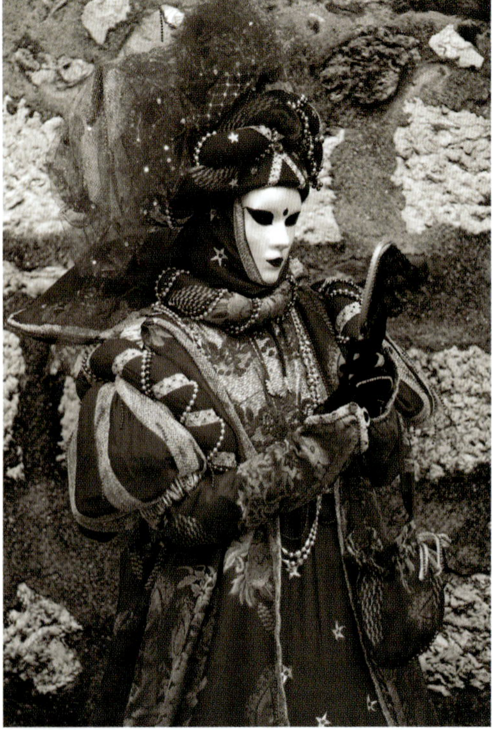

CARNIVAL

On a dreary day in February, the annual Venetian Carnival in Annecy, France, demanded extensive use of f/1.4, as the ambient light was extremely poor and flash would have created burnt-out highlights, especially on the mask.

50mm f/1.4 EX DG HSM ASP

Specifications (based on Sigma mount)

Lens construction: 8 elements in 6 groups
Angle of view: 46.8°
Diaphragm blades: 9
Min. aperture: f/16
Min. focusing distance: 45cm (17.7in)
Max. magnification: 1:7.4
Filter: 77mm
Dimensions: 84.5mm (W) × 68.2mm (L)
(3.3in × 2.7in)
Weight: 505g (17.8oz)
Mounts (HSM): Sigma, Canon, Nikon (D), Sony (D), Pentax, Four Thirds

Note: The appearance of lenses may differ depending on the camera mount.

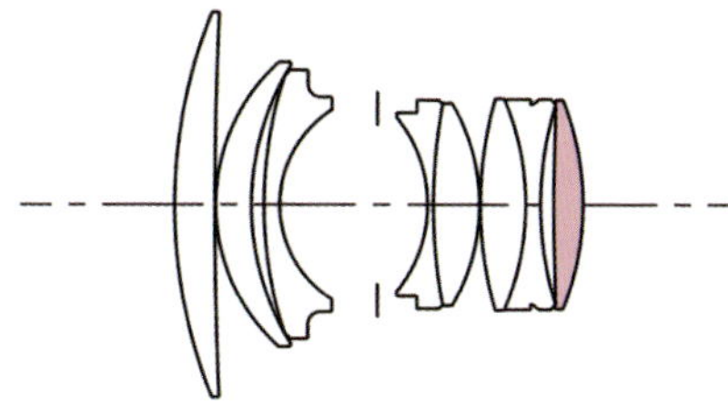

Sigma's fast, full-frame "standard" lens faces fierce competition from the camera manufacturers themselves, not least in terms of price. Both the Canon and Nikon versions are cheaper, the latter especially so, and I consider Canon's version to be unbeatable on the quality front. Both the Nikon and Canon models are also considerably lighter in weight than this lens, and use smaller filters. That said, the Sigma 50mm f/1.4 is still a joy to use.

If you prefer using lenses that feel substantial and well-made, with enough weight to provide the

LENS CONSTRUCTION

Aspherical lens

inertia that leads to less camera shake, you will almost certainly like this lens. Canon's website, incidentally, describes their own version of this lens as "robust," but it isn't a patch on the Sigma version in that respect. When it's mounted on the camera, it sits beautifully in the hand. Sigma's trademark rubber grip on the focusing ring provides sensitive fingertip control if you want to use manual focus or override the AF using the full-time manual focusing provided by the hypersonic motor (HSM).

The benefits of a shallow depth of field can be explored to the full with this lens. The maximum aperture of f/1.4 provides extremely

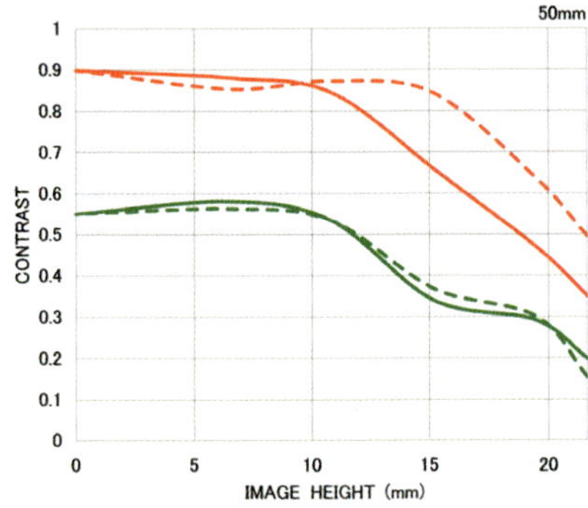

KEYBOARD
The maximum aperture of f/1.4 (below) gives very shallow depth of field. Compare this with the same setup at f/16 (opposite).

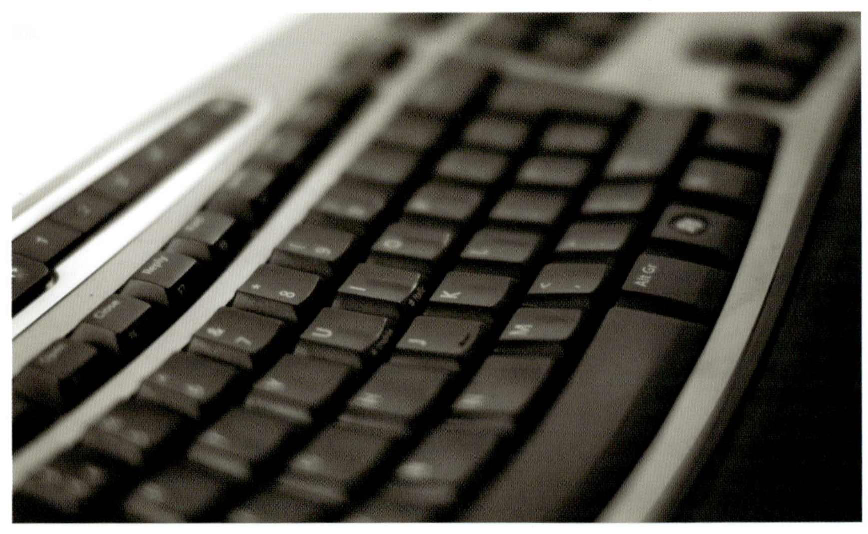

shallow depth of field (see images below) and lovely out-of-focus backgrounds for portraits.

Of course, on an APS-C camera body this lens has the same field of view (80mm at 1.6×) as the perennially popular full-frame portrait lenses. In addition, anyone stepping up from a slow zoom lens will be amazed at just how bright a viewfinder image is provided by such a fast lens, making it an excellent choice for low-light photography.

Autofocus in low light, and more importantly in low-contrast situations in low light, is fairly dependable, but it is all too easy to expect too much of fast lenses like this one. Because we can see so much more, and more clearly, in the viewfinder, we expect the lens/camera combination to "see" better too. However, there is always a limit to improved performance.

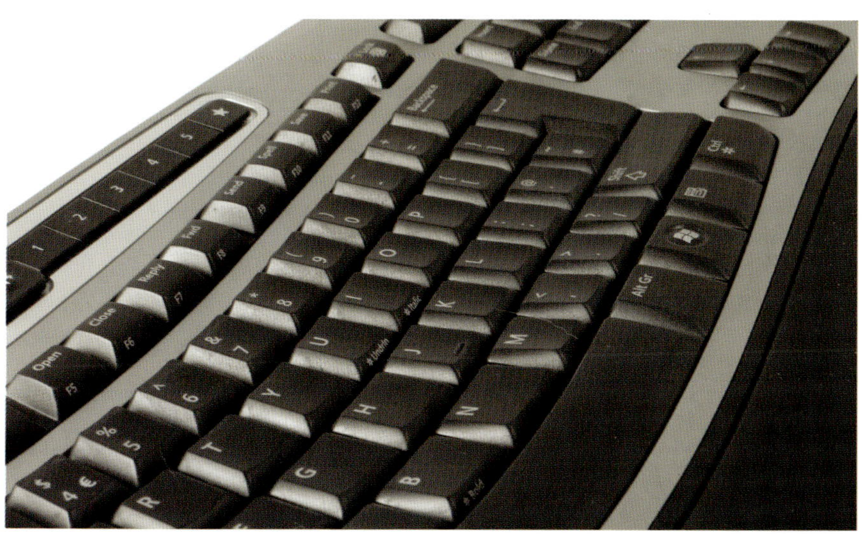

Photographing events

There is nothing quite as challenging, and therefore as rewarding when you are successful, as photographing events. In general, the time to set up your equipment, ponder the techniques you will use, and the wait until the light is just perfect, simply isn't there in the same way that it can be with landscape photography. Instead, event photography relies much more on intuition and the ability to seize the moment.

Equipment

Some degree of forethought is possible, though, starting with the decision about the equipment you will carry. Press photographers at major events will generally be seen carrying at least two camera/lens combinations, and often three—and it isn't because they enjoy carrying all that weight around. It's because many events offer opportunities for every type of lens, from fisheyes to mammoth telephotos. The average professional snapper at a major event will consequently have a small fortune hanging around his neck and off his shoulders—probably in the region of $30,000 (£20,000), or even more. Much of that cost will come in the form of top-of-the-range camera bodies and the fastest lenses money can buy. The good

news is that these are not essential requirements, though a single fast lens—even if it is an inexpensive f/1.8 standard or slightly wide lens—is always a good idea for when the light really fails.

Which lenses to choose will be determined largely by prior knowledge of how close to the action you can get. If you are able to mix with people, then a fairly wide angle—24mm full-frame, for example—is good for both crowd scenes and close-ups that accentuate the foreground. On a sunny day you will be able to work at ISO 100 and 1/500 at f/8, which will provide lots of depth of field and an adequate shutter speed. If you don't own a 1.4× or 2× converter, the longest focal length you use will almost certainly be the longest you own.

It is the standard to medium telephoto focal lengths that cause the most consternation, which is why manufacturers such as Sigma produce such a wide variety. If you can manage without Optical Stabilization, probably the best all-rounder is the 70–200mm f/2.8 II EX DG Macro, because it offers superb quality at maximum aperture, close focusing to a magnification ratio of 1:3.5, and it can take either the 1.4× or 2× converter into the bargain without sacrificing AF functionality. Although both Optical Stabilization and a fast maximum aperture are the ideal for photographing sporting events, and especially motorsports, if you have to choose one or the other, go for the fast maximum aperture, as this will be necessary for capturing fast-moving action. Hopefully, one day soon Sigma will add OS to the 70–200mm—enough people are certainly crying out for it.

Viewpoints

Whatever kit you decide to carry, the single most important factor is, in fact, your choice of viewpoints. This will determine how your images will stack up against all the other shots taken at the same event.

I remember vividly a busload of tourists at a famous landmark in Scotland. Being tourists, they each had a camera. Being completely unimaginative, they all filed off the coach, lined up against its side, and every one of them took an identical picture. Point taken?

Having determined several possible viewpoints in advance, usually in relation to the sun and always with the background in mind, it is important to investigate early on in the proceedings whether the reality matches up to the theory. Events that take place over the course of several days will make your life a lot easier. Any time you invest in checking out vantage points on the first day—provided

PIT STOP
Take the time to thoroughly scout your location and, if you're lucky, the good shots will fall into your lap.

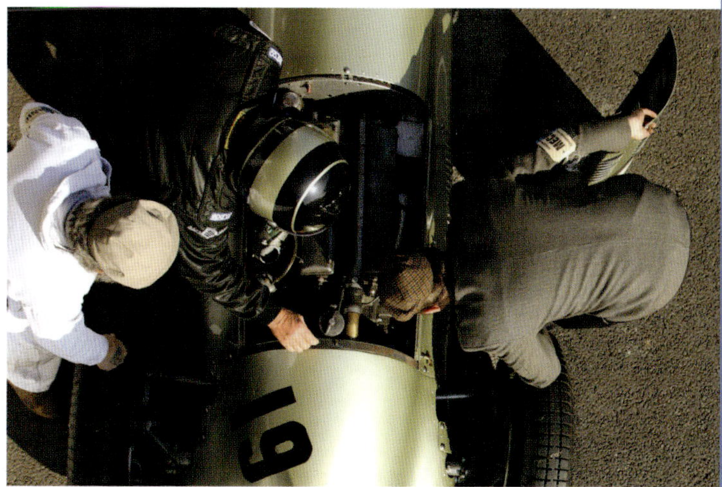

the weather holds, of course—will prove extremely valuable on the subsequent days.

Once you are in situ, ignore what others around you are doing and stick to your own plan of action. When capturing the horse racing scene below, I was the subject of some quizzical looks from all the photographers around me, who were using long telephotos. My 10–20mm lens was tiny by comparison, but I was the only one who captured an image like the one shown below.

Of course, sometimes fortune favors the brave. Having managed to attain a better viewpoint than other photographers at the same event, the motor racing image on the previous page just unfolded directly below me, and I know that no one else caught it because I was the only one there with a camera.

Community events can be just as much fun as major sporting events, but the same rule applies: viewpoint is everything. After that, it is a matter of intuition and technique, both of which will improve with practice.

The image opposite was one of a series taken when the Queen visited a tiny village that lies within her Duchy of Lancaster estate, at the time of her 80th birthday. It has been published several times, cropped in several different ways, and it makes the point that the spectators can be just as vital an ingredient as the principal characters.

HORSE RACING
Viewpoint is all: this striking image was captured using a diminutive 10–20mm lens.

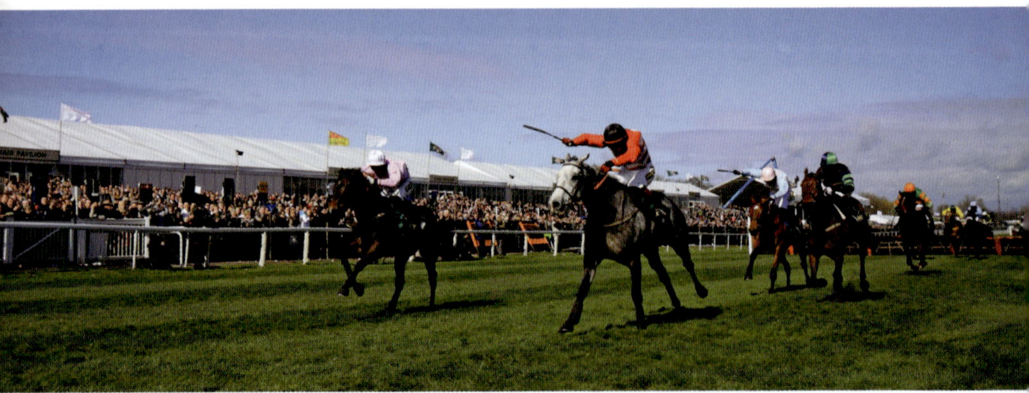

When framing an image, the supporting cast are often just as important as the major players.

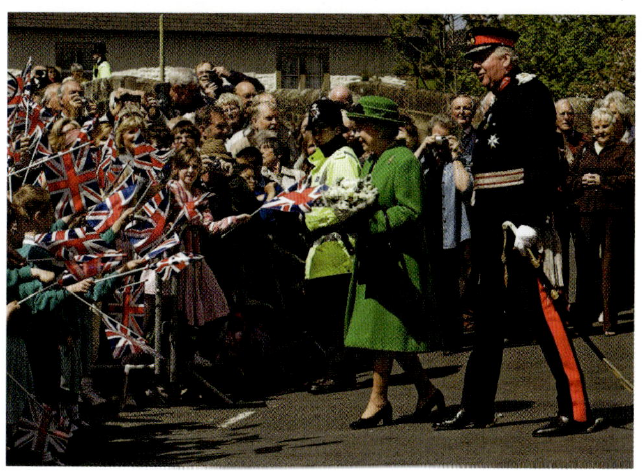

It isn't always possible to find that special viewpoint, of course, and one of the easiest types of event to photograph in this regard is an airshow. If you are used to mounting a longish lens on a monopod, you need to give some thought to the style of tripod ring you use. All lenses with a tripod ring are easily switched from landscape format to portrait (vertical) format if you leave the retaining nut a little slack. But shots of a flypast will almost certainly require you to take the camera and lens off the monopod. In this case, the hinged tripod ring of certain lenses can be opened completely, leaving the tripod ring on the monopod while quickly freeing up the camera and lens. Others, however, require the camera to be separated from the lens before the tripod ring can be removed, costing precious time.

Data storage

One parting shot, so to speak, is reserved for data storage. Do not underestimate how many memory cards you will require, especially if you're shooting at maximum file sizes. Shooting in excess of 500 images per day at a major event is easily done when using continuous drive and/or bracketing. Of course, if you have the facility for wireless file transfer to a laptop stored in a safe place, this isn't an issue. Otherwise you will require a good stock of memory cards or a portable storage device onto which you can periodically download your images.

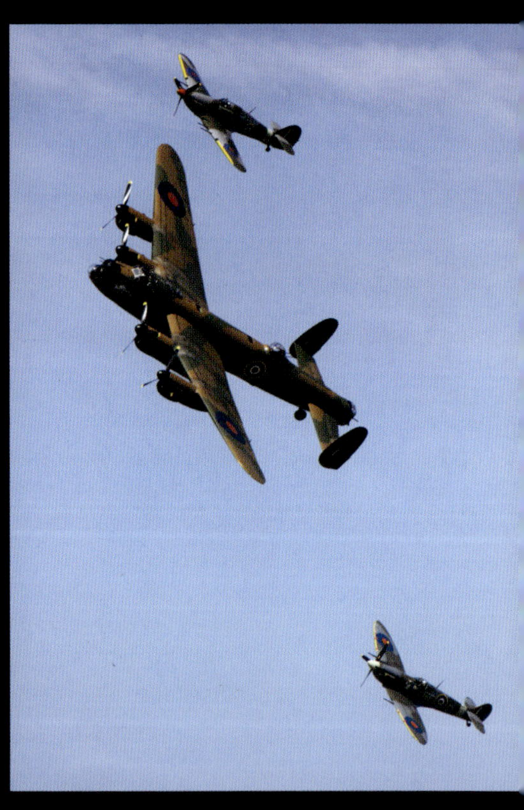

BATTLE OF BRITAIN FLIGHT
A Hurricane and Spitfire accompany the last airworthy Lancaster bomber in an airshow over southern England.

Settings
Focal length: 300mm
ISO: 200
Aperture: f/3.5
Shutter: 1/8000

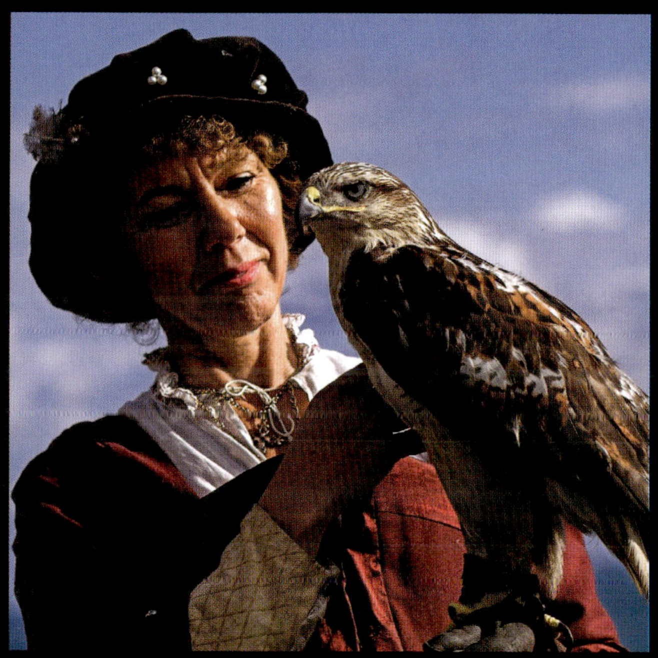

PECKING ORDER

When photographing events in which any kind of partnership exists—whether between man and machine or man and beast—it is important to demonstrate that relationship. This portrait of Wilhelmina, a ferruginous eagle native to the USA and bred in captivity in the UK, and her owner Sue Headon, is a good example. The ferocity of the eagle's stare is counterbalanced by Sue's tender stroking of its plumage, highlighting the close relationship between them.

Settings

Focal length: 85mm
ISO: 100
Aperture: f/4
Shutter: 1/2500

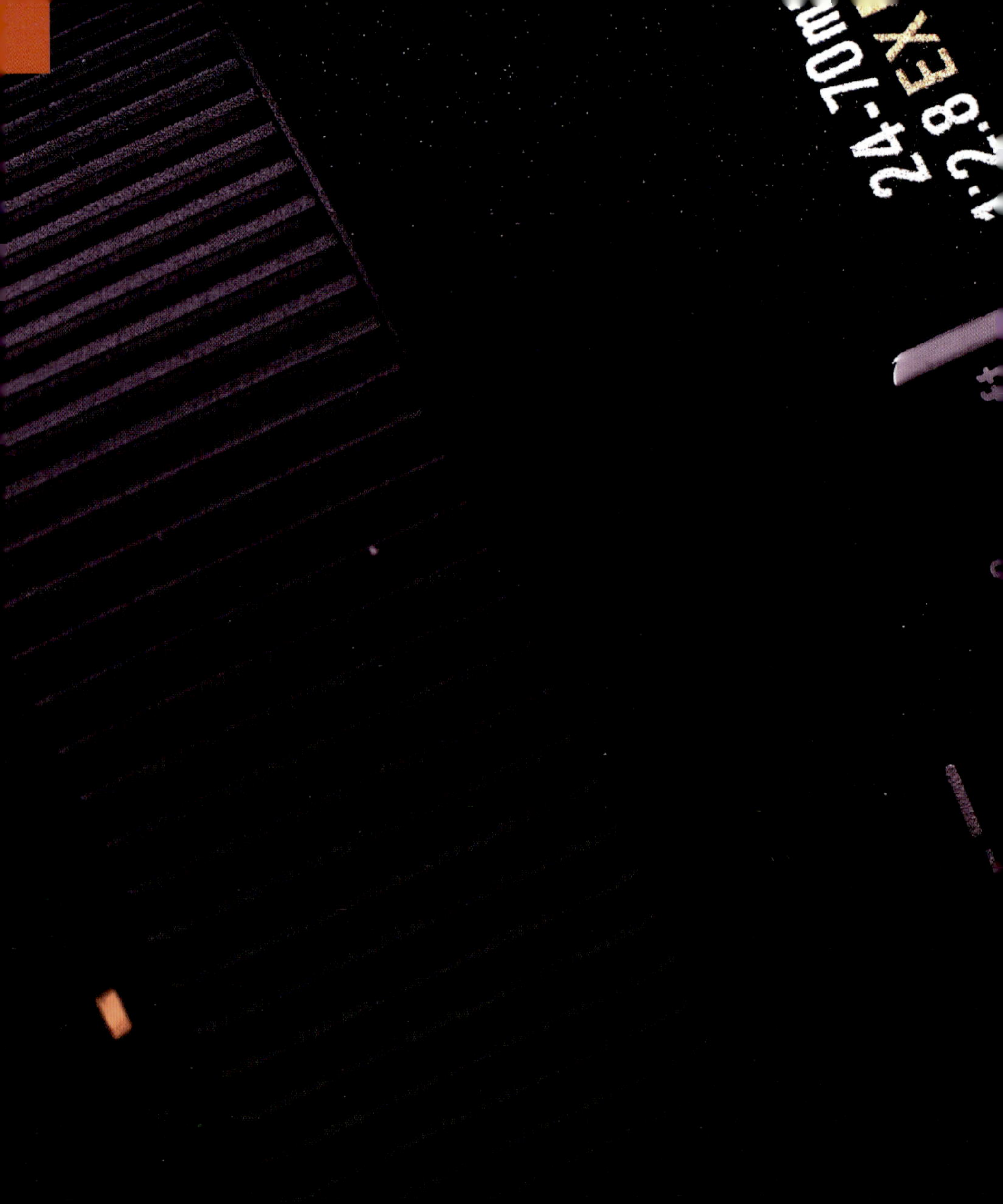

Chapter 6

A popular medley

This chapter covers a range of lenses, and indeed subject matter, that occupies what might be termed the middle ground. Everyone has a favorite zoom length, but remaining within your comfort zone can restrict the development of your photographic potential. This is a good place to start examining other possibilities.

Viewpoint and perspective

Most amateur photographers tend to shoot from a standing position. A far better approach is to put yourself on the same level as the subject. This benefits both the image and the relationship between photographer and subject, as it puts both on the same level, metaphorically and literally. This works especially well with smaller children. It is also important that the subject looks natural and engrossed in what they are doing. For this reason alone, I often capture the shot first and then ask the subject for permission. They rarely object.

Your choice of lens and perspective depends on the extent to which you wish your photography to be candid. A longer focal length gives you extra working distance so you can capture that natural look, but at the cost of the immediacy that comes from shooting close in with a wide-angle lens. A longer lens with a fast maximum aperture will also allow you to blur the background, which helps to minimize distractions and focus attention on the subject.

If, however, you favor using the wide-angle approach, then you will probably also need to develop one particular post-processing skill, that of cropping the image in order to remove minor distractions around the edge of the frame.

Photography and the law

With candid photography, you must always make sure you are aware of local restrictions relating to privacy, harrassment, and photographing people in a public place. It is always worth asking the subject's permission, retrospectively if need be, and explaining how the image will be used. Remember that in many countries, a person's image cannot be used to endorse a product unless a professionally worded model release has been signed.

In many parts of the world, taking photographs of the police, the armed forces, or sensitive locations could be classified as recording information that might be of use to terrorists. Photographing such subjects is not advised unless you have the full backing of an appropriate news agency.

24–70mm f/2.8 EX DG Macro ASP

Specifications (based on Sigma mount)

Lens construction: 14 elements in 13 groups
Angle of view: 34.3°–84.1°
Diaphragm blades: 9
Min. aperture: f/32
Min. focusing distance: 40cm (15.7in)
Max. magnification: 1:3.8
Filter: 82mm
Dimensions: 88.7mm (W) × 115.5mm (L)
(3.5in × 4.5in)
Weight: 715g (25.2oz)
Mounts: Sigma, Canon, Nikon (D), Sony (D), Pentax

Note: The appearance of lenses may differ depending on the camera mount.

With so many lenses available with moderate to huge zoom ranges, you might ask why this particular lens should stand out. The obvious answer is that, by keeping its functions relatively simple, it is able to perform them extremely well and at a consistently wide aperture. The widest zoom setting of 24mm still gives a broad view of sweeping vistas such as the one shown on page 118, which can be captured at f/2.8 in poor light or if shooting on a windy day demands a much higher shutter speed than normal. The inset image was shot at 70mm, though not from exactly the same position.

LENS CONSTRUCTION

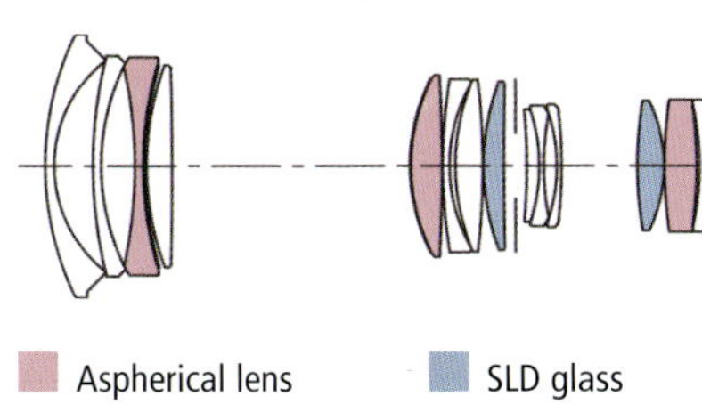

This lens utilizes Sigma's "clutch" mechanism, in which the focus ring is pulled or pushed to change from autofocus to manual focus, in addition to the AF/MF switch on the lens (for Sigma and Canon versions)

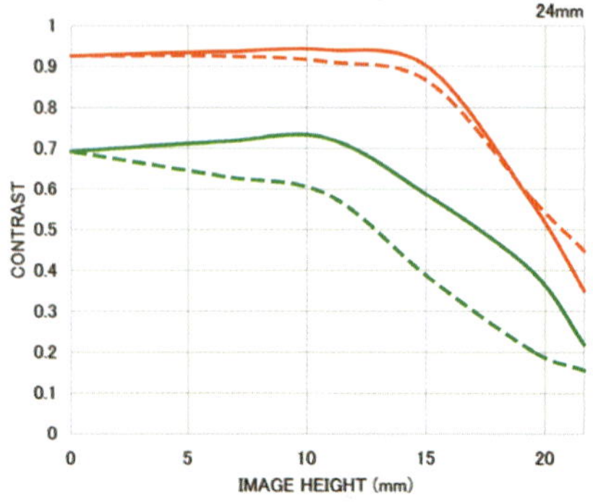

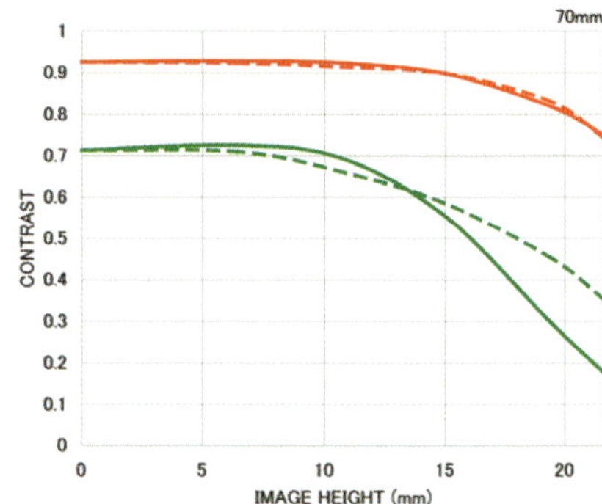

or the camera body. Note that even when the clutch mechanism is set to manual focus, if the AF/MF switch is still set to autofocus, the focusing ring will rotate, which could cause damage to the lens motor.

On an APS-C camera, the 70mm setting narrows the field of view sufficiently for some quite tight framing, if you can move a few steps nearer to your subject. Taking those few extra steps should become an ingrained habit, rather than relying on the zoom ring to allow you to stay where you are.

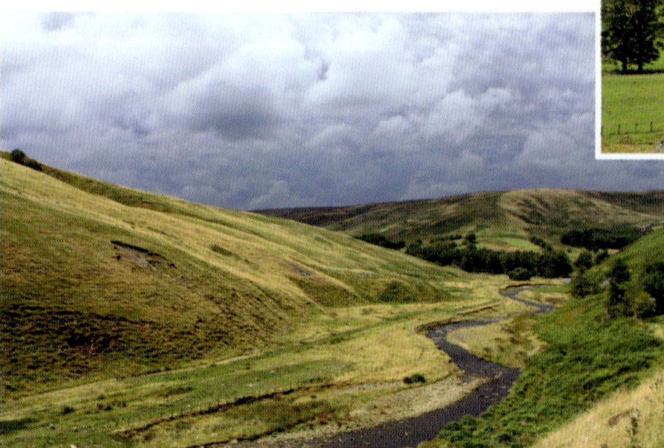

VISTA
This lens offers a broad view over a wide range of settings, from 24mm (main) to 70mm (inset).

118

Verdict

A solidly built full-frame lens that offers excellent contrast and resolution, even at its widest aperture, and which excels when fitted to a crop-sensor body. Fine detail is extremely sharp when the lens is rotated to its 70mm zoom setting, making it ideal for male portraits on either full-frame or APS-C cameras. At 82mm, glass filters will prove a little expensive and it is worth considering a rectangular filter system that can be used on different filter mounts using adapter rings.

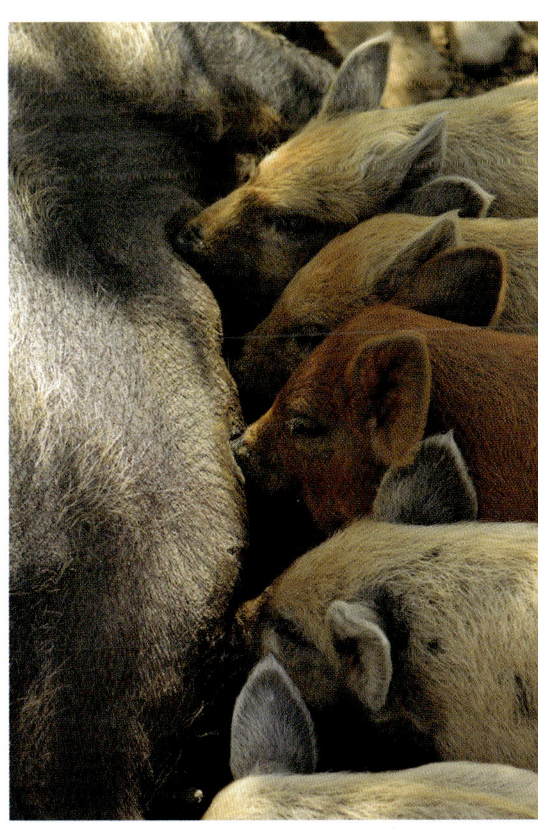

PIGLETS
The field of view narrows significantly at the 70mm setting on an APS-C camera.

24–70mm f/2.8 EX DG HSM IF ASP

Lens construction: 14 elements in 12 groups
Angle of view: 34.3°–84.1°
Diaphragm blades: 9
Min. aperture: f/22
Min. focusing distance: 38cm (15in)
Max. magnification: 1:5.3
Filter: 82mm
Dimensions: 88.6mm (W) × 94.7mm (L)
(3.5in × 3.7in)
Weight: 790g (27.9oz)
Mounts: Sigma, Canon, Nikon (D)*, Sony (D)*, Pentax*

*Camera body must support HSM for AF to work.

EISA European Lens 2009–2010

Note: The appearance of lenses may differ depending on the camera mount.

This is a delightful lens to use and, especially as it is relatively substantial in terms of weight, it feels very solidly made. Without the petal-shaped lens hood attached, the traditional EX matte finish is not especially evident, as most of the lens barrel is taken up by the non-slip focusing and zoom rings. The hood, as you might expect, can be reverse-mounted on the front of the lens for storage. Sharpness and contrast fare very

LENS CONSTRUCTION

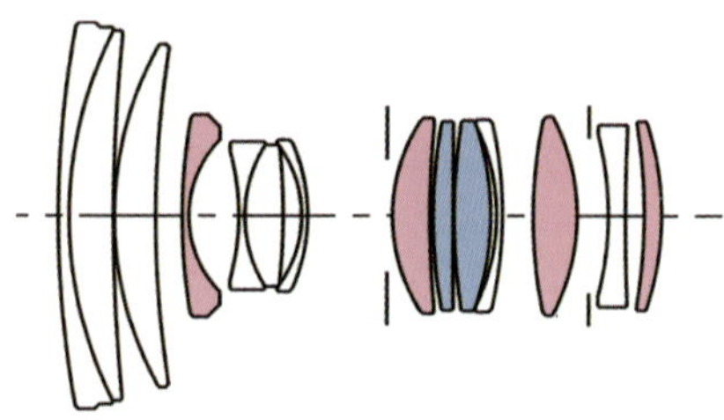

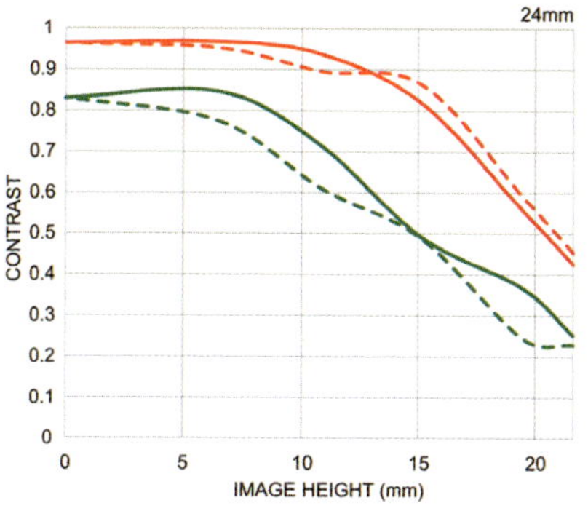

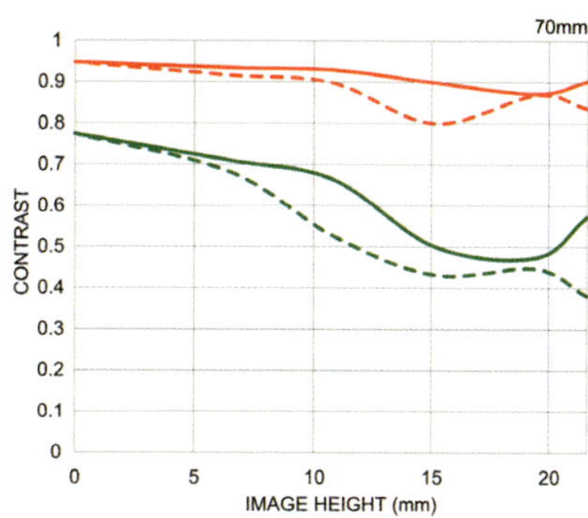

well throughout the zoom range and across all apertures, and the same characteristics are displayed equally at both 24mm and 70mm. In general, Sigma lenses have a tendency to perform better at the longer end of the zoom range, but as that range is quite limited on this particular lens, it isn't surprising that both wide and long zoom settings should be evenly matched.

Tested on a full-frame Canon body, center performance at 24mm was excellent at f/11 and even at f/2.8, though diffraction comes into play at f/22 with sharpness at the center dropping slightly to a subjective rating of very good.

Edge performance at 24mm matched center sharpness at f/22, but fell away slightly at f/11, though it was still extremely good. As for edge

sharpness at 24mm and f/2.8, we'll come back to that in a moment. At 70mm, both center and edge performance were very good at f/22, with f/11 showing excellent results right across the frame—the latter, in my opinion, being the optimum setting on a full-frame camera. Consistency of sharpness and contrast across the image, from the center to the edges and corners, is a tribute to Sigma's designers.

Testing edge performance at 24mm and f/2.8 raised an interesting phenomenon—one that I had not encountered before. On the lens I tested, center sharpness rated as excellent gradually gave way to a rating of very good, which was held consistently right up to a point about 4% of image width from the edge. At this point, sharpness dropped

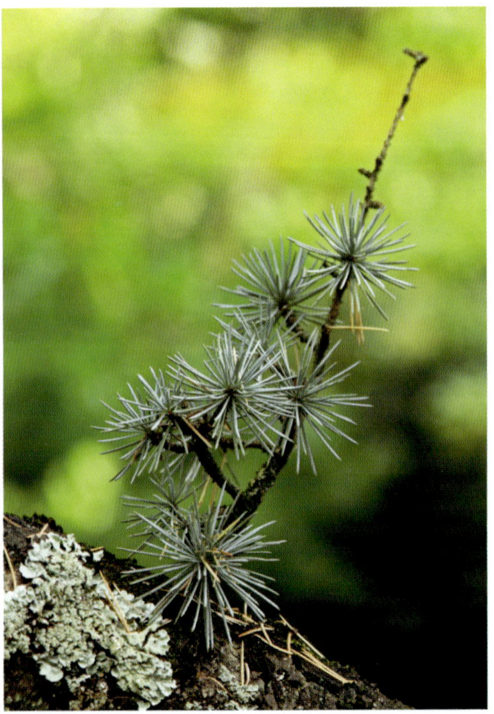

very suddenly to being soft for that last few percentage points of the overall width. Such a sudden transformation is quite unusual and isn't suggested by the MTF charts on page 121. However, it need not cause concern, as a full-frame camera is likely to produce such a large file that slight cropping will still leave a huge image at 350ppi. Obviously, with a crop-sensor body, this won't be an issue anyway.

LIMITS

Very few lenses behave perfectly in every situation, and it is always worth exploring the limits of a lens so that you can work to its strengths. Even with a lens that is soft at the edges, you can still obtain stunning images.

50–150mm f/2.8 II EX DC HSM IF APO CONV

Lens construction: 18 elements in 14 groups
Angle of view: 9.5°–27.9°
Diaphragm blades: 9
Min. aperture: f/22
Min. focusing distance: 100cm (39.4in)
Max. magnification: 1:5.3
Filter: 67mm
Dimensions: 76.3mm (W) x 140.2mm (L)
(3in × 5.5in)
Weight: 770g (27.2oz)
Mounts: Sigma, Canon, Nikon (D), Sony (D), Pentax

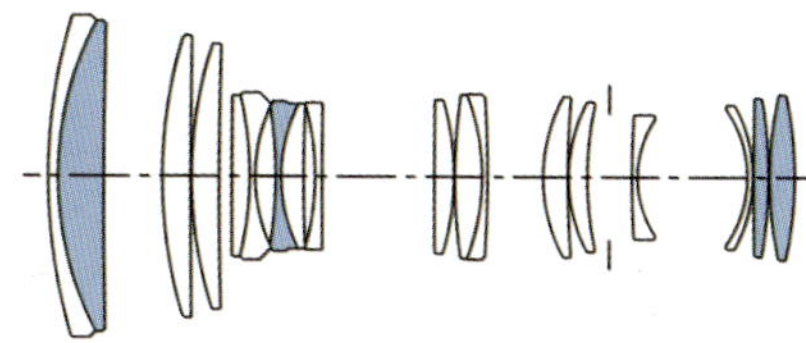

Note· The appearance of lenses may differ depending on the camera mount.

This is a simple and straightforward medium telephoto zoom for APS-C cameras, with a constant f/2.8 maximum aperture across the zoom range. It is an IF (inner focus) design so there is no lens extension, nor is there any when zooming. The front element does not rotate, so any type of filter or folder holder can be used, subject to the usual precautions concerning vignetting.

The zoom ring and the focusing ring are of equal width, with ribbed rubber grips that give a positive feel. The two grips are slightly different: the focusing ring at the front end of the lens has a narrower "tread."

LENS CONSTRUCTION

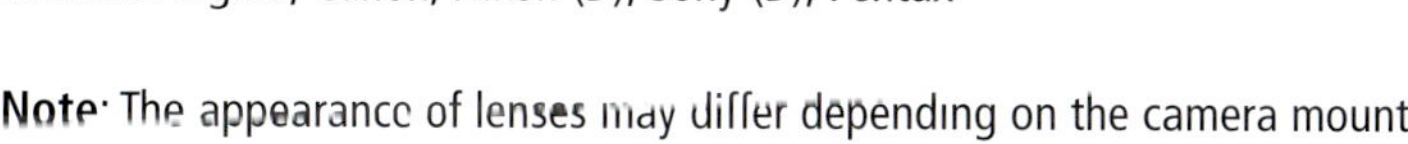

SLD glass

It may initially seem a disadvantage that this lens is longer and heavier than several other DC zooms that extend to greater focal lengths. Rest assured, it isn't—for several reasons. Its constant f/2.8 maximum aperture

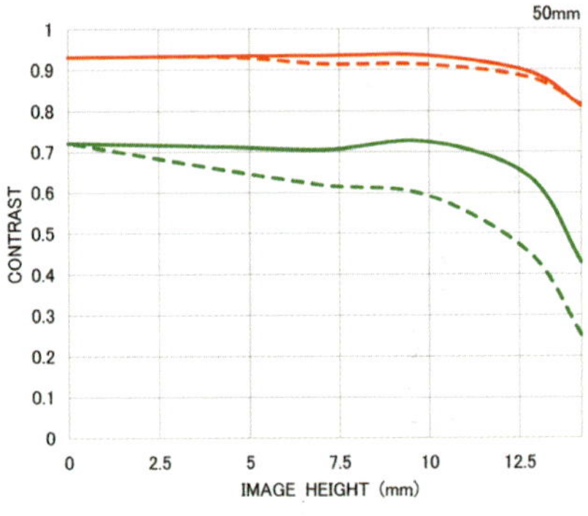

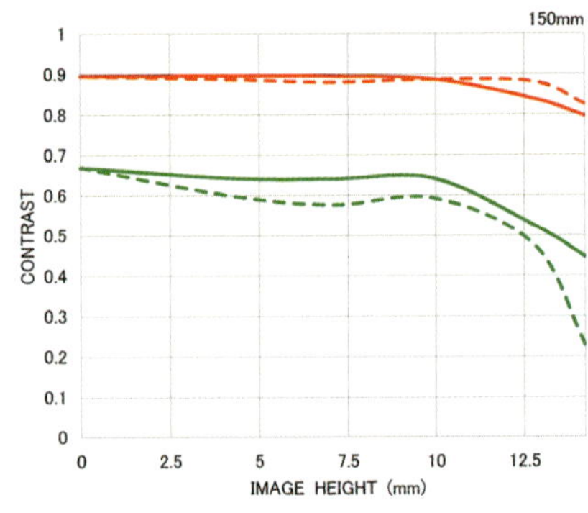

means a brighter viewfinder and consistent exposure across the zoom range, along with higher shutter speeds for action photos. Its contrast and resolution approach those of the excellent 150mm Macro. The out-of-focus background ("bokeh") that can be achieved with portraits is far better than that of longer, but slower zooms. And finally, this lens can accept both 1.4× and 2× converters, becoming either a 70–210mm f/4 or a 100–300mm f/5.6 in a moment without loss of autofocus.

ZOOM SETTINGS
These shots were taken at the 150mm (right) and 50mm settings (below).

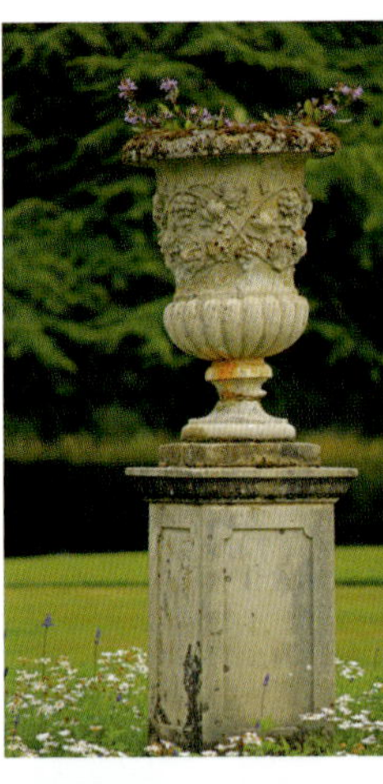

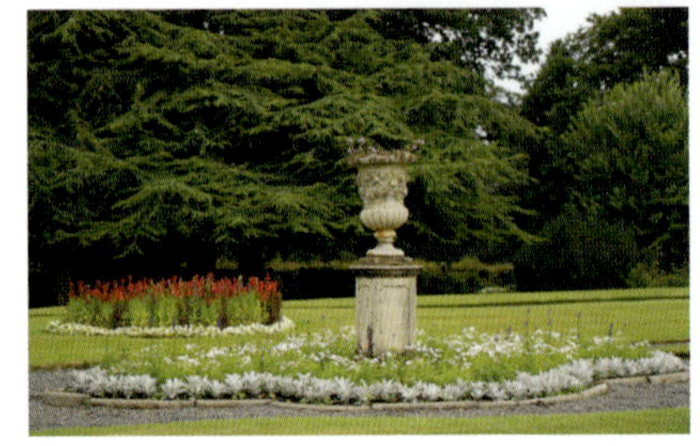

Verdict

A good choice for general-purpose photography, especially action and candid portraits, and particularly when paired with either of Sigma's two converters.

50–200mm f/4–5.6 DC OS HSM IF

Lens construction: 14 elements in 10 groups
Angle of view: 7.1°–27.9°
Diaphragm blades: 8
Min. aperture: f/22
Min. focusing distance: 110cm (43.3in)
Max. magnification: 1:4.5
Filter: 55mm
Dimensions: 74mm (W) × 102mm (L)
(2.9in × 4in)
Weight: 420g (14.8oz)
Mounts: Sigma, Canon, Nikon (D), Sony (D), Pentax*

*If Pentax body does not support HSM, autofocus will not function.

Note: The appearance of lenses may differ depending on the camera mount.

This is another new offering from Sigma and one that deserves some serious consideration. Physically, the lens is compact and relatively lightweight with a quality finish, despite not being an EX lens.

Handling and balance are good, though the supporting hand has to grip the zoom ring, as the focusing ring rotates during focusing. (The front element, however, does not rotate.) This issue can be a problem with many lenses when combined with certain camera bodies—and

LENS CONSTRUCTION

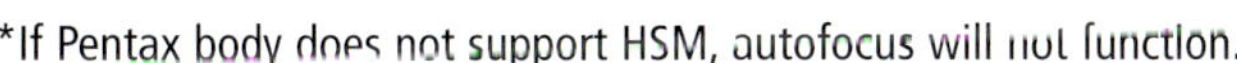

SLD glass

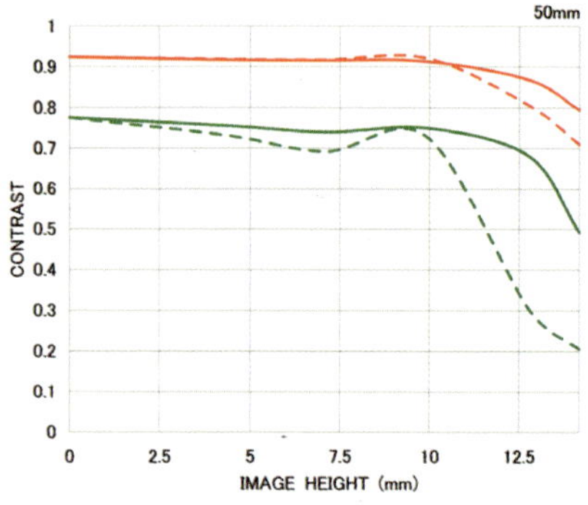

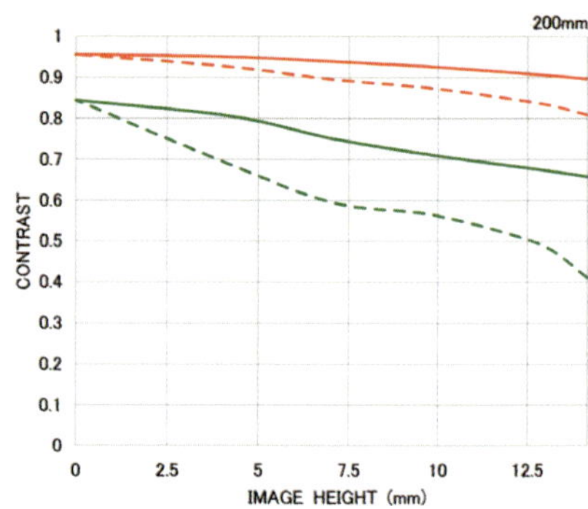

the blame has to be shared fairly equally between both camera and lens manufacturers. My own hands aren't particularly large, and I habitually use larger APS-C bodies (Canon EOS 40D and 50D) equipped with battery grips that

rarely pose handling issues, no matter which lens is used. This lens was also tested on the smaller EOS 500D, and the smaller body makes a huge difference. When supporting the lens close to the lens mount, the little finger and ring finger

OS AT 1/15 SECOND
In this image, a slow shutter speed blurred the flowing water.

OS AT 200mm
Tight framing and a sharp subject are easy to achieve with this lens.

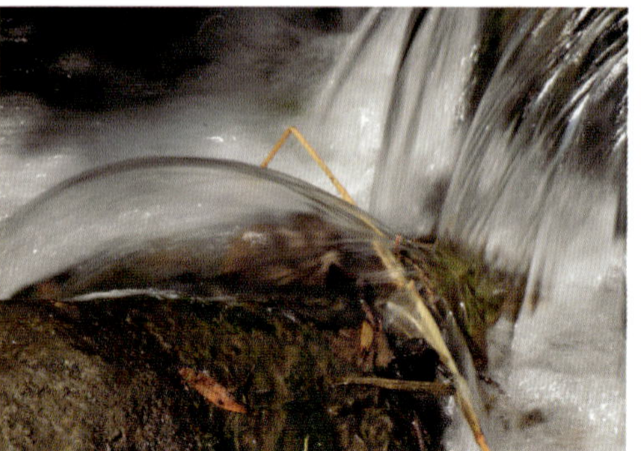

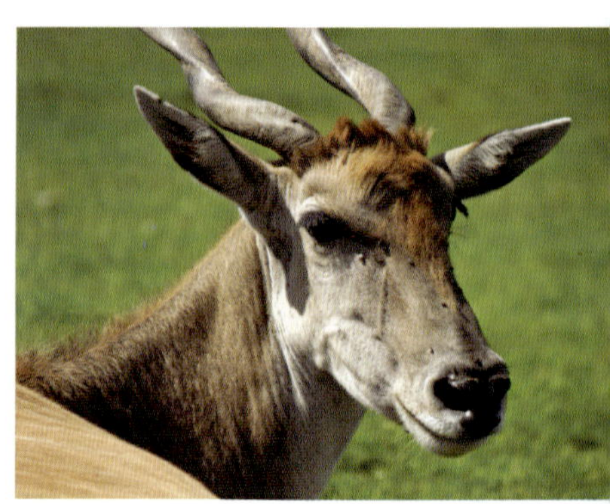

126

of the supporting hand regularly become entangled with the same two fingers of the right hand. The moral is this: take your camera body with you when shopping around and try before you buy.

However, it's important to focus on the positive attributes of this excellent lens. With only 25mm (1in) lens extension at 200mm, and no additional extension during focusing because of the IF design, the lens feels well balanced at all times. Both zoom and focusing rings work smoothly and provide non-slip rubber grips that permit fingertip control, while the AF/MF and OS switches have positive, firm click stops.

The four-stop optical stabilizer should, by rights, be the most impressive feature of this lens, but, good as it is, it is bettered by

the autofocus, which provided fast, accurate focus acquisition in astonishingly low-contrast, low-light situations without any sign of "hunting."

Verdict

Providing superb value for money, this lens outperformed expectations by a large margin. Coupled with the identically priced 18–50mm f/2.8–4.5 DC OS, it would meet the needs of many photographers who don't need a fast or full-frame lens or one that offers maximum image quality for bigger enlargements. Highly recommended in this price range.

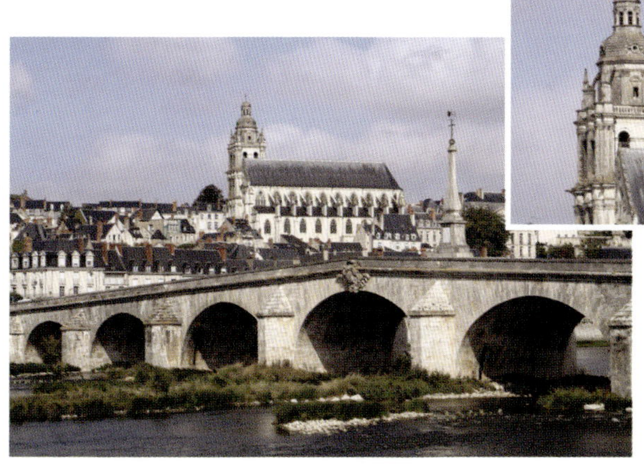

TRAVEL LENS
From townscapes at 50mm to isolating detail at 200mm, this is an extremely useful and lightweight zoom lens for traveling.

127

55–200mm f/4–5.6 DC HSM

Lens construction: 12 elements in 9 groups
Angle of view: 7.1°–25.5°
Diaphragm blades: 8
Min. aperture: f/22
Min. focusing distance: 110cm (43.3in)
Max. magnification: 1:4.5
Filter: 55mm
Dimensions: 71.5mm (W) x 87.1mm (L)
(2.8in × 3.4in)
Weight: 310g (10.9oz)
Mounts (HSM): Nikon (D)
Mounts (non-HSM): Sigma, Canon, Sony, Pentax, Four Thirds

Note: The appearance of lenses may differ depending on the camera mount.

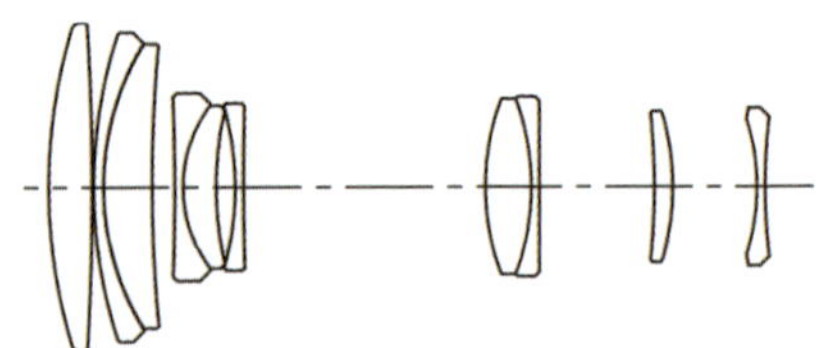

This is an extremely lightweight, compact, and portable lens. It is ideal for taking on vacation when you know that it will be sunny, or at least bright, so the slightly darker viewfinder that comes with using slower lenses isn't going to be an issue. Lens extension is only around 10mm (0.4in) at the minimum focusing distance, and when shifting from 55mm to the maximum 200mm, it is still only just over 3cm (1.2in), so you won't stand out in the crowd when capturing images of interesting characters in the local market.

LENS CONSTRUCTION

So, with such a lightweight lens and a very modest price tag, what sort of performance can you expect? Very consistent, is the answer. The lens performs better at the longer end of

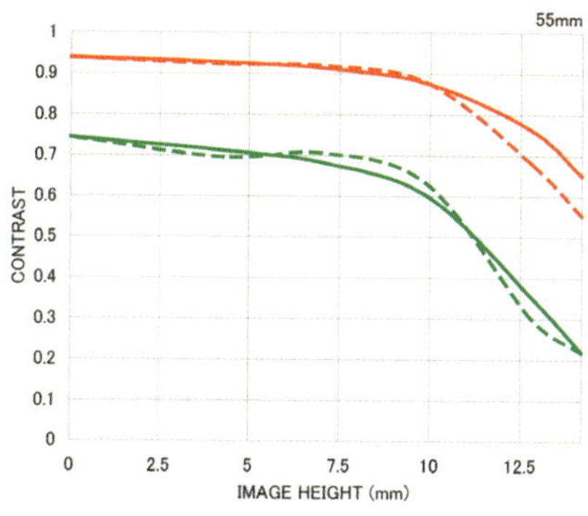

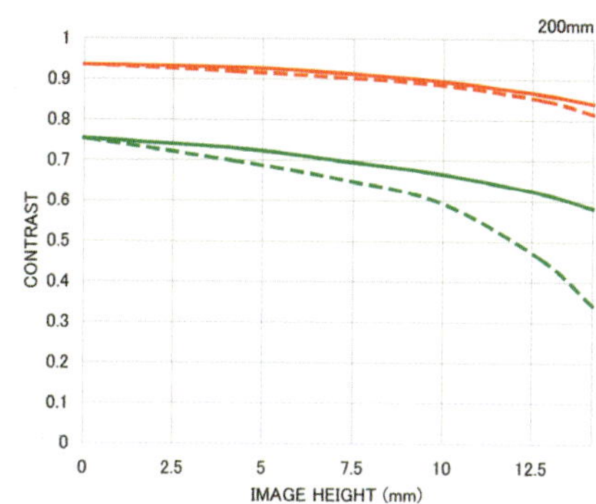

the zoom range than the wide end, which is not unusual. What is less common, however, is the provision of aperture settings down to f/32 at the 200mm end of the range (at the wide end, the minimum aperture is f/22). Used handheld, you will require a high ISO setting to make the most of f/32 in order to obtain a fast enough shutter speed to avoid camera shake.

Note that the lens rotates, which will affect the use of certain filters such as grads and polarizers.

Verdict

If your intention is to print regular enlargements of your holiday snaps and family outings, this compact yet flexible lens is good value for money —but you may want to increase the contrast parameter on your camera if you're shooting in anything less than bright sunlight. For the best results, position yourself so you can use a slightly longer focal length.

A POPULAR MEDLEY

70–200mm f/2.8 II EX DG Macro HSM IF APO CONV

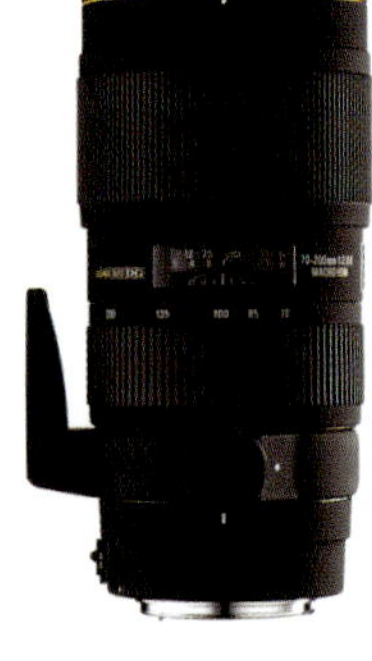

Specifications (based on Sigma mount)

Lens construction: 18 elements in 15 groups
Angle of view: 12.3º–34.3º
Diaphragm blades: 9
Min. aperture: f/22
Min. focusing distance: 100cm (39.4in)
Max. magnification: 1:3.5
Filter: 77mm
Dimensions: 86.6mm (W) × 184.4mm (L)
(3.4in × 7.2in)
Weight: 1345g (47.4oz)
Mounts: Sigma, Canon, Nikon (D), Sony (D)*,
Pentax (not SFX or SF7)*, Four Thirds

*Camera body must support HSM for AF to work.

Note: The appearance of lenses may differ depending on the camera mount.

This is the second generation of this lens and, having owned the first version, I needed no introduction to its merits. Optically, by making use of SLD and ELD glass, any aberrations are well corrected, and the Super Multi-Layer coating cuts right down on any possible flare. This is important in relation to the lens hood—of which more later. The 70–200mm f/2.8 sports the

LENS CONSTRUCTION

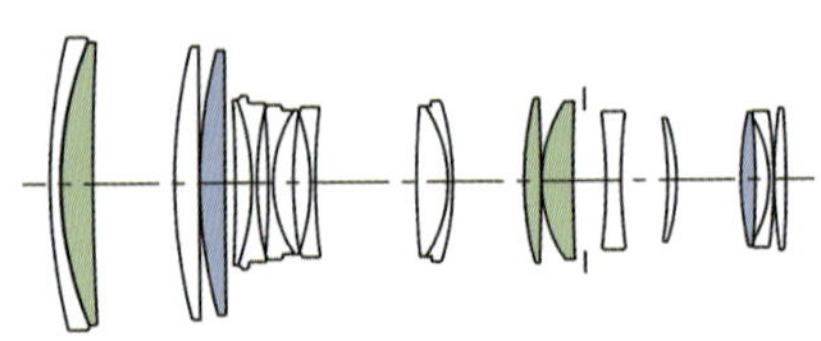

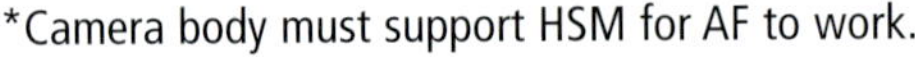

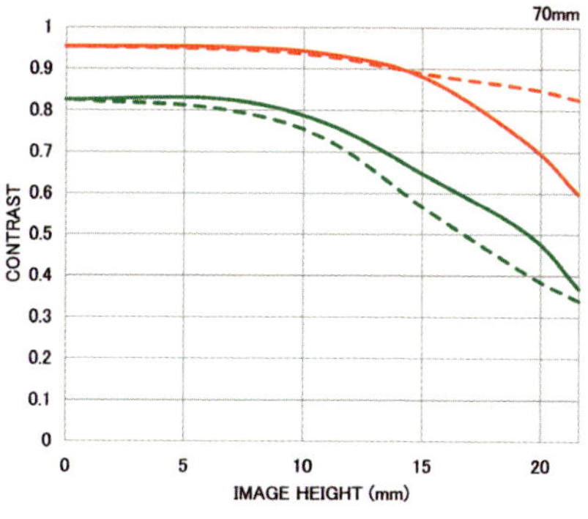

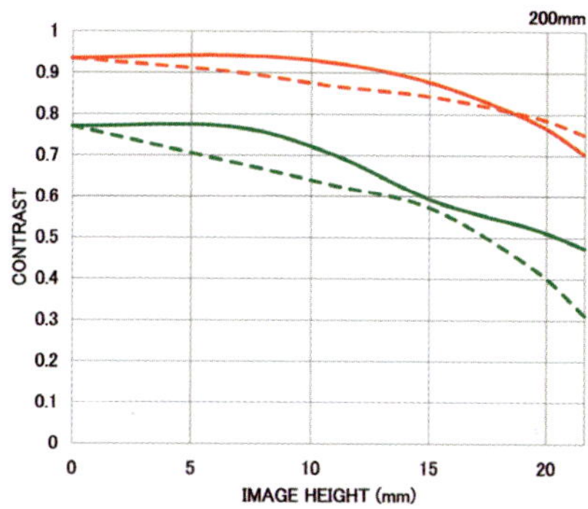

usual high-quality EX finish and is very well balanced, but there is a lot of glass encased in that lens barrel and the lens is therefore quite substantial in terms of weight. The ribbed rubber grips used for the zooming and focusing rings— both of which have just the right amount of resistance—make for very positive and confident handling. The AF/MF switch has a slightly longer travel than some of Sigma's other lenses and gives a very definite click when switching focus mode.

This lens is of IF design, so there is no lens extension when focusing and no rotation when using filters. The lens can easily be turned through 90° when using the

SHOW JUMPING
This shot was taken at the 200mm setting with the addition of a 1.4× teleconverter.

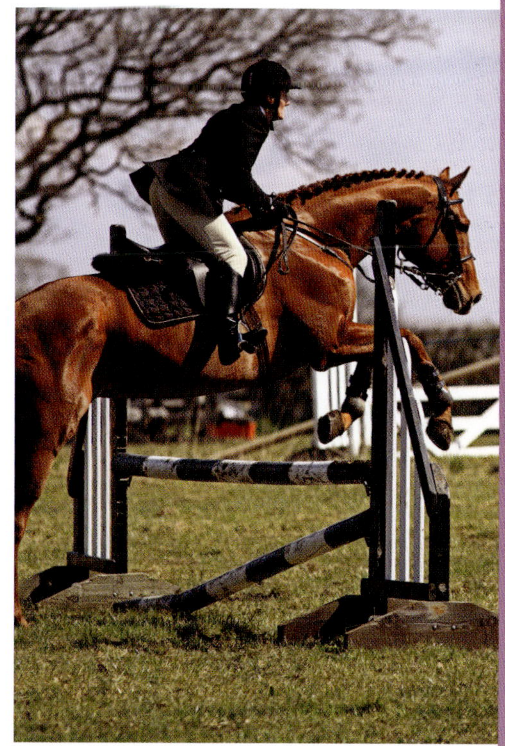

tripod collar (provided) on a tripod or monopod, and the lens barrel is marked with two white lines to line it up with the white line on the tripod collar for either landscape or portrait orientation.

Excellent images can be obtained even at the widest aperture, and even more so when the lens is used on a crop-sensor body, which will result in superb image quality when stopped down to f/4 or beyond. This means that in good light the 70–200mm f/2.8 can be used handheld with a low ISO rating and still produce publishing-quality images. For what is effectively, in terms of field of view, a 320mm f/2.8 at its longest focal length on an APS-C sensor body, that makes it a force to be reckoned with. It will also accept both 1.4× and 2× converters for a really long reach— but by this stage you will want to use some form of camera support.

Finally, the lens hood is deep and very effective, but I prefer to use the lens without it. For one thing, when it is reverse-mounted for storage, it obstructs your grip if you want to keep camera and lens ready for grab shots. But primarily, the extra length of the lens with the hood attached, especially if a converter is also being used, is just too much when juggling three bodies and their lenses, which is often the case with event photography. The hood also makes the lens look more imposing when shooting candids, and the advantage of a black telephoto lens, compared with a much more noticeable white lens if you're a Canon owner, tends to be lost. Without its hood and tripod collar, the lens makes it easier to melt into the background and the reach is long enough to be able to shoot candids from a little farther away in a crowded situation without being easily noticed.

Verdict

If you are keen on sports and event photography, this lens definitely warrants a place in your bag, along with a 1.4× converter, as you can confidently use it wide open, or almost so, to achieve great images. If you occasionally shoot close-ups, its 1:3.5 magnification and slightly longer working distance of 1m (3.3ft) to the focal plane is enough for subjects like butterflies—but if serious close-up work is your only requirement, it's perhaps not the ideal choice. In short, this is a superb lens for serious sports and events when high shutter speeds and wide apertures are the norm.

Photographing people

For many amateur photographers, the business of capturing people other than friends and family represents a significant hurdle at best and a complete mystery at worst. There are several reasons for this. First, the most popular subject for enthusiasts is undoubtedly landscapes—but with a definition of landscape photography that often excludes any human interaction with the land. Editorial photographers specializing in landscape work, on the other hand, regularly face tasks that include documenting conservation and changes in land management, so they often photograph people within the context of the landscape.

Second, photographing people tends to involve interaction with strangers, which often calls for a significant degree of confidence, both in oneself and in one's skill as a photographer. A lack of such confidence is a particular block when there is a need to manipulate the situation—the subject's pose, for example.

A third reason why many amateur photographers shy away from candid photography is because they are uncertain about their rights, the rights of the subject, and how images can and cannot be used. Of necessity, professionals have to cross these thresholds fairly early on. Thereafter, practice makes perfect.

The rich and famous

In all probability, most famous faces will be far more accustomed to being photographed than you can imagine —especially if they are appearing

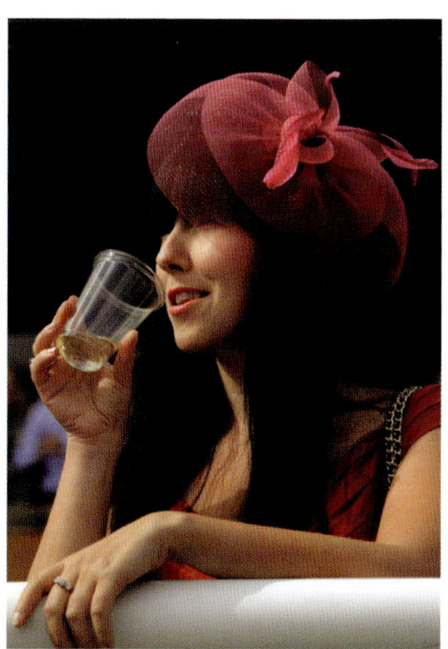

BACKDROP
If you are faced with elaborate detail, such as the hat in this image, try to place it against an uncluttered background.

at a public event. You are likely to be far more nervous than they are! It is always worthwhile capturing the obvious image, but also try to capture something slightly different, such as the unusual pose of a now elderly Sir Stirling Moss (right). I was enjoying privileged Press access to the area where this shot was captured, but it could easily have been shot by a member of the public from behind the fence.

One thing the rich and famous are unlikely to grant you is the time for a lengthy introduction and explanation of who you are and what you want. Frankly, they won't care who you are, and it's pretty obvious what you're after when you wave a camera in their face. Always sound respectful, but you can be brief and to the point: after all, they are expecting to be photographed.

Context

Isolating the subject from his or her environment, especially in travel photography, should only be done when the surroundings are detrimental to the desired effect of the image. Whenever possible, position the subject so that the viewer learns something about the subject's lifestyle. Compare the two images shown opposite. If the larger image had been a simple head and shoulders portrait, the image would have told us nothing about the subject's work or his position in society. In contrast, the second image, from a Venetian carnival, tells us a great deal about the situation and couldn't possibly have been taken at any other time, so a head and shoulders portrait was sufficient.

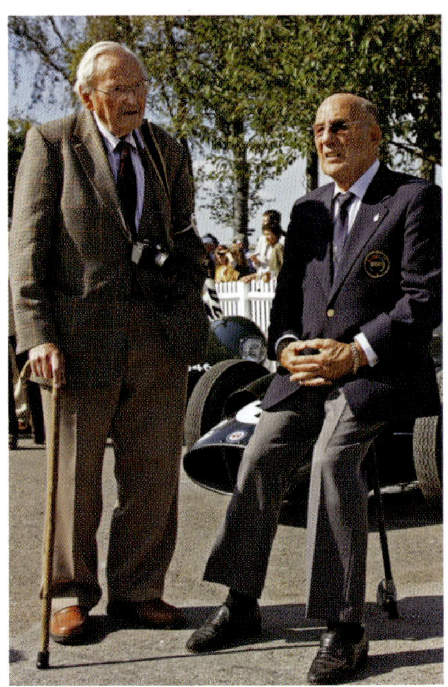

SIR STIRLING MOSS
Anyone can capture the most obvious images, so keep your eyes open for unusual situations such as this informal shot of the world-famous racing driver (right).

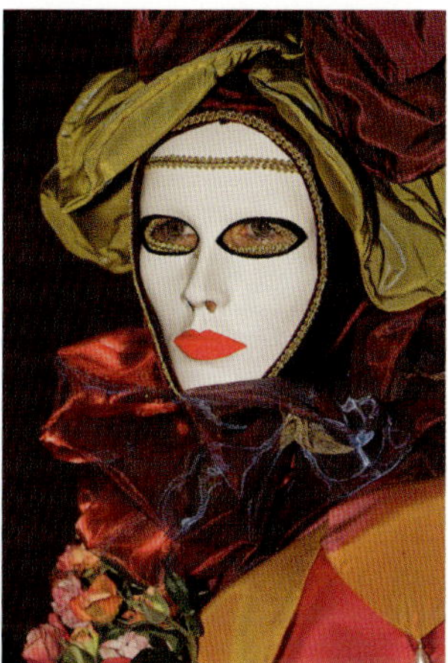

VENETIAN CARNIVAL

Festivals and carnivals are great opportunities to build up your collection of vibrant images, and a good time to practice shooting people.

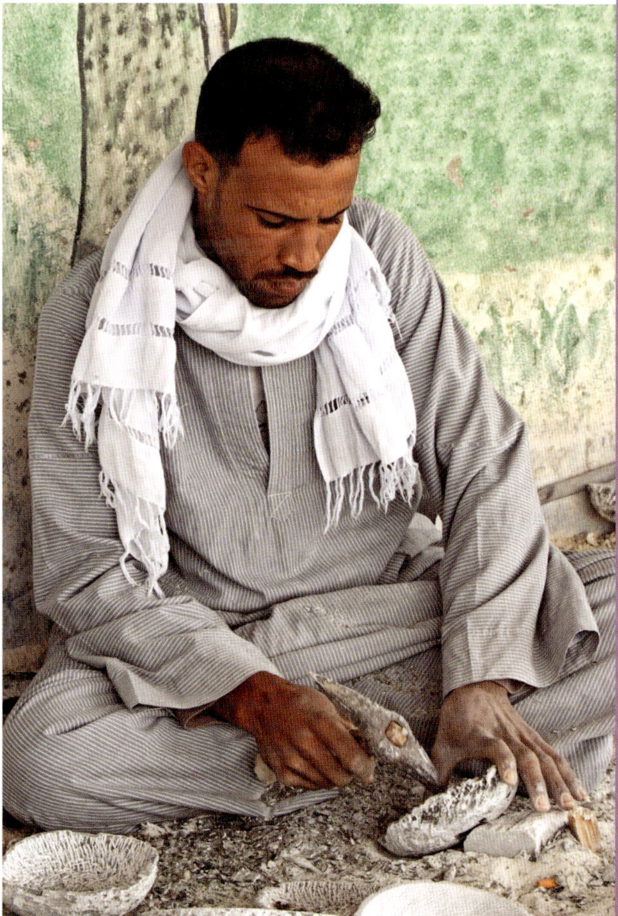

CONTEXT

When you are photographing people at their work, it is important to give the viewer a sense of what that job entails.

Tying the knot

At a wedding the focus is always on the happy couple, but there is also a wider relationship with the guests and even with the situation in which the ceremony takes place. Photographs can be taken quite discreetly even in church, but a high ISO setting is necessary.

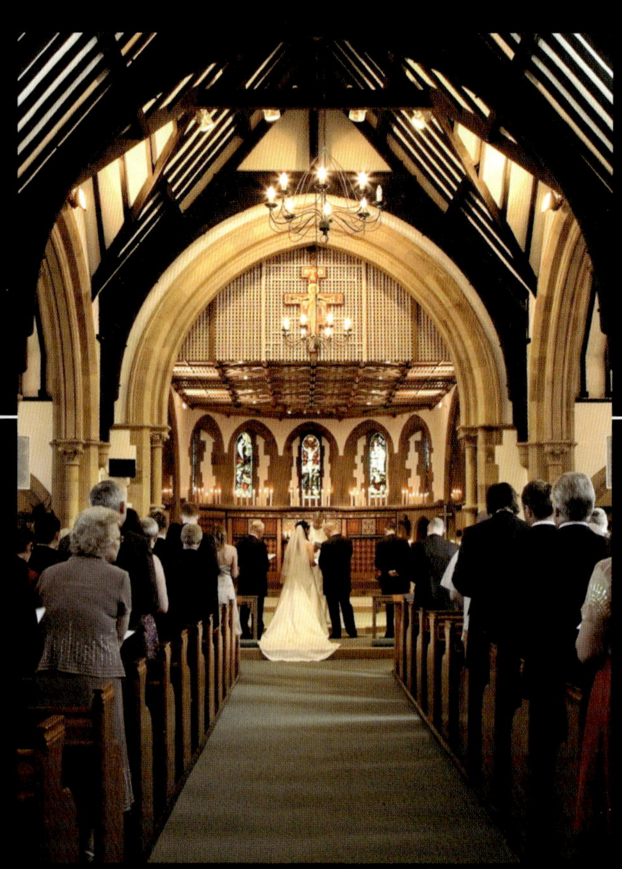

CEREMONY

Settings
Focal length: 24mm
ISO: 3200
Aperture: f/8
Shutter: 1/30

Statuesque

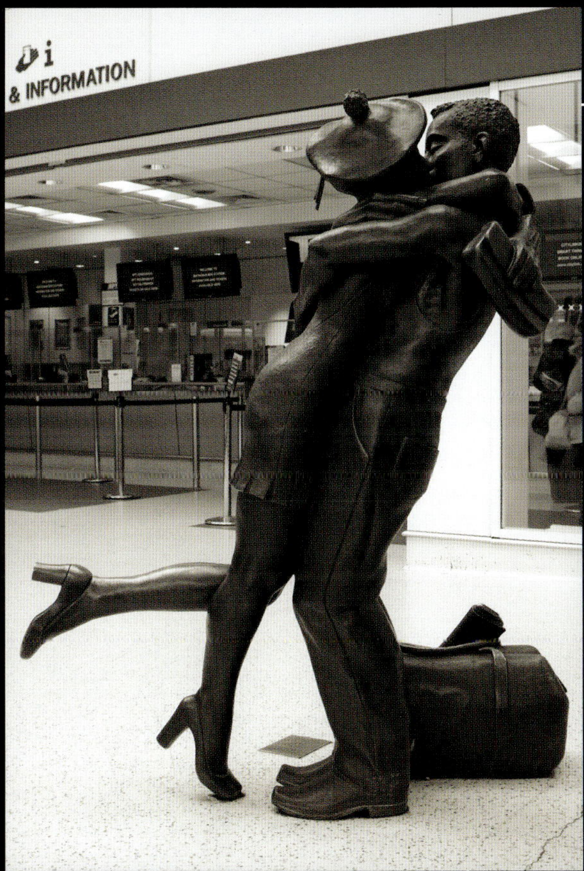

Settings
Focal length: 24mm
ISO: 400
Aperture: f/5.6
Shutter: 1/40

Portrayals of people can be as interesting a subject as the real thing. This unusual statue signifies a designated meeting point in a bus station concourse.

A POPULAR MEDLEY

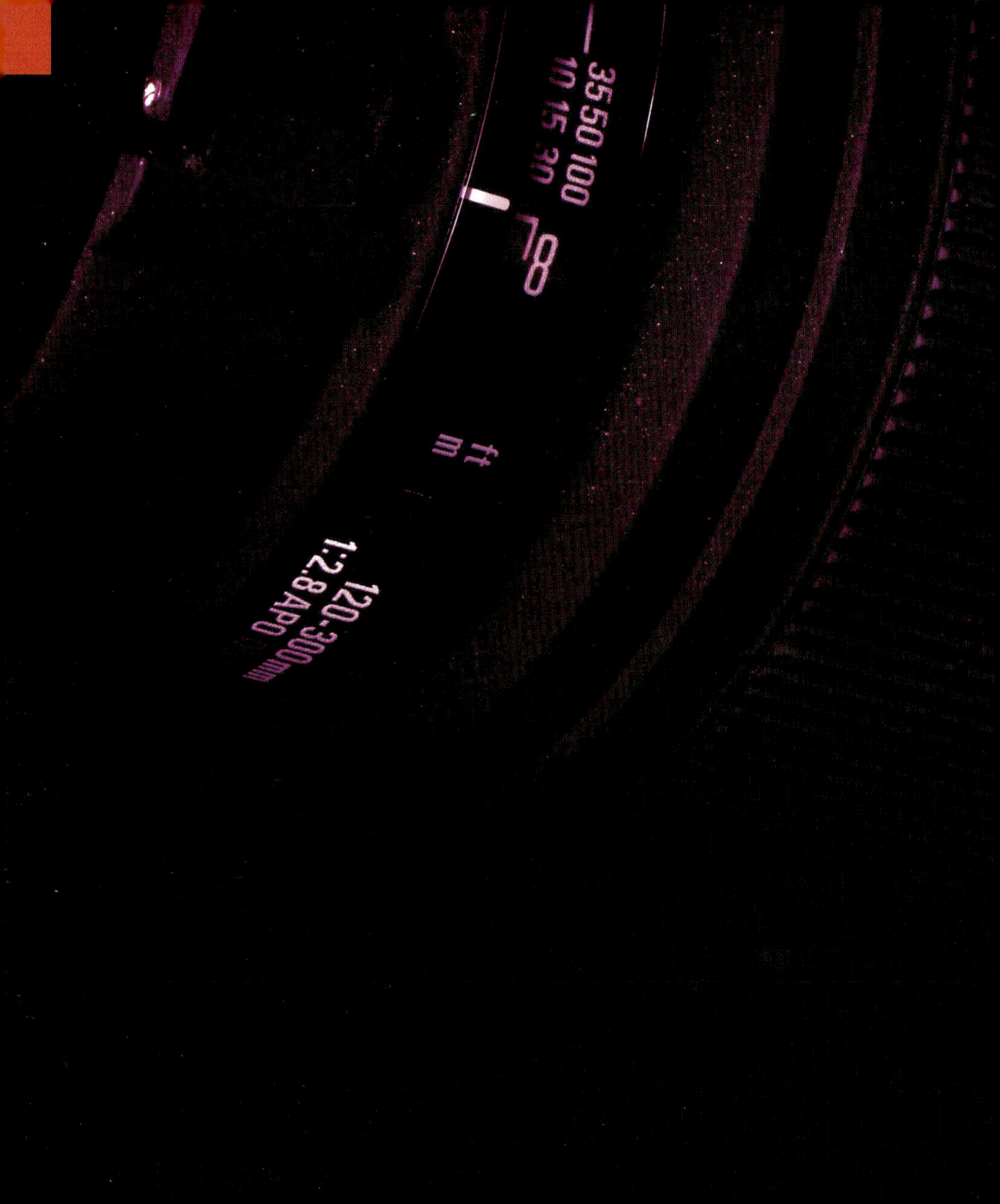
35 50 100
10 15 30
ft
m
120-300mm
1:2.8 APO

Chapter **7**

Zooms reaching 300mm

Of the six lenses in this category, only the 120–300mm f/2.8 has a fast maximum aperture. The 100–300mm f/4 is relatively fast for these focal lengths, unless you compare it with the expensive professional lenses produced by the major camera manufacturers. Both of these lenses benefit from having a constant aperture throughout the zoom range.

The remaining four, however, are relatively "slow." This does not refer to their focusing performance; rather, it relates to the extent to which the diaphragm opens up to allow light to reach the sensor. This is particularly true at the longer end of the focal length range, which is slower than at the widest focal lengths.

This slowness is not the hindrance it was a few years ago, because the current crop of DSLRs (Digital Single Lens Reflex cameras) have greatly improved performance at higher ISO speeds than was previously the case.

ISO speeds

The ISO (International Organization for Standardization) speed is a rating applied to the sensitivity to light of the sensor or film. A higher number indicates a greater sensitivity, which means that less exposure is needed— exposure being a combination of

the shutter speed and selected aperture. In short, low ISO speeds necessitate wider apertures and/ or slower shutter speeds. High ISO speeds permit smaller apertures— and therefore better depth of field—and/or faster shutter speeds.

The film user has to set the correct ISO setting on the camera for the specific type of film being used, as this determines the processing times used by the lab. The processing of the entire film can be adjusted by the lab if the film has been exposed at a different ISO than the one intended, whether intentionally or by accident. This is known as "push processing" when the film has been exposed at too high an ISO setting, or "pull processing" when the ISO setting has been reduced to a lower figure than intended by the film manufacturer. This will usually degrade the final image to some degree.

One of the huge benefits of digital photography is the ability to "process" each image individually. One image shot at ISO 6400 can be followed by another shot at ISO 100.

With film, higher ISO speeds lead to the appearance of "grain," which arises from the chemicals used and especially the small clusters of light-sensitive silver halide crystals suspended in gelatin, which together form the film emulsion. Whenever film is exposed at a higher ISO than was intended by the manufacturer, and processed accordingly, grain is likely to be more apparent.

Digital noise

Digital images suffer from the digital equivalent of film grain, which is referred to as "noise." The higher the ISO setting, the more noise may be evident in the final image. And just like film, whenever we deliberately or intentionally underexpose an image and try to rescue it in post-processing, the more likely it becomes that noise will appear in the final image.

The present generation of DSLRs boasts the ability to shoot at ISO speeds as high as 25,600. Compare that with film, where even specialized films of 3200 ISO can be hard to track down. These DSLRs usually offer a set ISO range with the added ability to "expand" the highest setting and sometimes also the lowest setting. The unexpanded ISO settings are referred to as "native" settings.

These menu-driven expanded ISO settings on DSLRs are not "native" to the camera. They are artificially created in just the same way as a lab can push-process a film that has been exposed at the "wrong" settings. As a result, images are subject to more noise than would be the case with a native ISO setting.

The millions of light-sensitive pixels that record the image produce a tiny electrical response when the exposure is taken (the terms used for the most popular forms of digital camera sensor, CMOS and CCD, actually relate to the way this process occurs rather than the way these sensors are physically manufactured). When ISO settings are increased on a digital camera, the electrical signals produced by these pixels are amplified. Unfortunately, unwelcome additional electrical signals—which are well controlled at low ISO speeds—are magnified at the same time. It is these stray signals that produce the noise in the final image, and the higher the ISO setting, the more this is evident— especially when ISO settings exceed their native boundaries.

Basically, a photograph is always a trade-off between the quality of the final image and the importance of the subject matter. When the subject is of absolute importance, image quality, though desirable, can be ignored—witness the appalling footage shot on cellphones and seen on the television news when a disaster occurs. Photographers all over the world, every day, do their utmost to combine the best of both.

28–300mm f/3.5–6.3 DG Macro IF ASP

Lens construction: 15 elements in 13 groups
Angle of view: 8.2°–75.4°
Diaphragm blades: 8
Min. aperture: f/22
Min. focusing distance: 50cm (19.7in)
Max. magnification: 1:3
Filter: 62mm
Dimensions: 74mm (W) × 86mm (L)
(2.9in × 3.4in)
Weight: 490g (17.3oz)
Mounts: Sigma, Canon, Nikon (D), Sony (D), Pentax

Note: The appearance of lenses may differ depending on the camera mount.

This is a budget full-frame lens with one-third life-size macro capability. Internal focusing means that there is no lens extension during focusing, but zooming makes up for this with a total extension of 77mm (3in) at the 300mm setting, which reveals magnification markings from 1:8.5 to 1:3 on the lens barrel.

At approximately 40°, the arc through which the focusing ring travels is one of the shortest you will find, which should make for very rapid autofocus. In practice, autofocus is indeed quick—except in very low-contrast situations,

LENS CONSTRUCTION

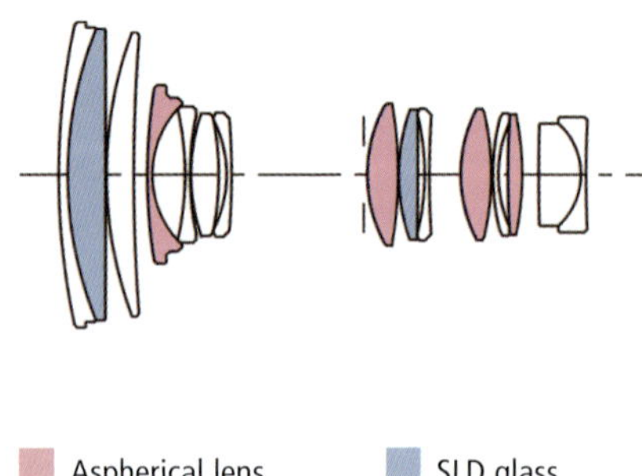

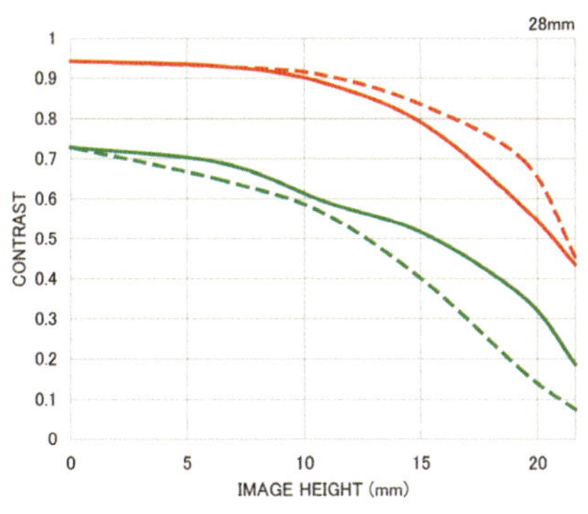

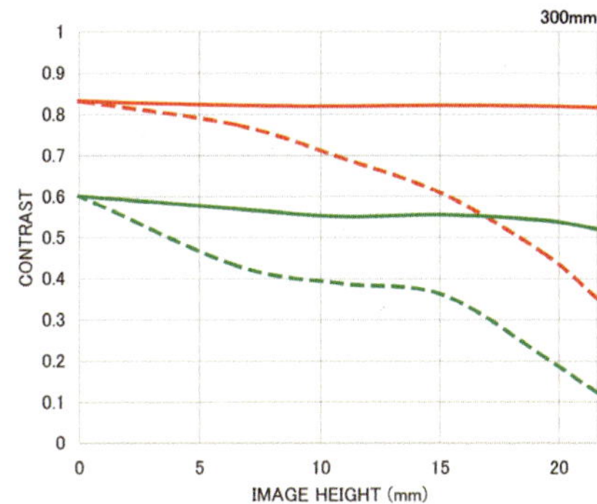

Depth of field (m): 28–300mm f/3.5–6.3 DG Macro at 200mm

Circle of confusion: 0.3333mm

Focused at	Aperture	6.3	8	11	16	22
0.5m	Near	0.497	0.496	0.495	0.492	0.489
	Far	0.503	0.504	0.506	0.508	0.511
1m	Near	0.99	0.99	0.98	0.98	0.97
	Far	1.01	1.01	1.02	1.03	1.04
3m	Near	2.94	2.92	2.89	2.85	2.79
	Far	3.06	3.08	3.12	3.17	3.24
5m	Near	4.85	4.81	4.73	4.63	4.49
	Far	5.16	5.21	5.30	5.44	5.64
10m	Near	9.45	9.31	9.06	8.72	8.28
	Far	10.62	10.80	11.17	11.74	12.66
infinity	Near	190	149	105	74	53
	Far	inf	inf	inf	inf	inf

ZOOMS REACHING 300MM

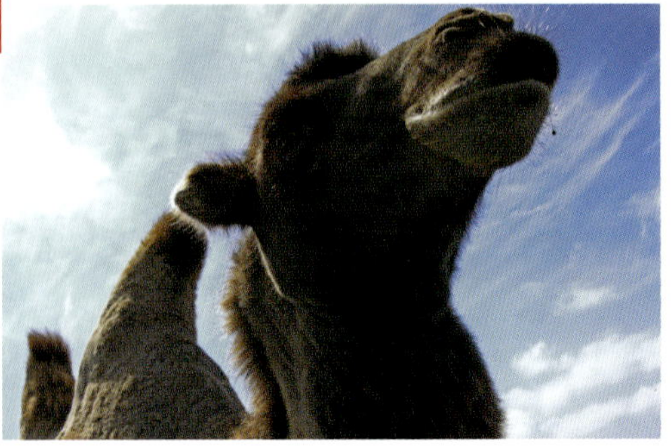

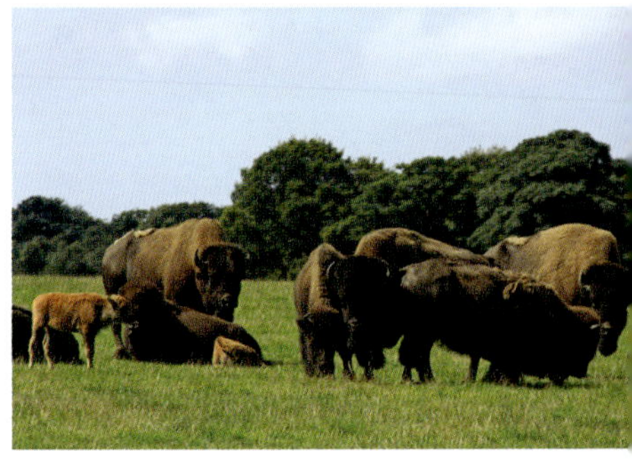

CAMEL
At its widest setting of 28mm, this lens is fast and responsive—as this camel can testify!

BISON
This shot was taken with a focal length of 195mm. This lens may "hunt" for focus when longer focal lengths are used.

especially with longer focal lengths, when the AF tends to "hunt." This is a limitation of the design and not a fault—Canon, for example, will only claim AF capability up to f/5.6 in any case.

However, before purchasing, consider the circumstances in which you may need to use this lens at or near its maximum focal length.

Verdict

Image quality at shorter focal lengths is best when there is strong foreground content. At longer focal lengths, contrast and sharpness are consistent, but don't have the same punch as an EX lens—but this lens is only half the price. If you are looking for a relatively inexpensive lens with a high zoom ratio, and are happy with 6 × 4in (15 × 10cm) or 7 × 5in (18 × 13cm) prints, this lens is worth investigating. However, if are using an APS-C camera, check out the new 50–200mm (see pages 125–7) with four-stop OS and HSM for a similar price. Alternatively, try the slightly more expensive 18–250mm (see page 83), which also offers a four-stop image stabilizer and HSM.

70–300mm f/4–5.6 APO DG Macro

Lens construction: 14 elements in 10 groups
Angle of view: 8.2°–34.3°
Diaphragm blades: 9
Min. aperture: f/22
Min. focusing distance: 150cm (59in)
95cm (37.4in) in Macro mode
Max. magnification: 1:2
Filter: 58mm
Dimensions: 76.6mm (W) × 122mm (L)
(3in × 4.8in)
Weight: 550g (19.4oz)
Mounts: Sigma, Canon, Nikon (D), Sony, Pentax (not SFX or SF7)

Practical Photography Best Buy Award May 2006

Note: The appearance of lenses may differ depending on the camera mount.

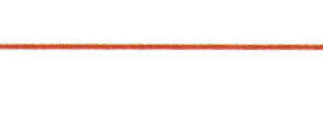

As a lightweight lens with a long reach, coupled with a wide-to-standard zoom, this is excellent value for money and perfect for traveling light around town, when out for a walk, or when on vacation.

The zoom ring on the sample provided was a little stiff, but a Nikon version owned by a friend was fine. By way of contrast, the focusing ring was a little too easy to turn when using manual focus and for macro work; when manual focus

LENS CONSTRUCTION

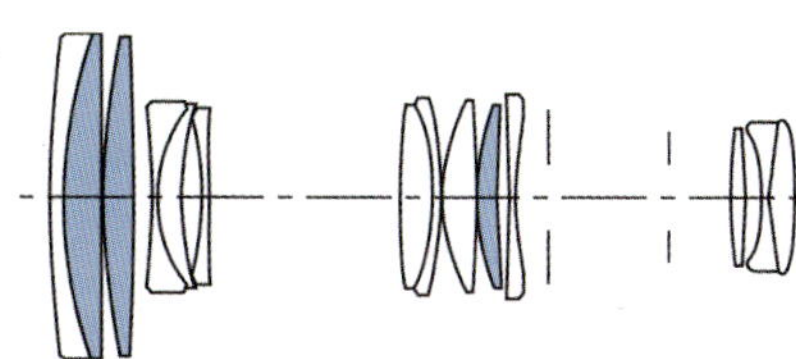

■ SLD glass

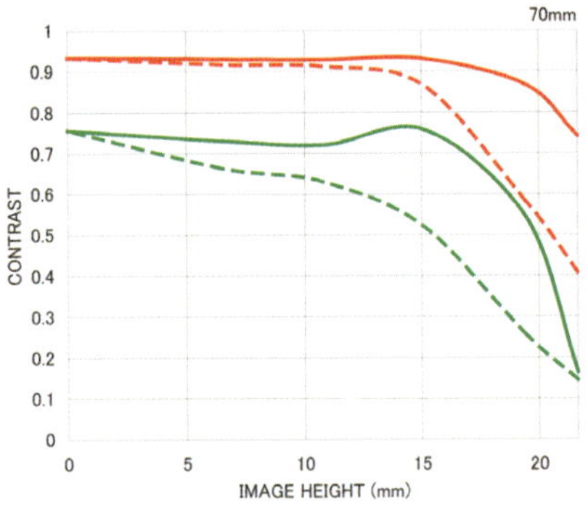

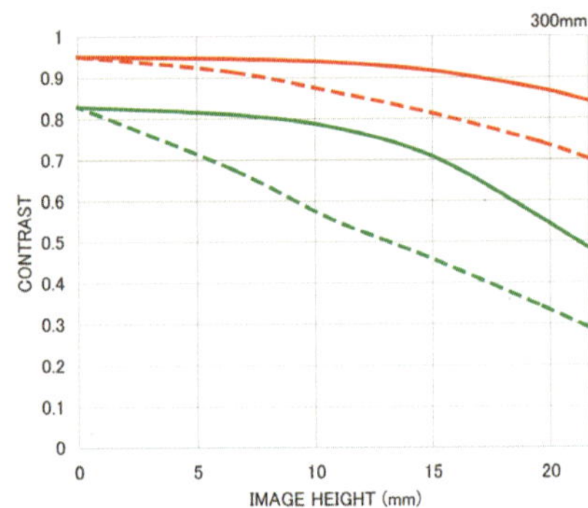

is used more frequently, investment in a focusing rack might be worth considering. Otherwise, the finish is good and the ribbed rubber grips for both the zoom ring (wide) and focusing ring (narrow) give excellent grip. Sigma also deserve praise for the additional subtle ribs around the lens barrel—an excellent touch that helps to ensure a safe grip no matter how you are handling the lens.

The red line around the lens, cheekily borrowed from Canon's L-series lenses, adds a touch of class, though unfortunately the same cannot be said for the lens hood, reverse-mounted for storage, which looks out of place on an otherwise smart piece of kit. The lens has a rotating lens barrel that affects the use of certain filters such as polarizers and graduated filters.

Eye-catching as the lens is, it is even more so when being used at its fullest extension. Although there is normally only a 1.7cm (0.7in) extension of the lens when changing focus from infinity to the minimum focusing distance, it is a different story when changing the zoom setting. Lens extension when zooming from 70mm to 300mm in "normal" mode is all of 5.3cm (2.1in). At the maximum zoom setting this will give you close-ups of one-quarter life-size, even without changing to macro mode using the small switch on the side of the lens.

The lens can be switched to macro mode when the zoom ring is set between 200mm and 300mm. The maximum front extension is then 8.5cm (3.3in), revealing the full range of magnification markings on the projecting lens barrel. Once in macro mode, it is impossible to turn the zoom ring back below 200mm. Neither can you slide the normal/macro switch back to its normal setting without first adjusting the focusing ring so that it is in the non-macro range of less than approximately 1:4 magnification—a good guide is the base of the long straight white line, which can be seen clearly in the image below.

Verdict

Given this lens's modest price tag, its Practical Photography award seems very appropriate. It is light in weight, easy to handle, and extremely versatile. Those looking to minimize expenditure, but still acquire a very worthwhile lens will certainly not be disappointed.

CAMERA SUPPORT

With extreme close-ups, tripod functionality is extremely important.

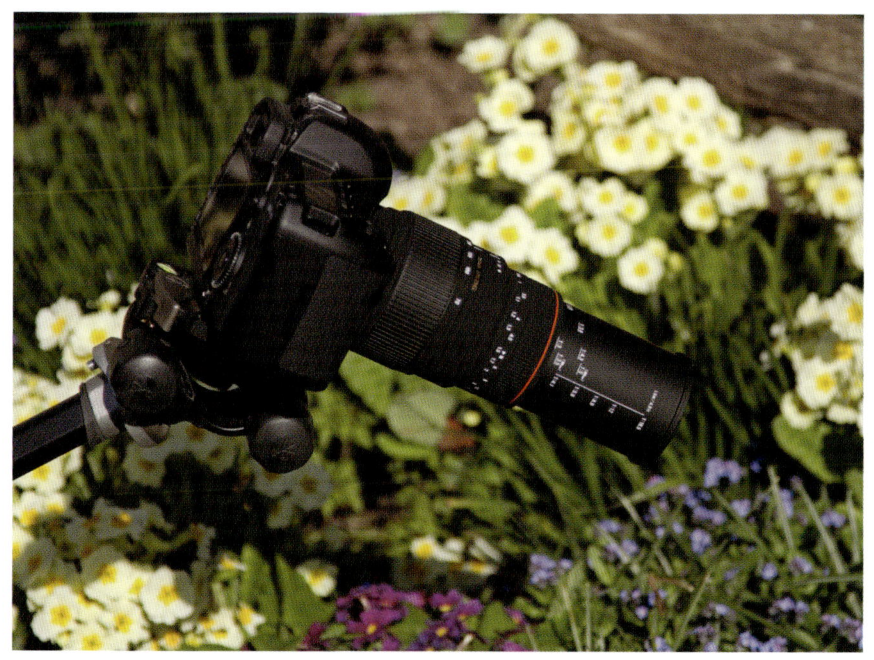

70–300mm f/4–5.6 DG Macro

Specifications (based on Sigma mount)

Lens construction: 14 elements in 10 groups
Angle of view: 8.2°–34.3°
Diaphragm blades: 9
Min. aperture: f/22
Min. focusing distance: 150cm (59in)
95cm (37.4in) in Macro mode
Max. magnification: 1:4.1 (1:2 in Macro mode)
Filter: 58mm
Dimensions: 76.6mm (W) × 122mm (L)
(3in × 4.8in)
Weight: 545g (19.2oz)
Mounts: Sigma, Canon, Nikon (D), Sony, Pentax

Note: The appearance of lenses may differ depending on the camera mount.

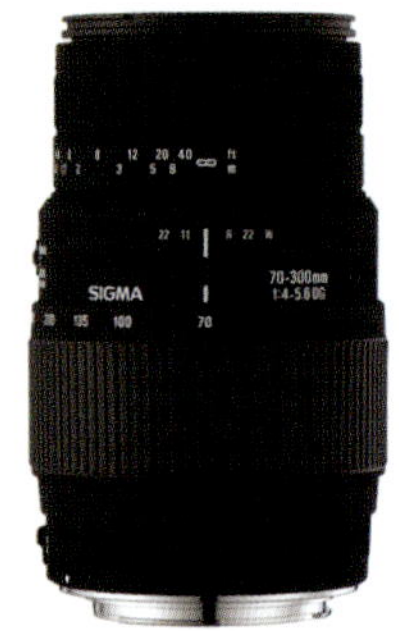

Inevitably, this lens will be compared to the more expensive—but still excellent value—APO version (see pages 145–7). This non-APO version of the lens is easily identified by the absence of a red line adorning the front end.

Other than that—and, of course, the absence of the SLD glass at the business end of the lens barrel—the specifications of the two lenses are identical. Okay, there's a 5g (0.2oz) difference in weight, but that isn't likely to influence your assessment of its suitability for your purposes.

LENS CONSTRUCTION

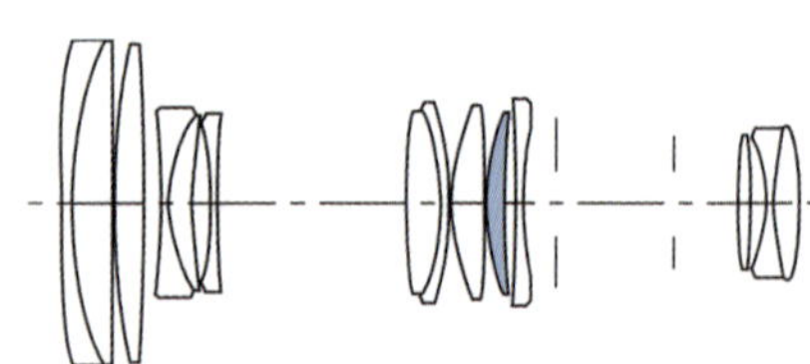

SLD glass

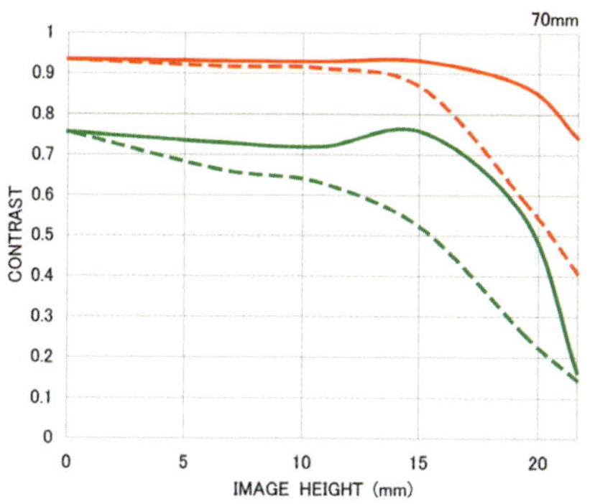

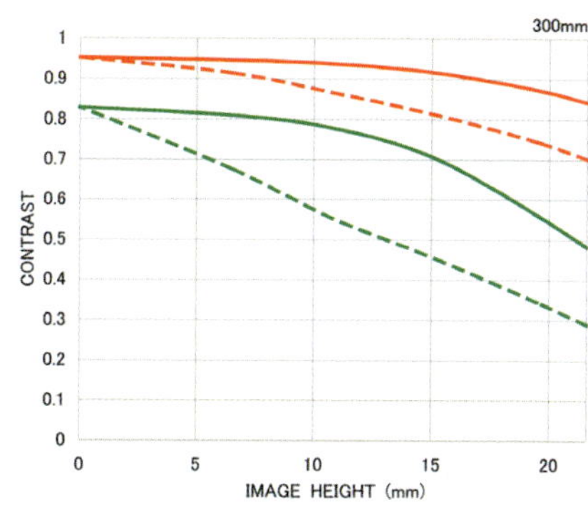

Depth of field (m): 70–300mm f/4–5.6 DG Macro at 135mm

Circle of confusion: 0.3333mm

Focused at	Aperture	4.4	5.6	8	11	16	22
1.5m	Near	1.488	1.484	1.478	1.469	1.457	1.440
	Far	1.512	1.516	1.523	1.532	1.546	1.566
2m	Near	1.98	1.97	1.96	1.94	1.92	1.88
	Far	2.03	2.03	2.05	2.07	2.09	2.14
3m	Near	2.94	2.92	2.89	2.85	2.80	2.72
	Far	3.06	3.08	3.12	3.17	3.24	3.35
5m	Near	4.83	4.78	4.69	4.57	4.42	4.22
	Far	5.19	5.25	5.36	5.52	5.77	6.16
8m	Near	7.54	7.42	7.21	6.92	6.56	6.11
	Far	8.52	8.68	9.00	9.49	10.28	11.67
infinity	Near	125	96	68	48	34	24
	Far	inf	inf	inf	inf	inf	inf

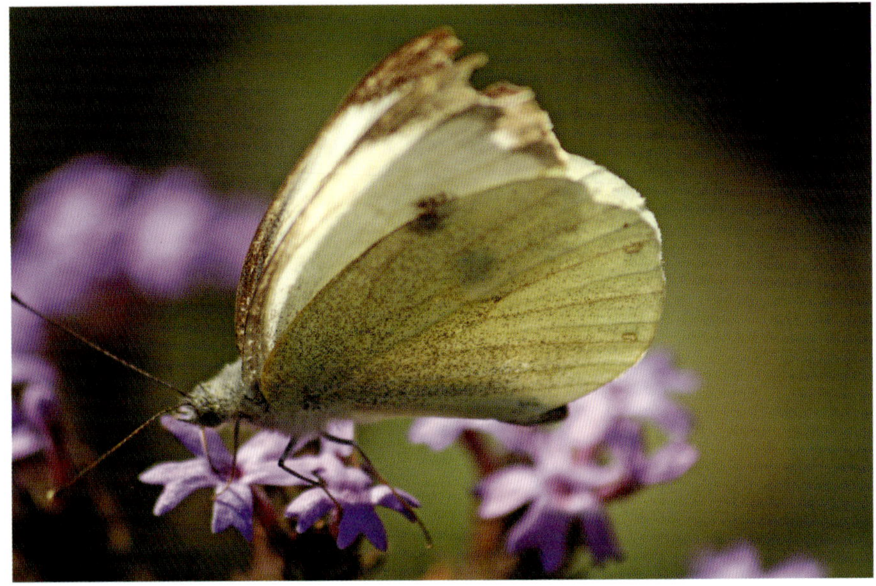

GATHERING NECTAR
This butterfly was photographed at the lens's maximum focal length of 300mm.

Verdict

This lens stands on a threshold beyond which some photographers will not want to stray, but others will be enthused by its possibilities. The former will be satisfied with images that will never be used large enough to warrant spending more—and this lens is very inexpensive given its flexibility. The latter, those who start out with budget in mind, but later want to improve their technique, will eventually be sufficiently inspired by their images to want bigger, better, longer, shorter, sharper... and will fork out more for the privilege. This is a lens to learn with, easy to use, and light to carry, but the APO version (see page 145) might tempt you to spend a little more.

70–300mm f/4–5.6 DG OS

Lens construction: 16 elements in 11 groups
Angle of view: 8.2°–34.3°
Diaphragm blades: 9
Min. aperture: f/22
Min. focusing distance: 150cm (59in)
Max. magnification: 1:3.9
Filter: 62mm
Dimensions: 76.5mm (W) × 126.5mm (L)
(3in × 5in)
Weight: 610g (21.5oz)
Mounts: Sigma, Canon, Nikon (D), Sony (D), Pentax

NEW

Note: The appearance of lenses may differ depending on the camera mount.

Announced only a matter of days before the manuscript for this book was submitted to the publisher, the 70–300mm f/4–5.6 DG OS is the third version of this immensely popular lens. The big news is that this version is equipped with the fourth generation of Sigma's Optical Stabilizer (OS), providing four stops of added stability. Conventional wisdom is that most people need to use a shutter speed that matches the focal length in use, i.e. 1/250 sec for a 250mm lens, or the same focal

LENS CONSTRUCTION

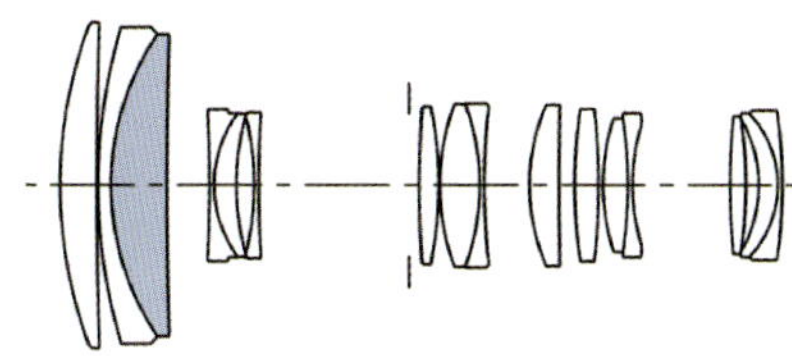

SLD glass

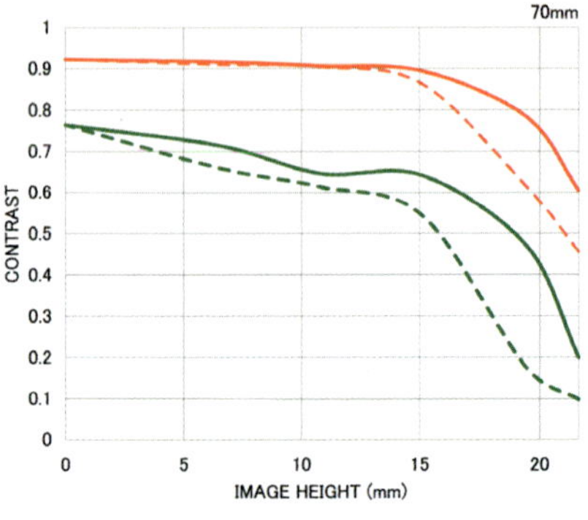

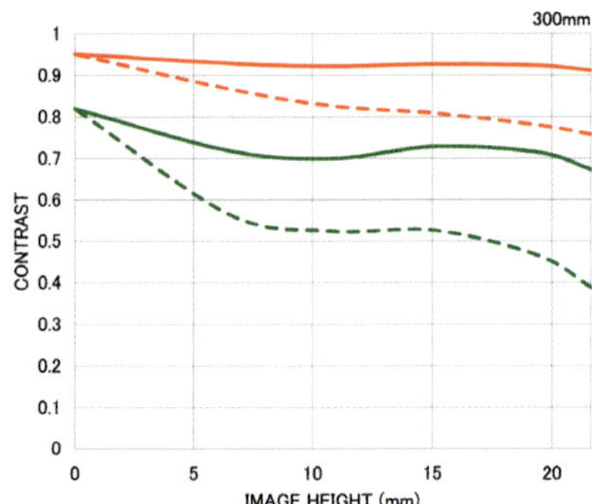

length setting on a zoom lens. With a four-stop OS facility, this can safely be reduced to 1/30 sec with no loss of quality due to camera shake.

At the widest zoom setting on this lens, this facility will open new doors for those who have never really tried their hand at low-light photography before. At 70mm, you would expect to use at least 1/70 sec—let's say 1/60 sec for convenience—but now it is possible with this lens to get away quite comfortably with just 1/4 sec. And that assumes that the outfit is being used handheld. If you are able to "borrow" some additional camera support in situ—such as using a wall to lean against or a fencepost to rest the camera on—then it is possible to find an additional couple of stops' worth of stability.

This version of the lens drops one of the SLD elements within the center of the lens in order to accommodate the OS function, but Sigma promise that it will still provide excellent aberration correction. However, due to time constraints, this lens could not be supplied in time to be tested for this book.

An important point for Sony and Pentax users is that the OS function of this lens can be used even if the camera body is equipped with an antishake function, though the in-camera stabilization must be disabled first—you cannot use both in combination.

Two important changes with this new version of the 70–300mm relate to the minimum focusing distance and the maximum magnification ratio. Due to the revised optical design necessary to incorporate the OS function, both of these features have had to be reduced slightly in specification. This current version has a minimum focusing distance of 150cm (59in) compared with 95cm (37in) on the other two versions, and this is available throughout the entire zoom range. The maximum magnification ratio is reduced from half life-size (1:2) to 1:3.9, rendering the lens still very useful for general close-up photography, but not quite as good for serious macro work.

ON THE WATER
Optical Stabilization is extremely useful when you are confined to a mode of transport that generates movement, whether messing about in boats or on safari.

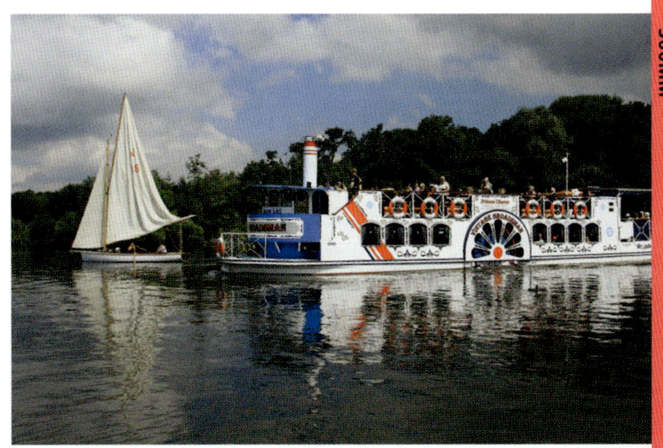

100–300mm f/4 EX DG HSM IF APO CONV

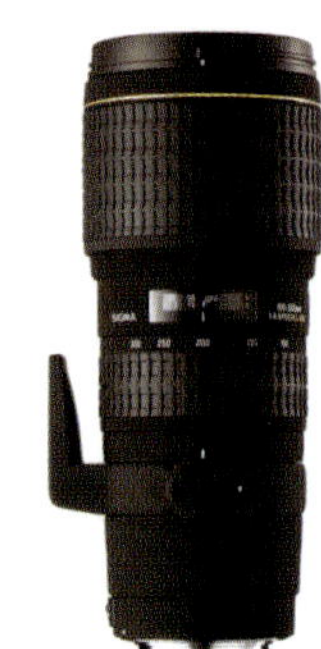

Specifications (based on Sigma mount)

Lens construction: 16 elements in 14 groups
Angle of view: 8.2°–24.4°
Diaphragm blades: 9
Min. aperture: f/32
Min. focusing distance: 180cm (70.9in)
Max. magnification: 1:5
Filter: 82mm
Dimensions: 92.4mm (W) × 226.5mm (L)
(3.6in × 8.9in)
Weight: 1440g (50.8oz)
Mounts (HSM): Sigma, Canon, Nikon (D)
Mounts (non-HSM): Sony (D), Pentax

Note: The appearance of lenses may differ depending on the camera mount.

This lens is well worth considering as a more flexible alternative to the 300mm f/2.8 prime lens. It is virtually the same length—actually 12mm (0.5in) longer if you ignore the lens hoods—and also has nine diaphragm blades, giving similar "bokeh" (the term used for out-of-focus backgrounds). The closest focusing distance is 180cm (70.9in) as against 250cm (98.4in), giving an improved maximum magnification ratio of 1:5 compared with 1:7.5 for the 300mm prime. Both will accept 1.4× and 2× converters.

LENS CONSTRUCTION

SLD glass

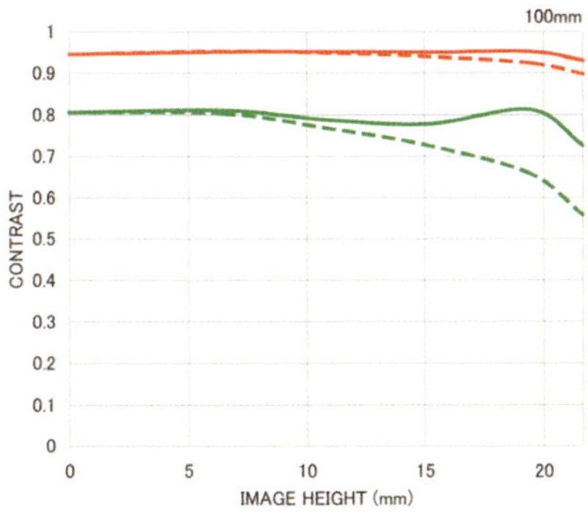

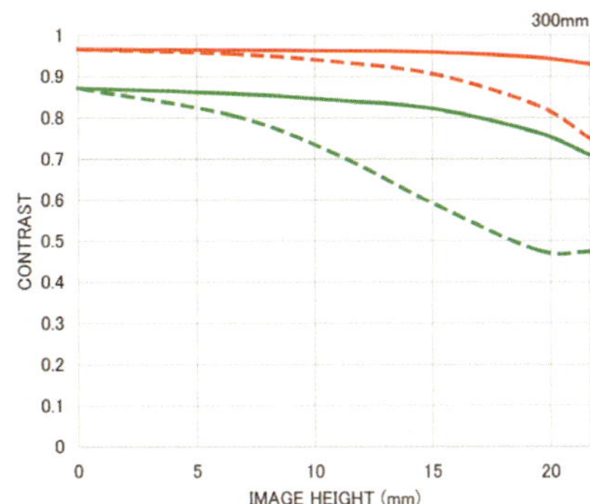

More importantly, this lens is much lighter than the 300mm prime lens and will leave your wallet considerably heavier too. However, there is a price to pay for saving all that money: one full stop, in fact. But unlike many zooms, this lens will perform supremely well at its widest aperture and does not require stopping down by one or even two stops for performance to be of real quality. This is borne out by the MTF charts (above) for both ends of the zoom scale, which show the kind of figures more commonly found with prime macro lenses.

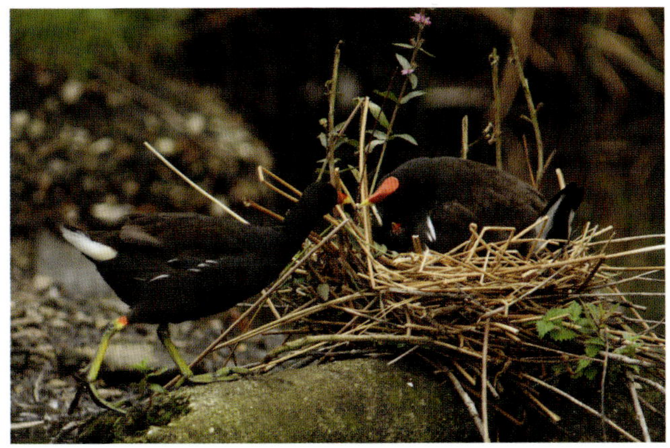

MOORHENS
These birds were photographed at the maximum focal length of 300mm with the addition of a 1.4× teleconverter.

ZOOMS REACHING 300MM

Verdict

Readers who have come across my camera guides will know that I possess the prime 300mm f/2.8 and sing its praises regularly. However, the one I own was an ex-demo model, serviced by Sigma and then purchased at half price. If I were setting out to buy such a lens today, I would have no hesitation in acquiring the 100–300mm f/4 instead. Its advantages, when weighed against the loss of a single stop compared with the 300mm f/2.8, make its choice inevitable unless the vast majority of the images you take are of high-speed action.

The lens sports the older-style rubberized grips, compared with more recent offerings from the EX range, which makes it look slightly dated, but, to be honest, I prefer these for fingertip control of both zoom and focus rings. Neither of these produces any lens extension, as the lens is an IF (inner focus) design. It also comes with a tripod ring that, unlike some of its larger siblings, is hinged so that the tripod ring can be removed without having to detach the camera first. When switching from a monopod to working handheld, or vice versa, at an event, this is an important consideration.

This lens also permits the use of front-mounted filters (82mm), unlike the 300mm prime lens, which only accepts single drop-in filters at the rear. Using more than one filter with this lens on a full-frame camera may cause some vignetting, but stacked filters can easily be used on crop-sensor bodies.

The lens hood, which can be reverse-mounted for portability, is 24mm (1in) narrower in diameter than that of the 300mm prime. That doesn't sound a great deal, but it makes the world of difference when it comes to arranging the partitions of your camera bag.

120–300mm f/2.8 EX DG HSM IF APO CONV

Specifications (based on Sigma mount)

Lens construction: 18 elements in 16 groups
Angle of view: 8.2°–20.4°
Diaphragm blades: 9
Min. aperture: f/32
Min. focusing distance: 150–250cm (59–98.4in)
Max. magnification: 1:8.6
Filter: 105mm
Dimensions: 113mm (W) × 271mm (L)
(4.4in × 10.7in)
Weight: 2600g (91.7oz)
Mounts: Sigma, Canon, Nikon (D)

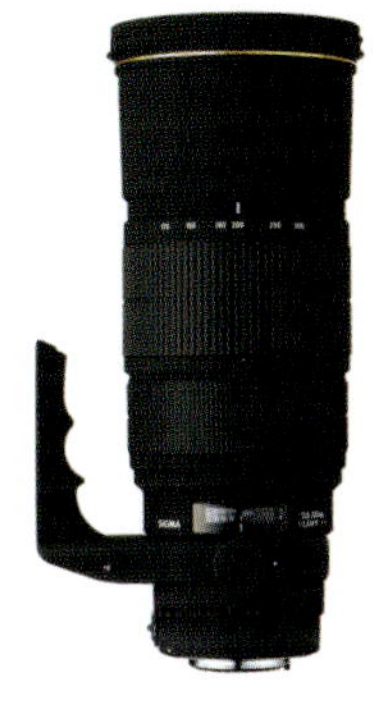

Note: The appearance of lenses may differ depending on the camera mount.

If you are a Sigma, Canon, or Nikon user, this lens has to be weighed against Sigma's prime 300mm f/2.8, the 100–300mm f/4, and perhaps even the 70–200mm f/2.8 with 1.4× converter. (Sony and Pentax owners will have to make do with one of the latter two lenses.) All four of these are EX full-frame lenses sporting internal focus, special low-dispersion lens elements, and a hyper-sonic motor, and will take both 1.4× and 2× converters. The main differences come down to cost, weight, length, flexibility in use, and image quality. Plus, of course, you have to consider

LENS CONSTRUCTION

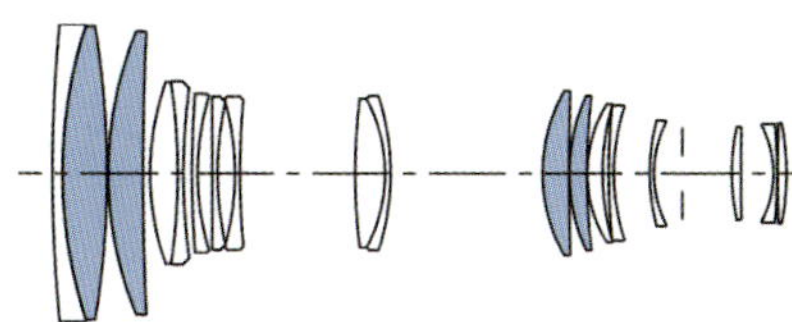

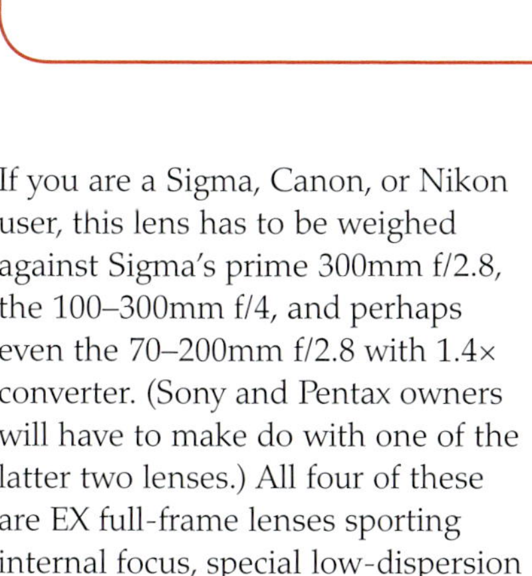
SLD glass

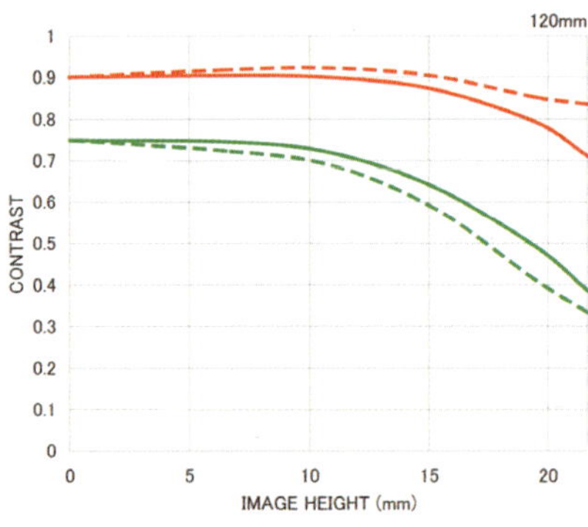

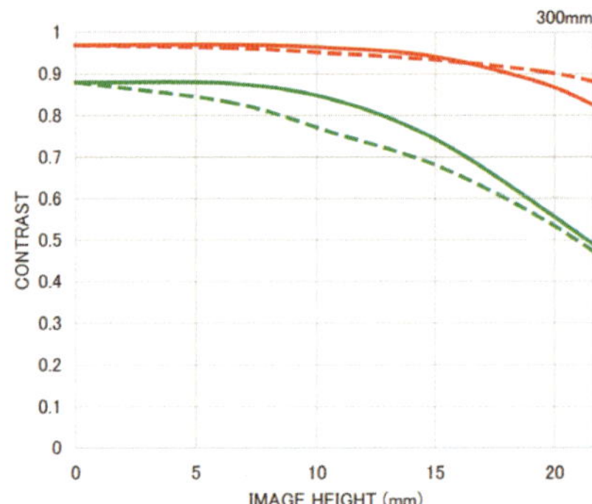

how the chosen lens will integrate with the lenses you already own.

In terms of retail price, the 120–300 f/2.8 and prime 300 f/2.8 are closely matched, with both the 100–300 f/4 and 70–200 f/2.8 costing less than half as much (even allowing for the added expense of a converter for the 70–200). Overall length is a factor that can largely be ignored as none of these four lenses is exactly discreet, but, for the record, the 120–300 is the longest by a couple of inches.

Weight, however, is a different matter. The lightest of this group is the slowest, the 100–300mm f/4, at 1440g (50.8oz). Next comes the 70–200mm f/2.8 at 1537g (54.2oz) including the 1.4× converter, followed by the prime 300mm at 2400g (84.7oz). The 120–300mm f/2.8 is the heaviest at 2600g (91.7oz).

All of which leaves the topics of flexibility in use and image quality. As you might expect, the fixed focal length 300 f/2.8 fares best of all when it comes to image quality, providing consistently high-quality results all the way from f/2.8. (In fact, I rarely use my own at anything other than the maximum aperture.)

The 70–200 f/2.8 is a first-class lens in its own right, but in this context it would have a converter added, placing it a debatable fourth. Of the remaining two, the 100–300 f/4 performs marginally better than the 120–300 f/2.8 at the wider end of the focal length range, but otherwise they are fairly evenly matched.

As for flexibility, the zooms are obviously the favorites, with the 100–300 f/4 being a serious contender among the big three,

158

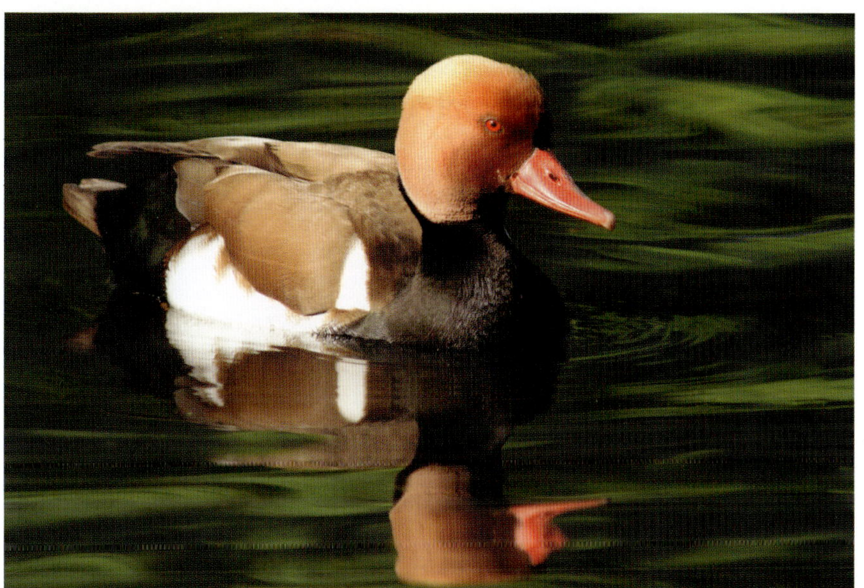

REFLECTIONS
This lens will accept both 1.4× and 2× converters. This shot was taken with a focal length of 300mm and a 2× converter.

despite being one stop slower, because its more manageable weight means that you might carry it with you more frequently. Of the four lenses examined, the most flexible solution is probably the 70–200 f/2.8 with the 1.4× converter, though that also means a loss of one stop. So just how important is it for you to have a maximum aperture of f/2.8 as against f/4? Only you can decide.

Verdict
The debate conducted here shows that it isn't always easy to choose which lens to purchase, and very often there is one overriding personal factor that dominates the proceedings. The 120–300mm f/2.8 is certainly an excellent lens, but it faces stiff competition from within Sigma's own ranks, depending on your own priorities.

Architecture (1)

The single biggest problem you will face with architectural shots is that of converging vertical lines, especially near the edges of the frame, and particularly with wide-angle and standard lenses. One solution to this is to use a longer focal length and to shoot from farther away. A slightly higher viewpoint in relation to the subject can also help when using a shorter telephoto. Both techniques were employed for the shot below.

GOZO, MALTA

Settings
Focal length: 70mm
ISO: 100
Aperture: f/5.6
Shutter: 1/160

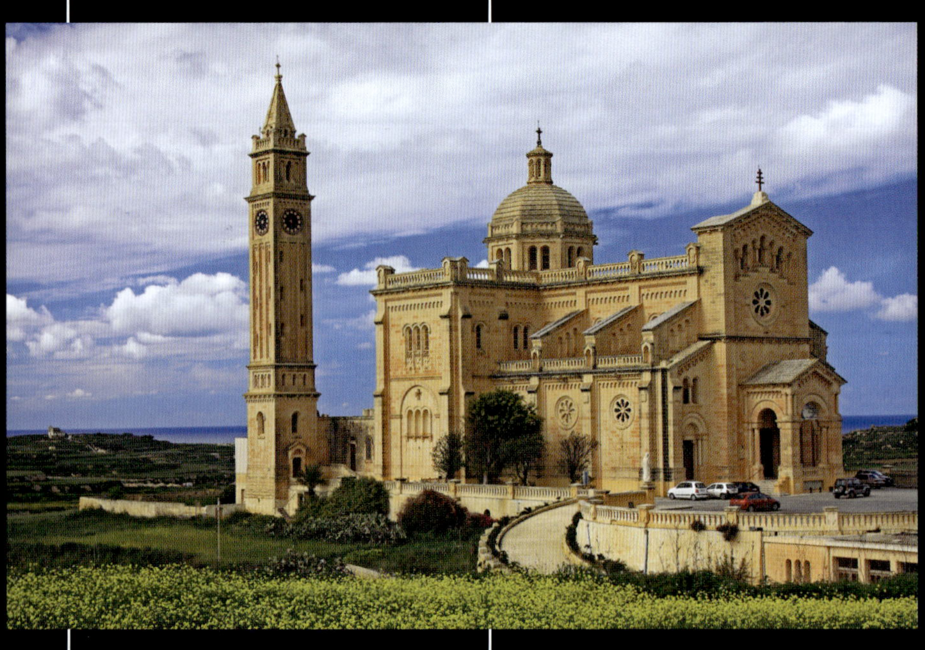

Architecture (2)

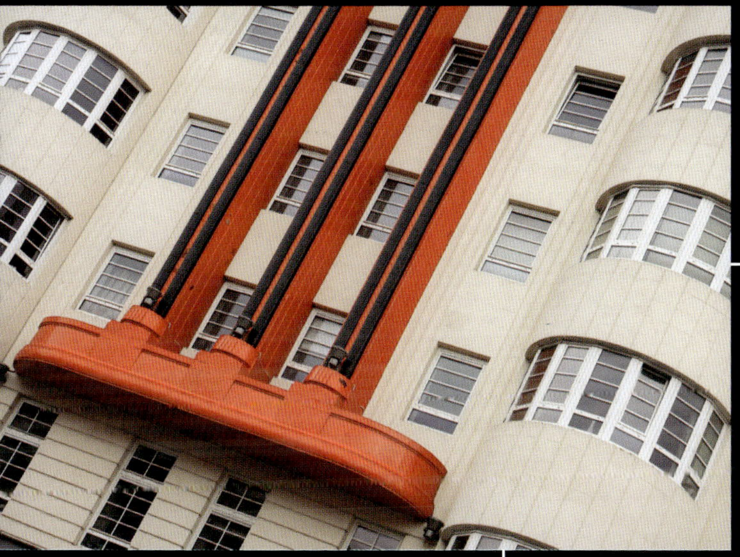

Settings
Focal length: 47mm
ISO: 100
Aperture: f/5.6
Shutter: 1/125

While shooting in the countryside may permit some choice with regard to viewpoint, as on the facing page, shooting in the confines of a city center rarely provides that option. Consequently, a completely different approach needs to be taken. This striking art deco building in the center of Glasgow had to be captured from a relatively short distance away at street level, so any conventional view would have suffered greatly from converging verticals. I took the decision to shoot just part of its facade and to rotate the camera to add to the graphic nature of the subject.

Silhouette (1)

In one sense, capturing a silhouette is simple because it only has two elements: the silhouette itself and the background. The first has line and shape, but no tonal detail to worry about, and the latter is simply a matter of color. So why do so many vacation snaps of sunsets not work?

I would suggest three reasons: people tend to get tunnel vision when viewing sunsets and don't consider the full image area; they put too much emphasis on the sky and not enough on the silhouette; and finally, they settle for one or two shots instead of paying attention to all the subtle changes that the scene goes through. In short, they get carried away.

When the sun drops below the horizon, lighting and color change with incredible speed. Five minutes after this shot was taken, the sea had lost its reflected color, the small breakers weren't discernible, and the tower was merging into the dark gray clouds on the horizon.

Before visiting a location that is likely to generate sunset images, look up the times of sunrises and sunsets for the dates concerned and what their respective compass directions will be. If a good sunset looks likely, set out early to locate a scene that will provide a strong silhouette. Meter readings should be taken constantly from the sky area, but without including the sun itself, as they change so fast.

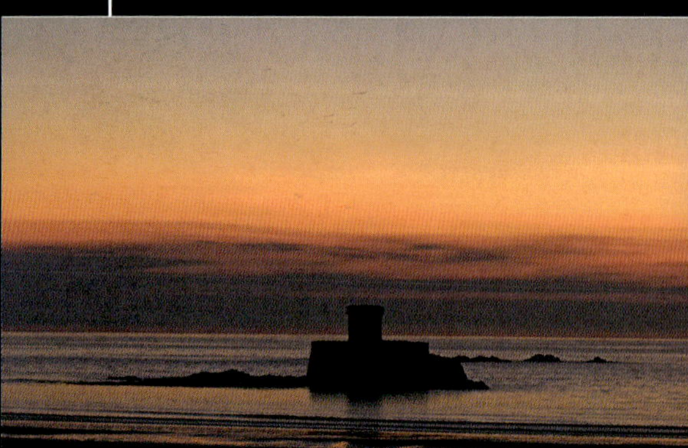

TOWER AT DUSK

Settings
Focal length: 85mm
ISO: 200
Aperture: f/5.6
Shutter: 0.4 sec

Silhouette (2)

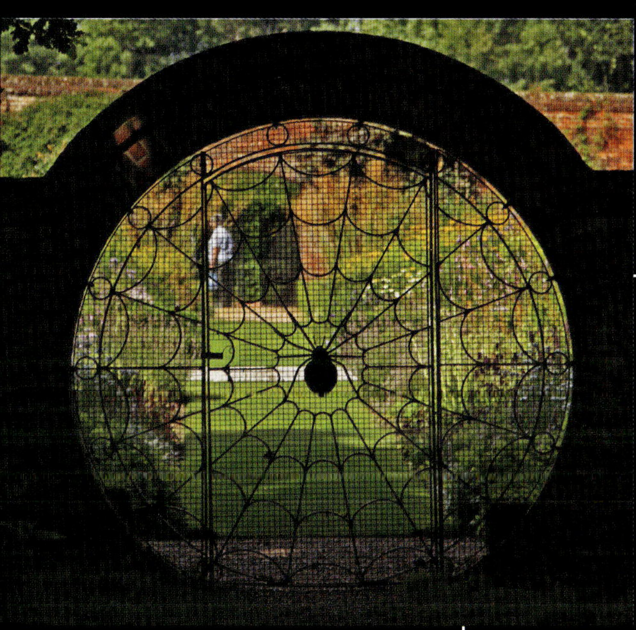

SPIDER GARDEN

This elaborate gate, featuring a
spider and its web, leads into a
walled garden at Hoveton Hall in
Norfolk, UK. Occasionally you will
come across an opportunity to apply
a technique in an unusual situation.
All that has been written on the
previous page about silhouettes and
metering from the sky (i.e. the
background) applies equally to this

Settings
Focal length: 82mm
ISO: 100
Aperture: f/4
Shutter: 1/500

shot. A meter reading was taken
from the garden beyond so as to
render that as the midtone, while
the wall and gate were allowed to
form a silhouette.

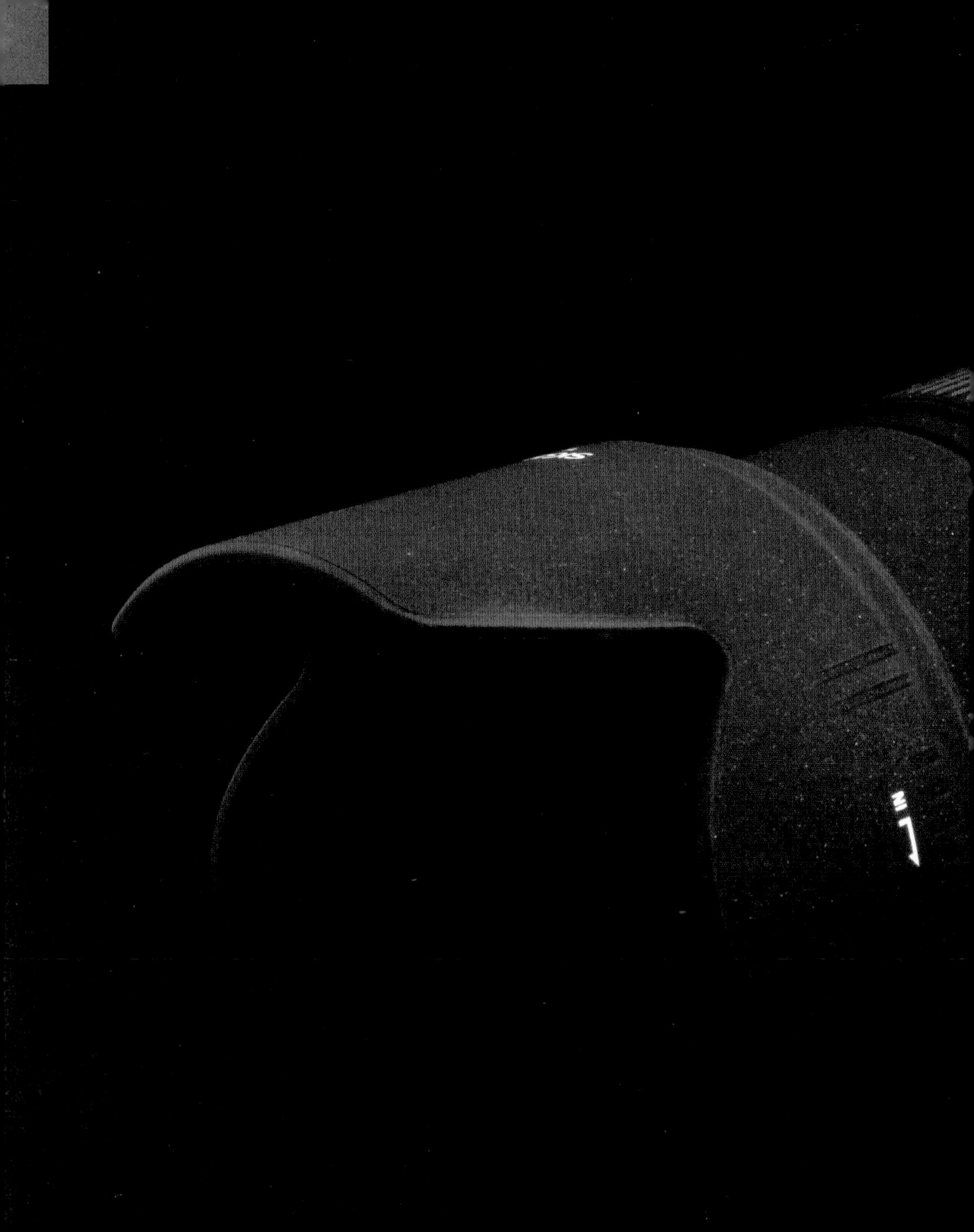

Chapter **8**

Zooms reaching beyond 300mm

None of the six lenses described in this chapter is light in weight, but several are surprisingly light on the wallet. Discount the 200–500mm f/2.8, which is so expensive that if you have to ask how much it is, you can't afford it. The 300–800mm f/5.6 is not quite as expensive, but still costs in the region of $10,000 (£7,000) at the time of writing. However, all the others can be found with prices that move the decimal point one place to the left, making them extremely good value for money.

The 50–500mm f/4-6.3; the now discontinued 80–400mm f/4.5-5.6; its replacement, the optically stabilized 120–400mm f/4.5-5.6; and the 150–500mm f/5–6.3—also stabilized—all weigh in at less than a kilogram (2.2 pounds). This means that they are too heavy to leave permanently mounted on the camera, but light enough to carry at a specific event.

Canon produce only one lens that would fall into this category, and Nikon only offer two, one of which also costs several thousand dollars. Telephoto lenses from these manufacturers, zooms as well as primes, are nearly all fixed focal length lenses with constant apertures. Alongside optical stabilization and fast maximum apertures, this is one of the features that raises the purchase price. But most of the photographers you see sporting these long, fast telephotos have not had to put their hands in their own pockets, as the lenses will have been purchased by their publication or agency. In short, Sigma have much of the amateur and semiprofessional market to themselves.

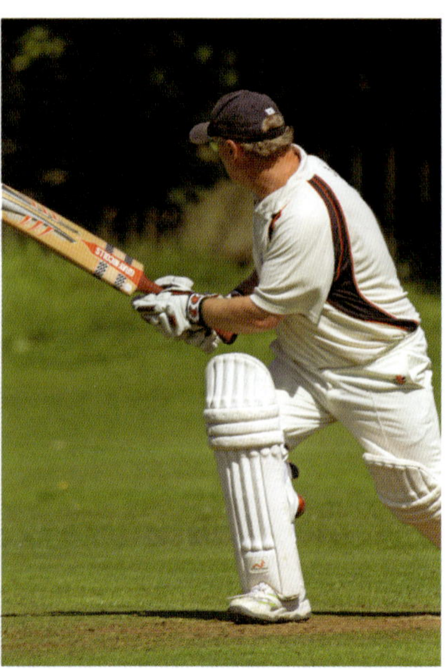

CRICKET
This image was shot with the 300–800mm f/5.6 lens at 800mm. The focal length could have been increased even more by fitting a converter.

50–500mm f/4–6.3 EX DG HSM APO RF CONV

Lens construction: 20 elements in 16 groups
Angle of view: 5°–46.8°
Diaphragm blades: 9
Min. aperture: f/22
Min. focusing distance: 100–300cm
(39.4–118.1in)
Max. magnification: 1:5.2
Filter: 86mm
Dimensions: 95mm (W) × 218.5mm (L)
(3.7in × 8.6in)
Weight: 1840g (64.9oz)
Mounts (HSM): Sigma, Canon, Nikon (D), Four Thirds
Mounts (non-HSM): Sony, Pentax (not SFX or SF7)

Note: The appearance of lenses may differ depending on the camera mount.

With a quoted weight of 1840g (69.4oz), this lens in fact weighs 2048g (72.2oz) when the lens hood and tripod collar are added, making it a bit of beast to carry around. However, it is just as much of a beast when it comes to eating up all sorts of image opportunities, as you can see from the two images on page 168, one at each end of the focal length range (both images were shot on an APS-C body). Given that you can also use either the 1.4× or 2× converter, albeit with manual

LENS CONSTRUCTION

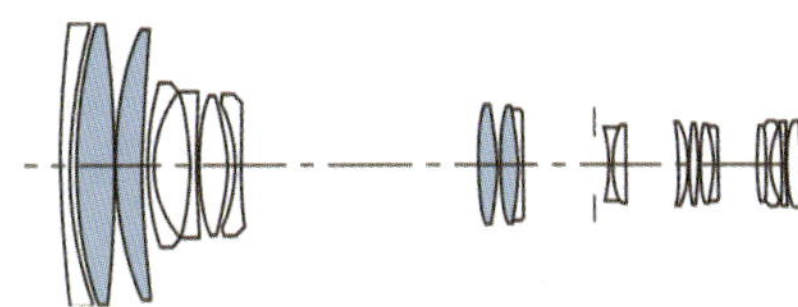

SLD glass

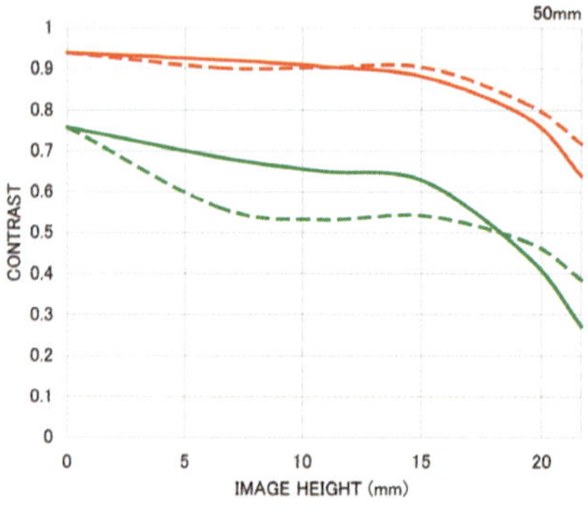

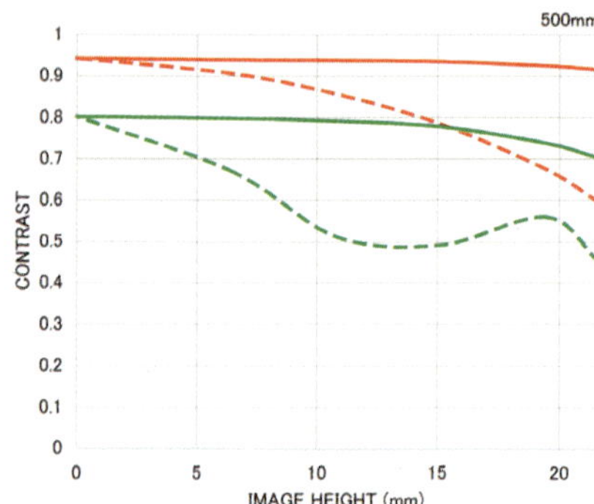

focusing being the only option, this lens manages to pull in detail which is way beyond what the human eye can discern.

Just what sort of pulling power does this 10× zoom provide? The answer is shown below, with both 50mm (left) and 500mm (right) shots taken from the same camera position. Camera technique, however, has to be spot on at the longest focal lengths, and image quality will depend more on how stable you can keep the camera and lens than it will on the optics. The lens extension at 500mm is almost

10× ZOOM RATIO
From 50mm (left) to 500mm (right) in the flick of a wrist, this lens offers all sorts of possibilities.

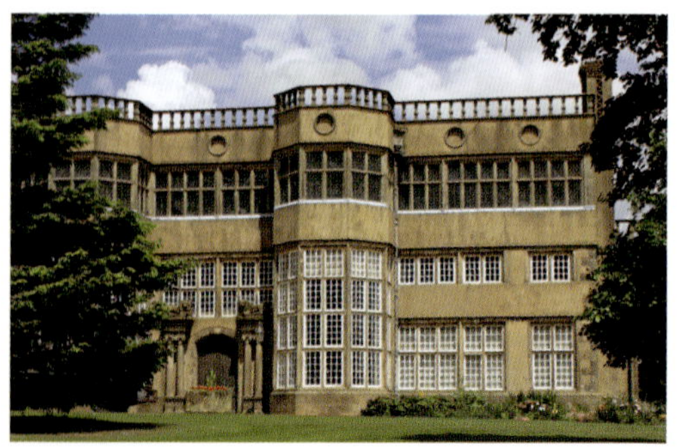

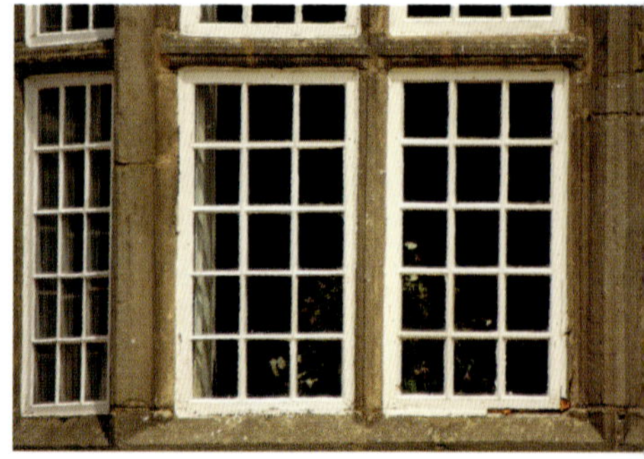

168

9cm (3.5in) and it is heavy, too. Even on a tripod, the slightest vibration causes the image to wobble alarmingly and, especially with the lens hood attached, wind will be another factor to watch out for. Ironically, the more rigid the tripod, the more it picks up vibration from passing traffic as well, so attention to your surroundings is as important as paying attention to the viewfinder.

Manufacturing quality and finish are excellent, as you would expect from the EX range. The tripod collar is not hinged so cannot be removed without detaching the lens from the camera—but I don't see this as the sort of lens which will be swapped around from being used handheld to being mounted on a tripod or monopod, so it's not a big issue.

The lens can be locked at the 50mm position to prevent zoom creep and the same switch has to be deployed when mounting a converter. There is no confusion over this because the lens will only lock at 50mm, whereas the zoom ring has to be rotated to the CONV mark (roughly 135mm) or

beyond before the switch will move positively and enable you to fit the converter. That said, I would prefer that the switch didn't move at all when it shouldn't (i.e. between the 50mm and CONV settings). Instead, it makes an itty-bitty movement and an itty-bitty click, which could be misinterpreted as the full positive switch movement when shooting under pressure.

Verdict
If you are planning to shoot from a stable platform, whether it's trackside with a monopod or in a bird hide, the sheer range of this lens makes it worthy of consideration, not to mention the quality APO glass and sturdy finish. A wide maximum aperture is now less necessary for sporting events, given the strides made in reducing noise at higher ISO settings, so this lens will suit many more shooters than it would have done a couple of years ago.

80–400mm f/4.5–5.6 EX DG APO OS RF CONV

Lens construction: 20 elements in 14 groups
Angle of view: 6.2°–30.3°
Diaphragm blades: 9
Min. aperture: f/32
Min. focusing distance: 180cm (70.9in)
Max. magnification: 1:5
Filter: 77mm
Dimensions: 95mm (W) × 129mm (L)
(3.7in × 5in)
Weight: 1750g (61.7oz)
Mounts: Sigma, Canon, Nikon (D)

DISCONTINUED

Note: The appearance of lenses may differ depending on the camera mount.

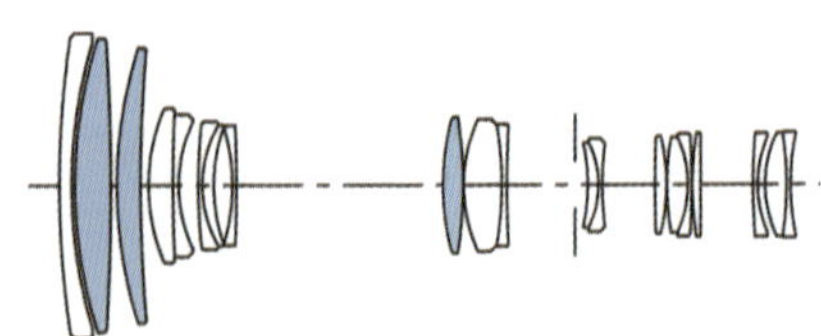

With its zoom set at 80mm, a position that can be locked to prevent zoom creep, this lens is still relatively compact and easy to handle. The positions of the zoom ring and the focus ring are reversed, with the zoom ring being farthest forward. At 80mm, the balance of the lens is such that the supporting hand still tends to find the focusing ring—but when zoomed to 400mm, which extends the lens by 85mm (3.3in), the supporting hand needs to be farther forward, finding the

LENS CONSTRUCTION

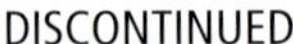

SLD glass

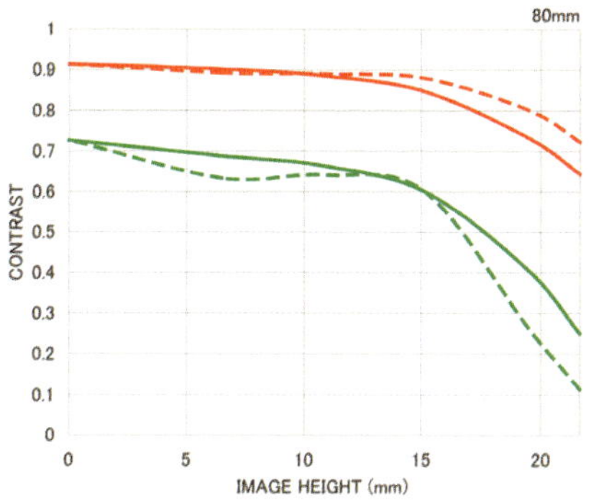

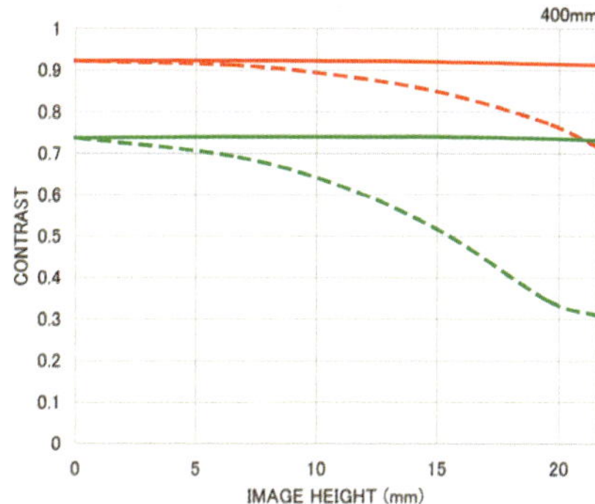

zoom ring instead. This can be a little confusing at first. A consistent alternative is to support the lens by holding the substantial grip that forms part of the tripod collar, though the thumb position is a little uncomfortable.

The tripod collar itself does not sit in a groove around the lens. Instead, it slides onto the rear of the lens barrel and is seated by rotating it over two positioning pins before tightening the knurled locking nut. The collar is not hinged and can only be attached as described above, which means that it cannot be attached or detached while the lens is mounted on a camera body.

The three separate switches on the lens—zoom lock, AF/MF, and Optical Stabilizer—are all the same size, and are firm and positive. All three are positioned on the left of the lens barrel within easy reach of the fingers of the supporting hand.

The Optical Stabilizer, according to Sigma, is good for two stops. This means that it is possible to shoot images with a shutter speed two stops slower than would normally be the case in terms of camera shake. It does not, of course, make any difference to subject blur caused by movement of the subject itself.

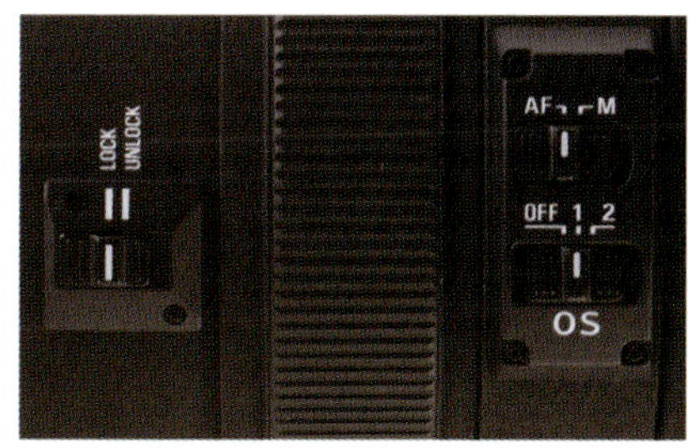

In practice, the claim of a two-stop improvement is perhaps a little conservative, and three stops would be nearer the mark. It is not possible to verify this objectively, of course, because so much depends upon handling technique.

The OS switch has three settings: Off, Position 1, and Position 2. Position 1 should be selected for normal use. Position 2 is used to combat vertical movement only, while panning in situations where the subject is moving horizontally to the camera. The Optical Stabilizer comes into play when focus is achieved, taking about one second to stabilize the image, producing a small amount of noise as it does so.

This lens can be used with either the Sigma 1.4× converter or the 2× version, but autofocus capability may be lost owing to the effective increase in maximum aperture.

PANNING
Position 2 on the OS switch should be selected when panning, so that the Optical Stablizer only combats vertical camera movement.

Verdict
Performance is excellent and the DG coatings combined with a deep lens hood virtually eliminate any chance of flare. Build quality is also excellent and typical of the EX range, though the lack of flexibility in use of the tripod collar is a disappointment. Fully extended to 400mm, the lens is appreciably longer and its handling characteristics change, so potential purchasers are encouraged to handle the lens before purchase. This lens has now been superseded by the 120–400mm version opposite.

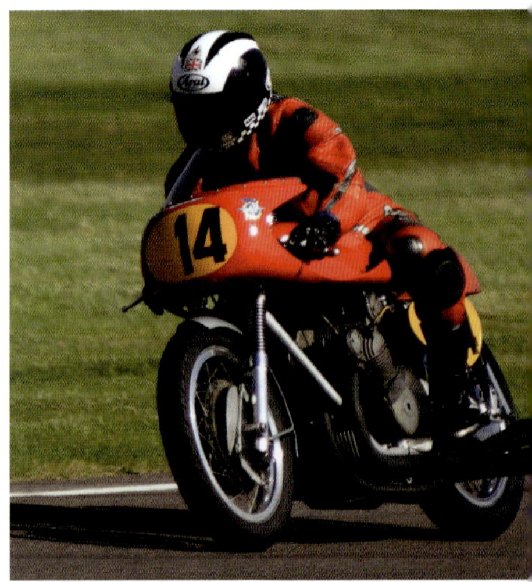

120–400mm f/4.5–5.6 DG OS HSM APO RF CONV

Specifications (based on Sigma mount)

Lens construction: 21 elements in 15 groups
Angle of view: 6.2°–20.4°
Diaphragm blades: 9
Min. aperture: f/22
Min. focusing distance: 150cm (59in)
Max. magnification: 1:4.2
Filter: 77mm
Dimensions: 92.5mm (W) × 203.5mm (L)
(3.6in × 8in)
Weight: 1750g (61.7oz)
Mounts: Sigma, Canon, Nikon (D)
Sony and Pentax versions are available without the OS function.

Note: The appearance of lenses may differ depending on the camera mount.

This is the big brother of the now discontinued 80–400mm on pages 170–2, and much that is written there applies to this version. Its weight remains the same, but lens extension at 400mm is reduced by 2cm (0.8in) to 6.5cm (2.6in), which improves the balance marginally, though the overall length is slightly greater. Focusing is internal, so there is no extension of the lens barrel, nor is there any rotation. Minimum focusing distance is reduced by 30cm (11.8in), which means that the maximum magnification ratio also benefits, from 1:5 to 1:4.2.

LENS CONSTRUCTION

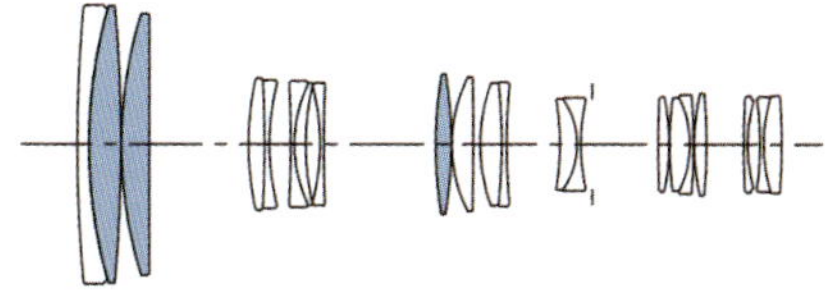

SLD glass

The MTF charts show impressive results across the range, in controlled conditions. In real life, it handles a good range of tones extremely well, but benefits from a bit of extra contrast in post-processing.

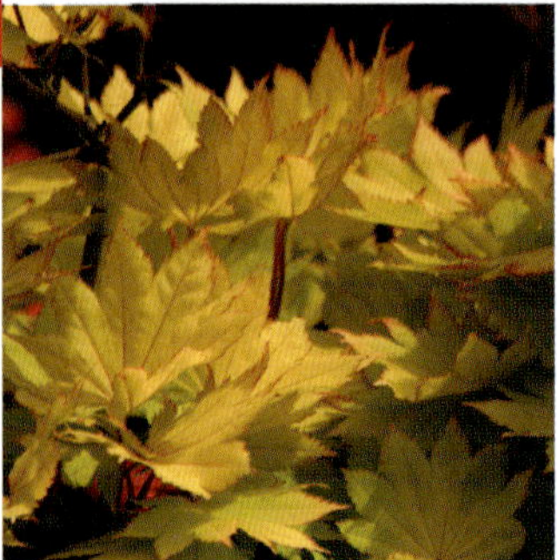

MAPLE LEAVES
Shot handheld using OS at 400mm and 1/400 sec at f/8.

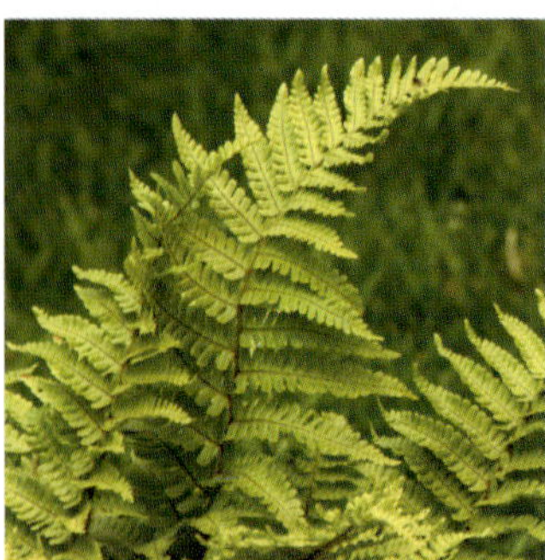

FERNS
Shot handheld using OS at 400mm and 1/30 sec at f/16.

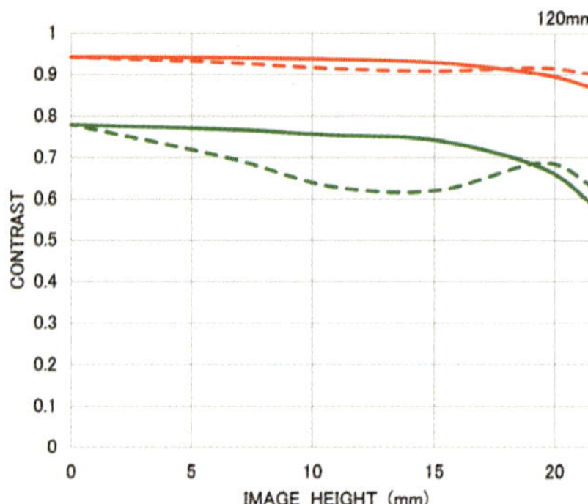

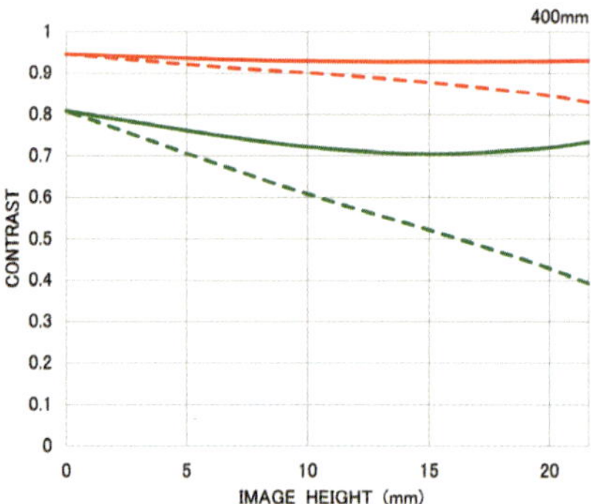

Verdict

Although the weight is a bit of a handful at first if you aren't used to lenses like this, using the OS facility quickly restores confidence. It also has to be remembered that when using a lens such as this at an event, it may actually replace two or more prime lenses and a second body, possibly with additional battery grip—and that alone makes it well worthy of consideration. Image quality is excellent and OS means that you can make the most of that quality in most situations without the aid of a tripod.

174

150–500mm f/5–6.3 DG OS HSM APO RF CONV

Specifications (based on Sigma mount)

Lens construction: 21 elements in 15 groups
Angle of view: 5°–16.4°
Diaphragm blades: 9
Min. aperture: f/22
Min. focusing distance: 220cm (86.6in)
Max. magnification: 1:5.2
Filter: 86mm
Dimensions: 94.7mm (W) × 252mm (L)
(3.7in × 9.9in)
Weight: 1780g (62.8oz)
Mounts: Sigma, Canon, Nikon (D)
Sony and Pentax versions are available without the OS function.

Note: The appearance of lenses may differ depending on the camera mount.

The third longest of Sigma's zooms in terms of reach, it is not much heavier than the 120–400mm (see pages 173–4) and, although it is 4.9cm (1.9in) longer when fully extended, I found it to be better balanced even with the additional 6.5cm (2.6in) at its maximum 500mm zoom setting.

Although the lens was initially tested mounted on a monopod, this and the tripod ring provided were quickly dispensed with in favor of working handheld and making occasional use of whatever support was available. To that end, the four-stop stabilizer worked a treat.

LENS CONSTRUCTION

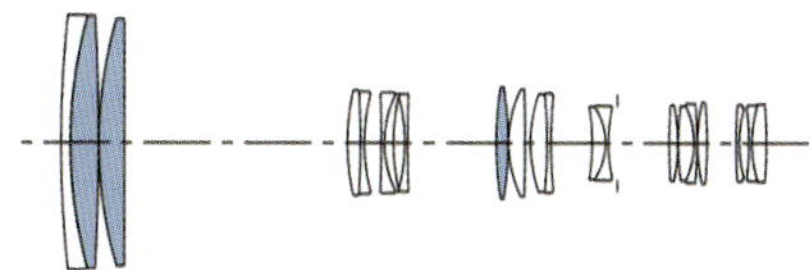

SLD glass

The tripod ring is not of hinged design, so the lens has to be taken off the camera in order to remove it. Front-mounted filters can be used, although only the less common size

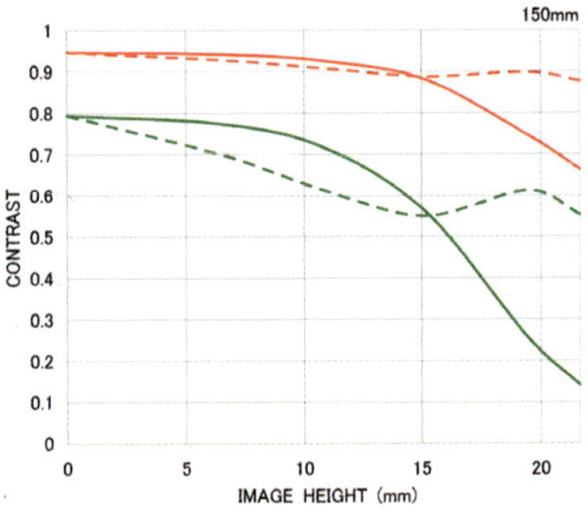

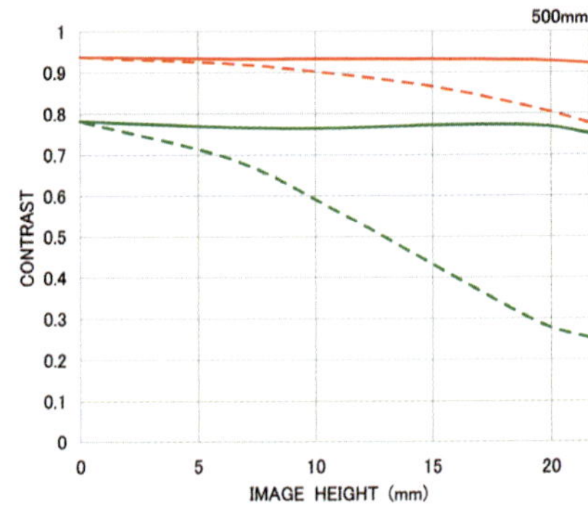

of 86mm. Otherwise, the lens design is as you might expect, including a locking switch to prevent zoom creep, which can lock the lens at its 150mm setting. The OS switch offers two settings, with Mode 2 being used when panning.

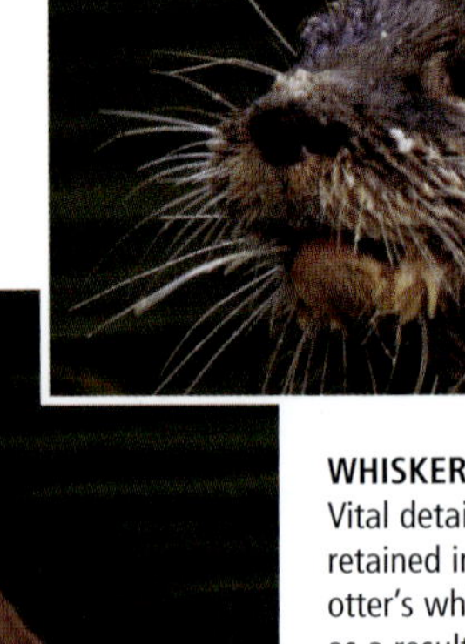

WHISKERS
Vital detail was retained in this otter's whiskers as a result of using the OS function.

In use, there is no need to stop the lens down from its maximum aperture unless huge enlargements or better depth of field are needed, as it performs extremely well at its widest aperture in conjunction with the OS system. In addition, the HSM's full-time manual override means that minor manual tweaks can be made after AF has done its job.

This lens will accept both 1.4× and 2× converters (except Pentax version), but this will take the effective maximum aperture into the realms of manual focus only.

Verdict
This lens typifies what Sigma does best—offering a product that simply isn't matched by the camera manufacturers or other independent lens producers; which has all the benefit of OS and HSM; and, to top it all, has a price that would knock spots off the competition—if there was any. Incredible value for money if you can live with an ISO setting a couple of stops faster.

MUD PACK
Despite the beauty treatment covering much of its face, this rhino's weathered hide is revealed in all its detail at settings that may well be typical when using this lens: ISO 400 and 1/500 at f/9 using the Optical Stabilizer.

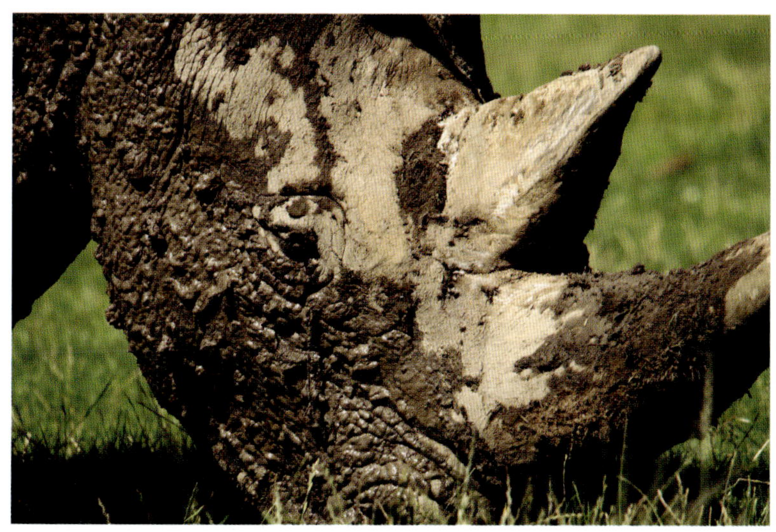

200–500mm f/2.8 EX DG IF APO CONV

Lens construction: 17 elements in 13 groups
Angle of view: 5°–12.3°
Diaphragm blades: 9
Min. aperture: f/22
Min. focusing distance: 200–500cm
(78.7–196.9in)
Max. magnification: 1:7.7
Filter: 72mm rear
Dimensions: 236.5mm (W) × 726mm (L)
(9.3in × 28.7in)
Weight: 15,700g (553.8oz)
Mounts: Sigma, Canon, Nikon (D)

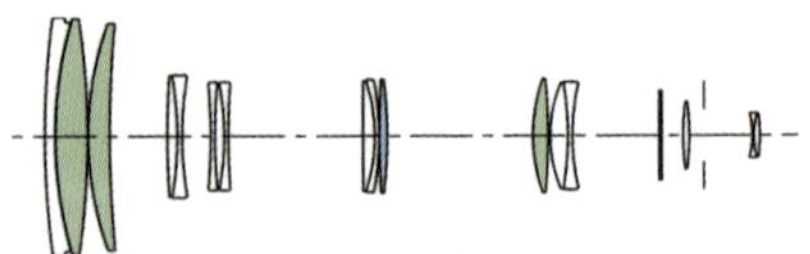

Note: The appearance of lenses may differ depending on the camera mount.

This lens is BIG. In fact, on internet forums it has acquired the nickname "Bigma." Launched in 2008, it has its own lithium-ion battery to power both zoom and focusing, and is yet another world first for Sigma: never before has a 500mm lens for photographers been made available with an f/2.8 maximum aperture.

It is mainly suited to working in a fixed position in a hide, or trackside during a sports event, and demands a substantial tripod and tripod head.

In addition to using Special Low Dispersion glass in its construction, the 200–500mm also has several

LENS CONSTRUCTION

Extraordinary Low Dispersion glass elements to correct optical aberrations, plus a Super Multi-Layer lens coating to reduce flare and ghosting. Filters can be inserted at the rear of the lens—including polarizing filters,

178

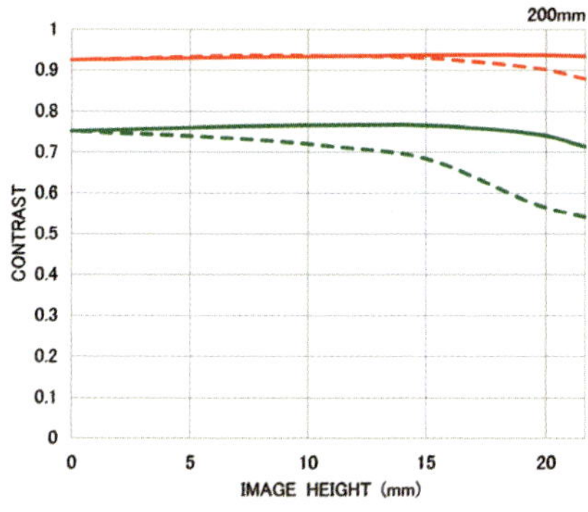

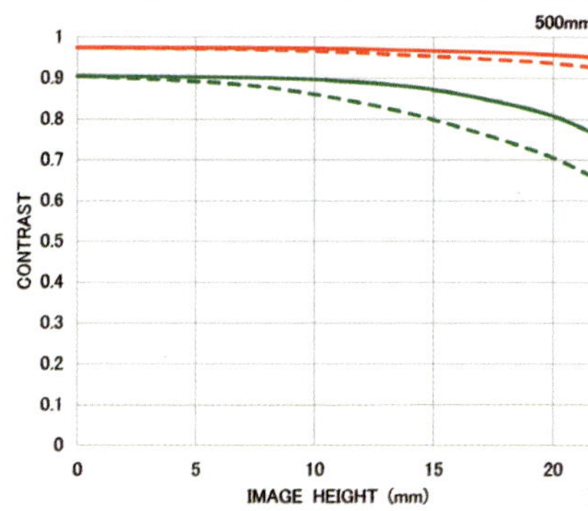

MTF Charts 200–500mm (Shown with 2× converter)

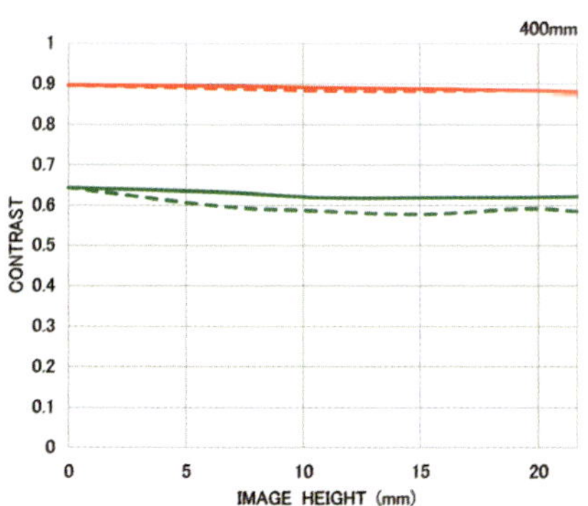

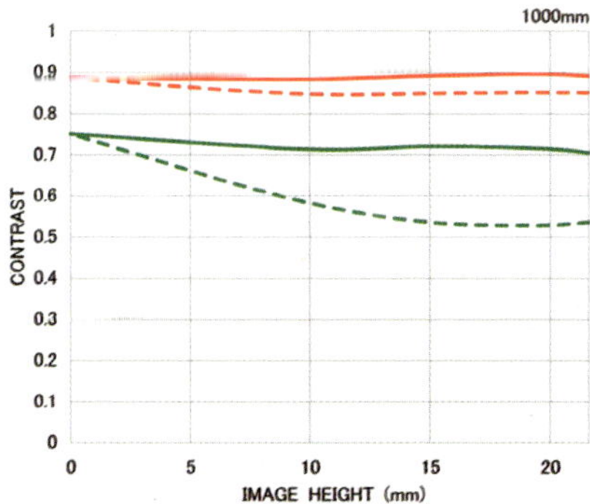

which can still be rotated. A built-in LCD panel displays focusing distance and focal length information.

A dedicated APO Teleconverter 2× EX DG II is supplied as standard, and its exclusive design minimizes any potential image degradation. When this is used with the 200–500mm, it becomes a 400–1000mm f/5.6, maintaining full AF functionality.

Verdict

Redefining the whole meaning of the term "specialized lens," the 200–500mm f/2.8 will find favor with a handful of professionals, while the rest of us watch quietly from the wings, in nothing less than a state of awe.

300–800mm f/5.6 EX DG HSM IF APO CONV

Specifications (based on Sigma mount)

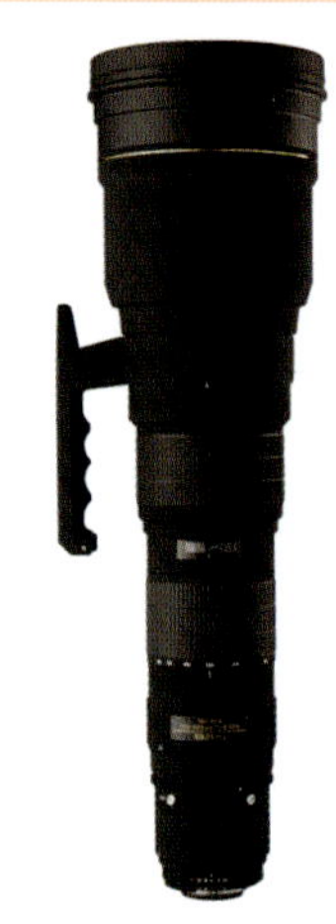

Lens construction: 18 elements in 16 groups
Angle of view: 3.1°–8.2°
Diaphragm blades: 9
Min. aperture: f/32
Min. focusing distance: 600cm (236.2in)
Max. magnification: 1:6.9
Filter: 46mm rear
Dimensions: 156.5mm (W) × 544mm (L)
(6.2in × 21.4in)
Weight: 5880g (207.4oz)
Mounts: Sigma, Canon, Nikon (D), Four Thirds

Note: The appearance of lenses may differ depending on the camera mount.

This lens would represent a huge investment. However, for sports and event photographers it is certainly worthy of serious consideration, as it offers a zoom range unmatched by the main camera manufacturers' own products. With the addition of a 1.4× or 2× converter, it becomes a 420–1120mm f/8 or 600–1600mm f/11, which should suit birdwatching enthusiasts too, though AF will be lost at these effective apertures.

The lens comes with a substantial carrying case, which would be improved greatly by providing

LENS CONSTRUCTION

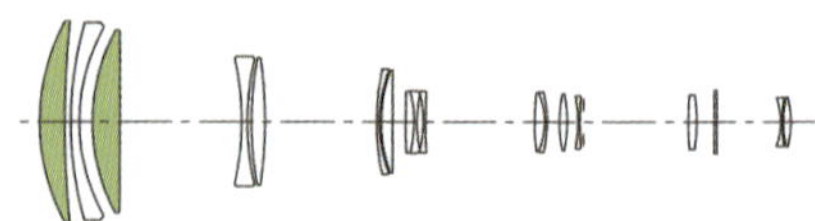

■ ELD glass

backpack-style shoulder straps and waistbelt like the Lowepro Lens Trekker. One good point about it, however, is that it is long enough

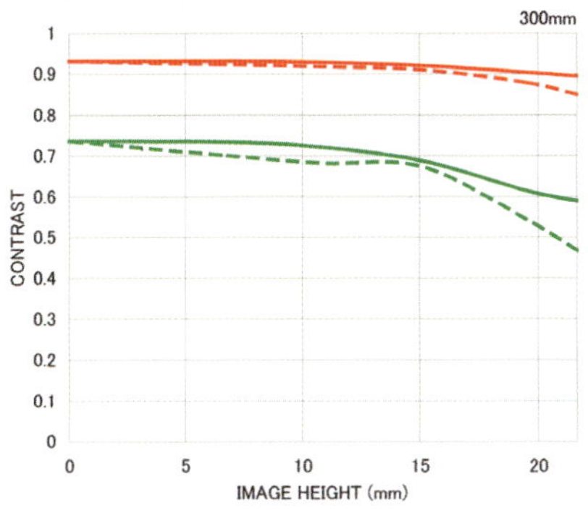

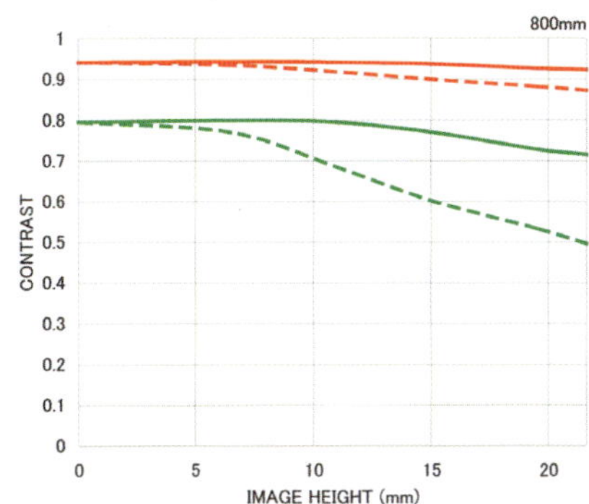

to permit the camera to be carried while the lens is fitted. Filters are restricted to the 46mm drop-in type.

Like a fish out of water until it is mounted on a monopod, the lens is surprisingly maneuverable in use. The option to pull back to 300mm to locate the subject before zooming back out again makes life a lot easier.

At around 80m (87.5 yards), a standing figure will fill the frame in portrait format, though capturing moving subjects requires anticipation, smooth reactions, and a high frame rate. Depth of field is obviously limited and in practice would appear to be less generous than is suggested by the published depth of field tables to be found on Sigma USA's website. Consistent quality is delivered across the zoom range at a constant aperture with good contrast. With HSM providing

full-time manual focusing, the fast, quiet, and reliable AF can be tweaked slightly at any time, though this proved unnecessary in a wide range of situations, with the AF holding focus very well on a moving subject.

Verdict

This lens is in a class of its own. Its zoom capability and price give it a real edge against the competition.

Photo essays

The great thing about digital photography is that you can fire off as many shots as you like at no extra cost. This makes it ideal for what I refer to as "stalking the subject" when I am compiling a group of images on a single theme. When a number of images are used together, whether framed as a group on a wall in your home or published in a magazine, they are described as a photo essay.

When I come across a good photographic situation, I always want to make the most of it and produce a variety of usable images. But I also find that stalking the subject gradually hones my ideas and the shots I obtain usually get better as I go along. However, it is usually still necessary to obtain a straightforward establishing shot

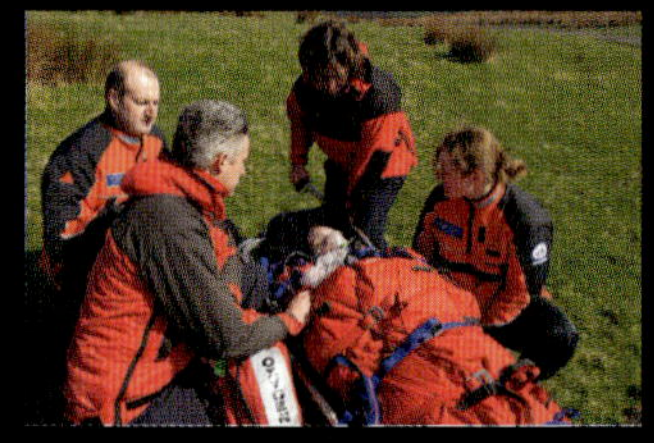

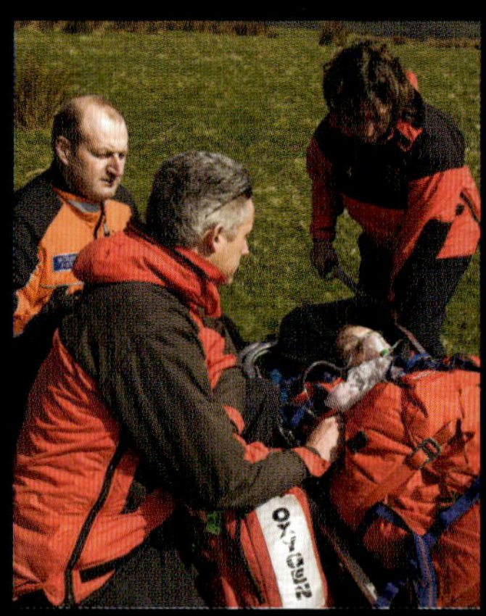

CROPPING
The landscape format image (top) captures the details of the team dealing with a rescue victim, but it all looks too relaxed. I achieved a greater sense of urgency by careful cropping into portrait format—note how each rescuer's line of sight focuses on the victim's face, increasing the intensity. The vital oxygen bottle also achieves more prominence in the frame.

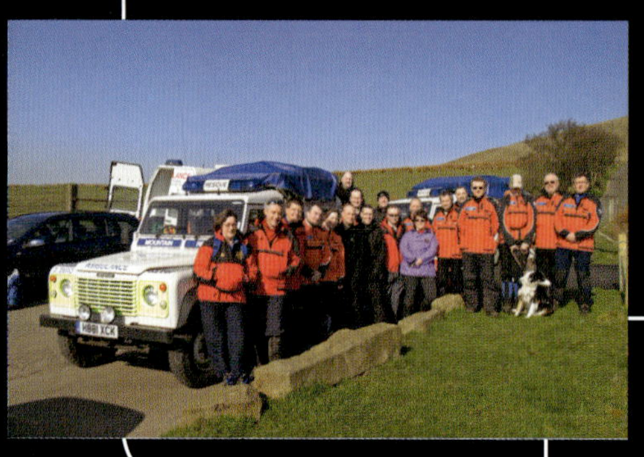

MOUNTAIN RESCUE TEAM
The establishing shot encompasses the whole subject and places it in context.

PORTRAIT FORMAT

I often shoot as many portrait format frames (vertical orientation) as I do landscape format, especially for magazine use. By encouraging the dog handler to allow her search and rescue dog to climb onto her knee, both achieve equal prominence and look like a team. It is also a pose that suits the vertical format perfectly.

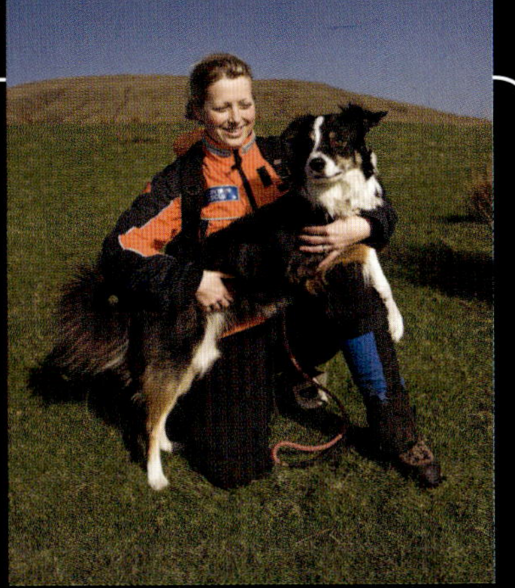

that acts as an introduction—just like the first paragraph in an essay. This image may be no more than a technically competent record of the subject or it may involve setting up a photo such as the group shot shown opposite.

These pictures were to be used to illustrate a magazine feature on my local mountain rescue team, and the image of the group had to be captured early in the day before everyone dispersed into the hills to carry out their various duties.

With this frame in the bag early on, I could concentrate on the individuals and their particular responsibilities, and any drama that the day might bring.

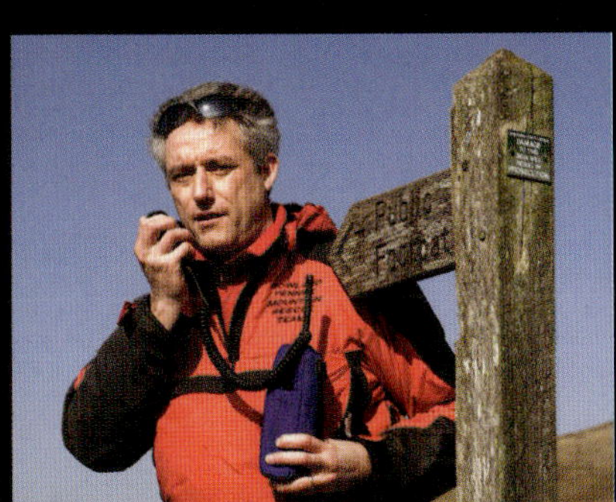

General settings

Focal length: 20mm
ISO: 400
Aperture: f/8
Shutter: 1/800

CONTEXT

Radio communication was all-important in this context. The question was how to dramatize it? I opted for a lower viewpoint to add subtle prominence to the subject and positioned him tight up against the signpost. This directs the eye into the image in quite dramatic fashion.

Street photography

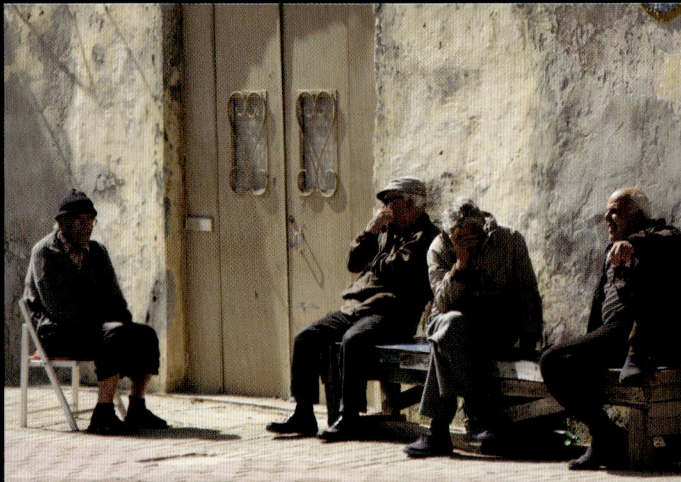

EXPRESSIONS
Like many candid opportunities, this scene was encountered quite by chance. The camera was in standby mode, already set up for the unexpected, and only needed partial pressure on the shutter release to activate it.

This style of photography requires considerable care with regard to people's privacy, but can be both exhilarating and rewarding. The laws governing privacy vary from country to country and you should make yourself aware of them before starting out.

For example, in some countries, it is permissible to photograph people in a public place provided it is not a situation in which the subject has a reasonable expectation of privacy, the photograph or its treatment is not defamatory, and the image is not used to advertise or market a specific product or service. In others, the law states that every individual owns the rights to his or her own image, and a photographer can be sued if permission has not been obtained, even when the subject has been photographed in a public place.

Settings
Focal length: 85mm
ISO: 100
Aperture: f/4
Shutter: 1/1000

Positioning the subject

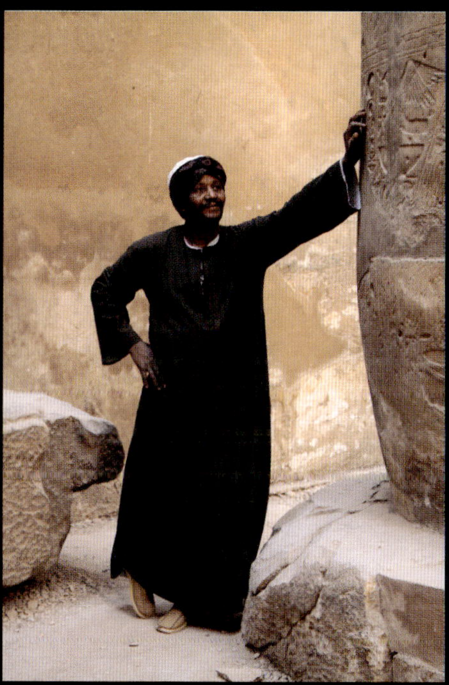

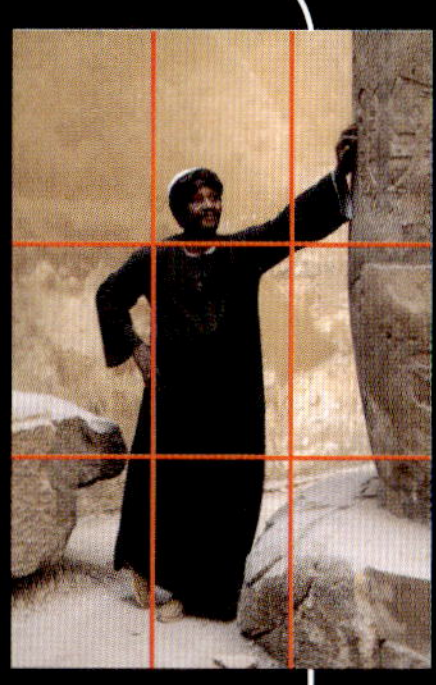

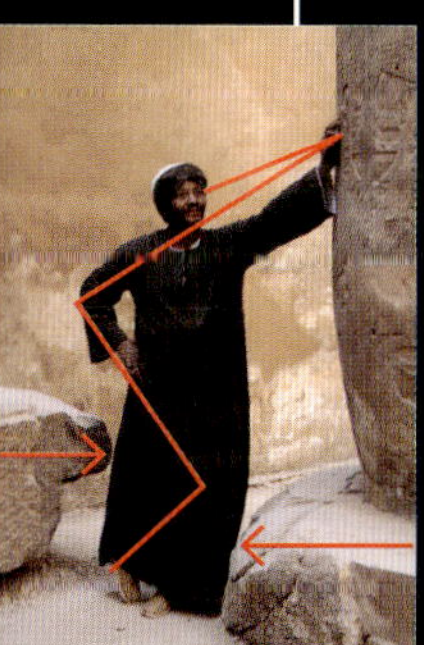

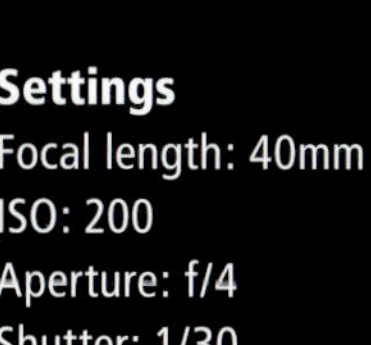

Settings
Focal length: 40mm
ISO: 200
Aperture: f/4
Shutter: 1/30

The main subject in this image is obviously the man, but the column with its hieroglyphs is also of secondary importance. The first inset image shows how this subject occupies the frame when it is divided into thirds. Of more importance, in terms of dynamics, are the lines shown in the second inset image. Note how the blocks of stone at the bottom of the image act as "stoppers" that help to concentrate the eye on the central figure. (The one on the left also lies on a "third.") The diagonal lines also help to keep the eye centered on the main subject, with a strong diagonal formed by the arms traveling almost through the face to meet his line of sight where his hand rests on the pillar and its strongest hieroglyph.

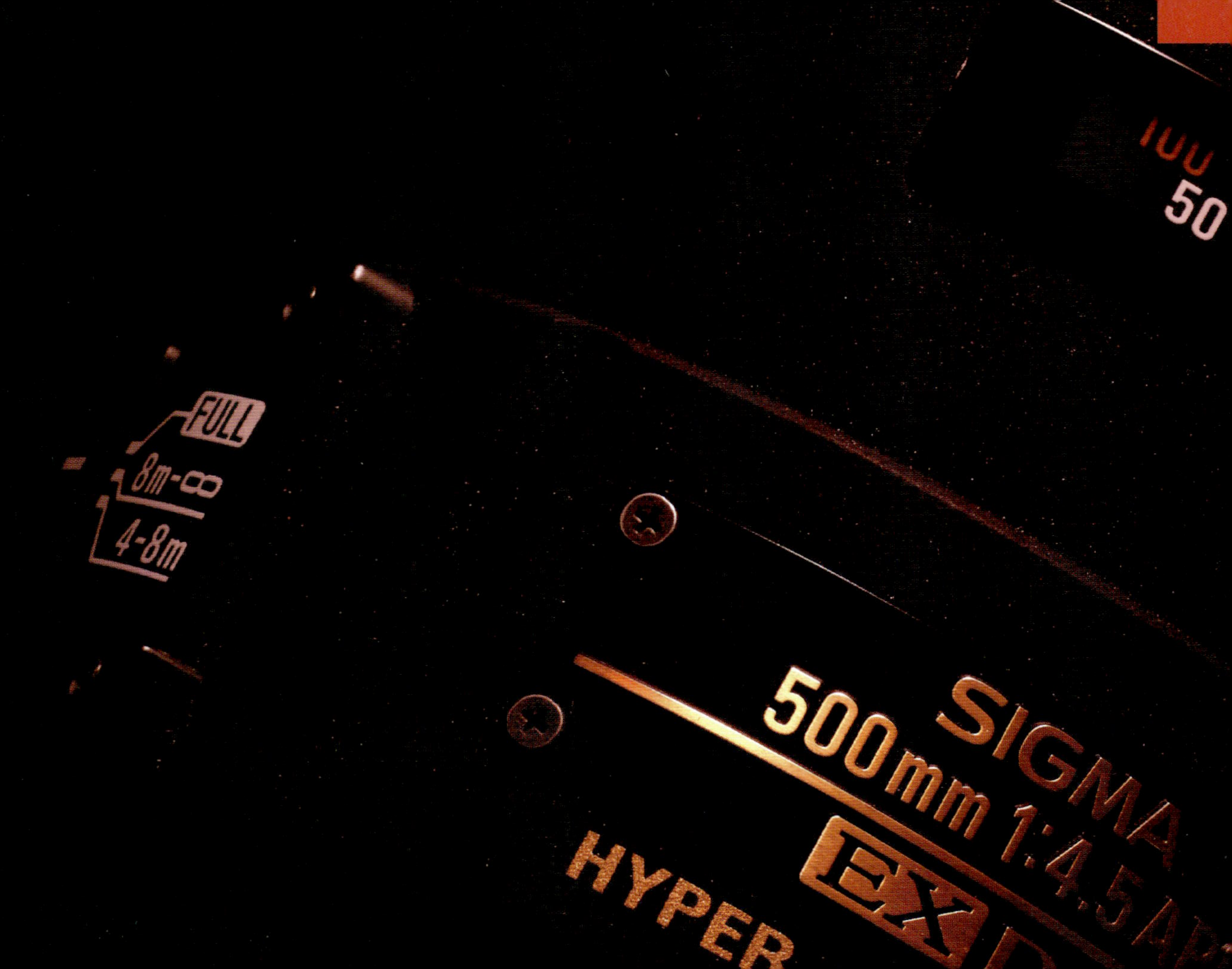
100
50
FULL
8m-∞
4-8m
SIGMA
500mm 1:4.5 AP
EX
HYPER

Chapter 9

Prime telephoto lenses & converters

If a wider maximum aperture and especially outright image quality are your main concern, prime—or fixed focal length—lenses are still a cut above the rest, never mind the numerous improvements that have been made to zoom lenses in recent years. The reason for this is simple enough: the prime lens design needs to perform just one set of tasks, while zoom lenses are required to suit a wide range of purposes.

Each of Sigma's prime telephoto lenses makes use of Extraordinary Low Dispersion glass, and a quick glance at their respective MTF charts tells a story of superb contrast and resolution across the frame, corner to corner, in each case—even with full-frame cameras.

In normal circumstances, it is worthwhile advocating the use of full-frame lenses on APS-C cameras because the slight deterioration in quality toward the edge of the frame is cropped out with the smaller sensor. Frankly, with Sigma's fixed focal length lenses, it wouldn't make any difference anyway, because there simply isn't any fall-off in quality to speak of.

There is also the issue of the maximum aperture to consider, especially if teleconverters are to be used. In the case of the 300mm lens, having a maximum aperture of f/2.8 is very important. Why? Because autofocus will not be retained if the effective aperture of any lens/converter combination exceeds f/5.6.

The two-stop loss when the 2× converter (or one-stop loss with the 1.4× converter) is fitted to the 300mm means that AF is fully retained. However, when these are added to the two longer focal lengths, manual focus becomes the order of the day. At such focal lengths, however, manual focus really isn't difficult, as the depth of focus is so shallow that the subject jumps in and out of focus quite sharply anyway.

1.4× and 2× EX DG APO teleconverters

Both of the current generation of Sigma teleconverters make use of apochromatic lens design to maximize image quality. However, neither can be fitted to every lens in the lineup. The table on pages 190–1 details the compatibility options available. To fit the teleconverter, attach it to the lens first. Then mount the lens/converter combination onto the camera. Any other sequence may result in malfunction.

Caution!

Converters can only be used on certain lenses. If the lens is incompatible, there is a danger of its rear element being damaged by contact with the converter. For compatible Sigma lenses, see pages 190–1. For compatible lenses from other manufacturers, refer to the manufacturer's website.

1.4× converter

Specifications

Elements/groups: 5/3
Coupling range: f/2.8–f/32
Dimensions: 68.5mm (W) × 19.5mm (L) (2.7 × 0.8in)
Weight: 143g (5oz)

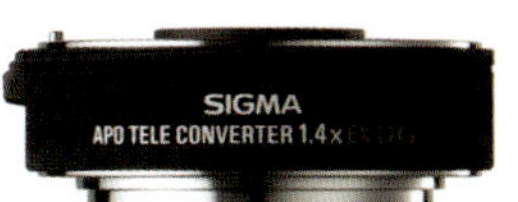

2× converter

Specifications

Elements/groups: 6/5
Coupling range: f/2.8 - f/32
Dimensions: 68.5mm (W) × 52mm (L) (2.7 × 2in)
Weight: 234g (8.3oz)

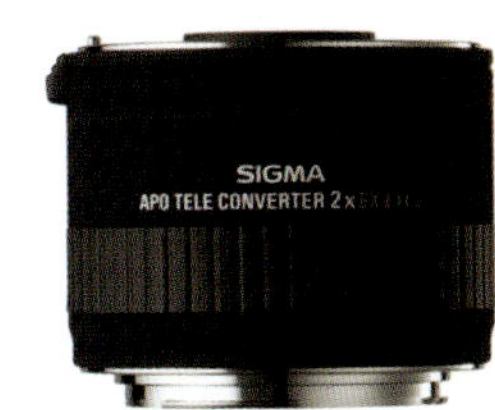

1.4× and 2× converter compatibility

Lens compatibilty	Converter	Effective focal length	Effective aperture
150mm f/2.8 EX DG Macro	1.4×	210mm	f/4
150mm f/2.8 EX DG Macro	2×	300mm	f/5.6
180mm f/3.5 EX DG Macro	1.4×	252mm	f/4.9
180mm f/3.5 EX DG Macro	2×	360mm	f/7
300mm f/2.8 EX DG	1.4×	420mm	f/4
300mm f/2.8 EX DG	2×	600mm	f/5.6
500mm f/4.5 EX DG	1.4×	700mm	f/6.3
500mm f/4.5 EX DG	2×	1000mm	f/9
800mm f/5.6 EX DG	1.4×	1120mm	f/8
800mm f/5.6 EX DG	2×	1600mm	f/11
50–150mm f/2.8 II EX DC	1.4×	70–210mm	f/4
50–150mm f/2.8 II EX DC	2×	100–300mm	f/5.6
50–500mm f/4–6.3 EX DG*3	1.4×	140–700mm	f/7.3–8.8
50–500mm f/4–6.3 EX DG*3	2×	200–1000mm	f/10.4–12.6
70–200mm f/2.8 II EX DG	1.4×	98–280mm	f/4
70–200mm f/2.8 II EX DG	2×	140–400mm	f/5.6
80–400mm f4.5–5.6 EX OS	1.4×	112–560mm	f/6.3–7.84
80–400mm f4.5–5.6 EX OS	2×	160–400mm	f/9–11.2
100–300mm f/4 EX DG	1.4×	140–420mm	f/5.6
100–300mm f/4 EX DG	2×	200–600mm	f/8
120–300mm f/2.8 EX DG	1.4×	168–420mm	f/4
120–300mm f/2.8 EX DG	2×	240–600mm	f/5.6
120–400mm f4.5–5.6 DG OS	1.4×	168–560mm	f/6.3–8
120–400mm f4.5–5.6 DG OS	2×	240–800mm	f/9–11
150–500mm f/5–6.3 DG OS	1.4×	210–700mm	f/7–8.8
150–500mm f/5–6.3 DG OS	2×	300–1000mm	f/10–11
200–500mm f/2.8 EX DG	2×*4	400–1000mm	f/5.6
300–800mm f/5.6 EX DG	1.4×	420–1120mm	f/7.8
300–800mm f/5.6 EX DG	2×	600–1600mm	f/11.2

Focus function	Max. macro ratio
AF *1	1:4.1
MF	2:1
AF*1	1.4:1
MF	2:1
AF	1:5.4
AF	1:3.8
MF*2	1:5.5
MF	1:3.9
MF	1:6.3
MF	1:4.4
AF	1:3.8
AF	1:2.7
MF	1:3.7
MF	1:2.6
AF	1:5.6
AF	1:3.9
MF	1:3.6
MF	1:2.5
AF	1:3.6
MF*2	1:2.5
AF	1:6.1
AF	1:4.3
MF	1:3
MF	1:2.1
MF	1:3.7
MF	1:2.6
AF	n/a
MF	1:4.9
MF	1:3.5

Notes

For Canon, Nikon, and Sigma AF cameras, autofocus operates from 119.4cm (47in) to infinity. Manual focus must be used from 45.7cm (18in) to 119.4cm (47in). For Minolta and Pentax AF cameras, manual focus only can be used.

*1 With 1.4×, manual focus is necessary at closest focusing distances.

*2 MF for all cameras, except Canon EOS 3 and EOS 1V, which can use autofocus with this combination.

*3 Zoom control range is limited to 100–500mm when the teleconverters are used with this lens.

*4 This lens uses a dedicated 2× converter, not the standard 2× converter.

Corrected effective aperture will be displayed on the camera's digital display, and TTL exposure will be normal, when these teleconverters are used with the lenses listed.

300mm f/2.8 EX APO DG HSM IF CONV

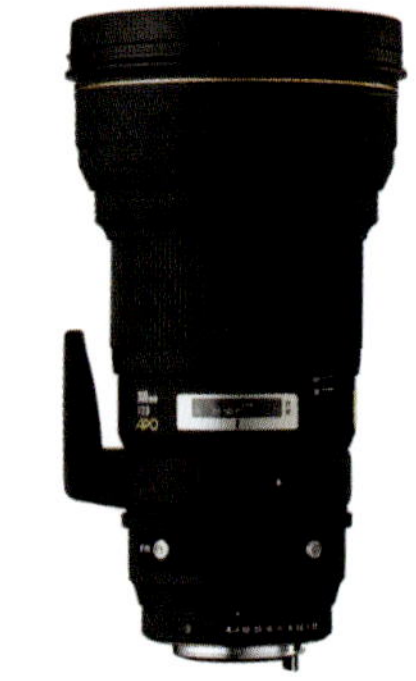

Lens construction: 11 elements in 9 groups
Angle of view: 8.2°
Diaphragm blades: 9
Min. aperture: f/32
Min. focusing distance: 250cm (98.4in)
Max. magnification: 1:7.5
Filter: 46mm rear (drop-in)
Dimensions: 119mm (W) x 214.5mm (L) (4.7in × 8.4in)
Weight: 2400g (84.7in)
Mounts (HSM): Sigma, Canon, Nikon (D)
Mounts (non-HSM): Sony, Pentax (not SFX or SF7)

Note: The appearance of lenses may differ depending on the camera mount.

Probably the most versatile of Sigma's longer lenses, and a great deal less expensive than the equivalent offerings from the major camera manufacturers, this is a superb performer by any standard.

This lens makes extensive use of Extraordinary Low Dispersion glass at the front end. Sharpness and contrast are excellent, and both are sustained from corner to corner.

The lens has been designed with action and sports photography in mind, when the highest shutter speeds invariably mean working

LENS CONSTRUCTION

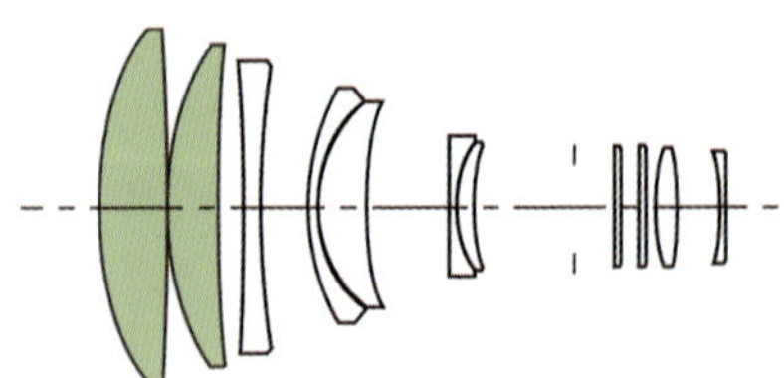

ELD glass

with the lens at its maximum aperture, or close to it. I have owned this lens for years and never used it any narrower than f/5.6.

MTF Chart 300mm

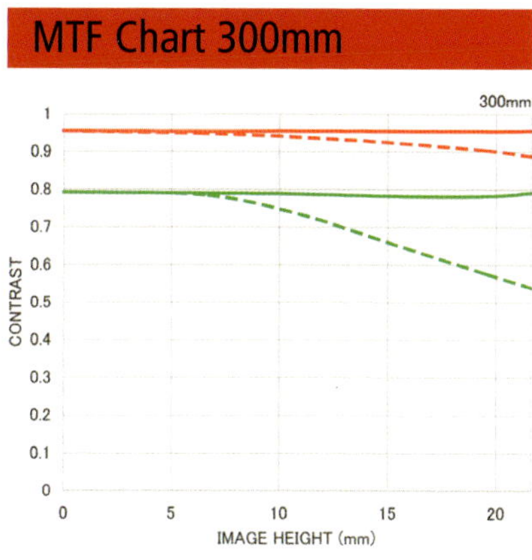

The tripod ring is hinged, enabling it to be removed quickly and easily for working handheld, when despite its weight, the lens is easy to control. In fact, it is even easier when panning than stationary.

It comes with a very substantial lens hood that can be reversed for carrying, but the addition of the hood makes a huge difference to the space needed in your camera bag. With such a huge front element to gather all that light, it takes drop-in filters, reducing the cost, but also the range of filters that can be used.

Depth of field (m): 300mm f/2.8 EX APO DG HSM

Circle of confusion: 0.3333mm

Focused at	Aperture	2.8	4	5.6	8	11	16	22	32
2.5m	Near	2.494	2.492	2.488	2.483	2.476	2.467	2.453	2.435
	Far	2.506	2.508	2.512	2.517	2.524	2.534	2.549	2.570
5m	Near	4.97	4.96	4.95	4.93	4.90	4.86	4.80	4.73
	Far	5.03	5.04	5.05	5.07	5.11	5.15	5.22	5.31
10m	Near	9.89	9.85	9.80	9.70	9.59	9.43	9.21	8.92
	Far	10.11	10.16	10.22	10.32	10.45	10.65	10.95	11.40
20m	Near	19.56	19.40	19.16	18.83	18.38	17.80	17.01	16.03
	Far	20.46	20.64	20.92	21.33	21.94	22.86	24.30	26.69
50m	Near	47.29	46.35	44.99	43.20	40.90	38.04	34.62	30.72
	Far	53.04	54.28	56.28	59.37	64.38	73.11	90.51	136.57
infinity	Near	865	629	445	315	223	158	112	79
	Far	inf	inf	inf	inf	inf	inf	inf	inf

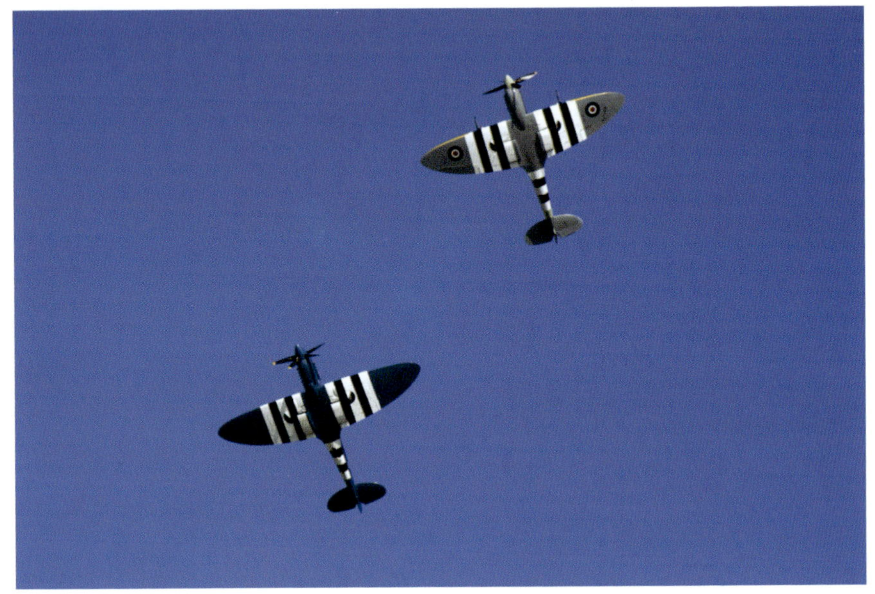

BRACE OF SPITFIRES
Captured handheld at f/3.5 during an air display, these Supermarine Spitfires are pin-sharp against a perfect blue sky.

Verdict

This is a first-class lens in every respect and a worthwhile investment for anyone interested in outdoor events and action photography where a longer reach is required. I can find only one possible reservation: Sigma really need to produce a stabilized version quickly to catch up with the camera manufacturers' versions.

Coupled with either the 1.4× or 2× converter, you also have a very manageable 420mm f/4 or 600mm f/5.6 (672mm f/4 or 960mm f/5.6 equivalent field of view on APS-C) without significant loss of image quality and without losing autofocus functionality.

500mm f/4.5 APO EX DG HSM IF CONV

Lens construction: 11 elements in 8 groups
Angle of view: 5°
Diaphragm blades: 9
Min. aperture: f/32
Min. focusing distance: 400cm (157.5in)
Max. magnification: 1:7.7
Filter: 46mm rear (drop-in)
Dimensions: 123mm (W) × 350mm (L)
(4.8in × 13.8in)
Weight: 3150g (111.1oz)
Mounts (HSM): Sigma, Canon, Nikon (D)
Mounts (non-HSM): Sony, Pentax (not SFX or SF7)

Note: The appearance of lenses may differ depending on the camera mount.

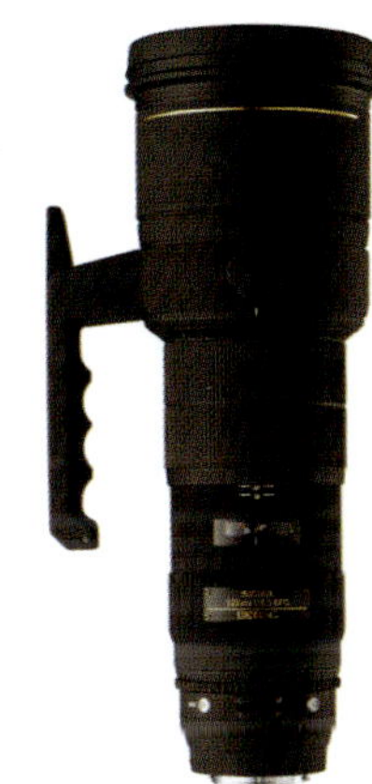

A substantially heavy lens, the 500mm f/4.5 is easily mastered when it is mounted on a monopod, but this highlights what is perhaps the lens's only weak point: the tripod ring cannot be removed for those times when the lens would be rested on an object such as a fence post, or when using it handheld. However, it does rotate completely when the locking knob is loosened and can be swiveled out of the way—essential during manual focusing, as the tripod ring's grip is in line with the ribbed rubber focusing ring.

LENS CONSTRUCTION

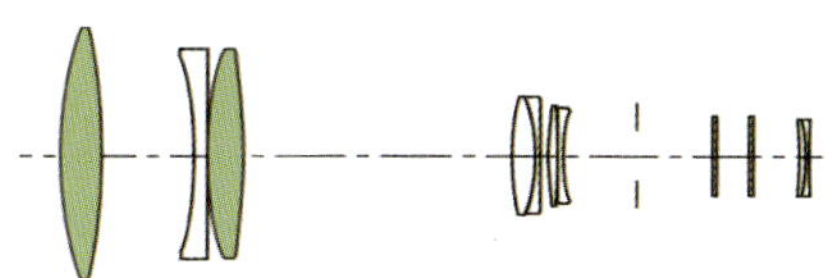

ELD glass

That minor grumble aside, the lens performs magnificently and provides enough working distance for photographing shy wildlife—with the exception of smaller birds and animals, which require either a converter or a switch to a longer focal length. With either the 1.4× or 2× converter, autofocus will almost certainly be lost, no matter which camera is being used.

A focus limiting switch on the side of the lens provides a choice of three settings: 4–8m, 8m to infinity, or the full range, and the HSM-controlled focusing is both fast and quiet, even on the full-range setting. Image quality is excellent across the board, but, in truth, it is more dependent on shutter speed and holding technique than the quality of the optics themselves. The combination of the large lens hood, which can be reversed for carrying, and a new multi-layer coating, along with two ELD elements, makes for sharp, high-contrast images with well-controlled flare and chromatic aberration.

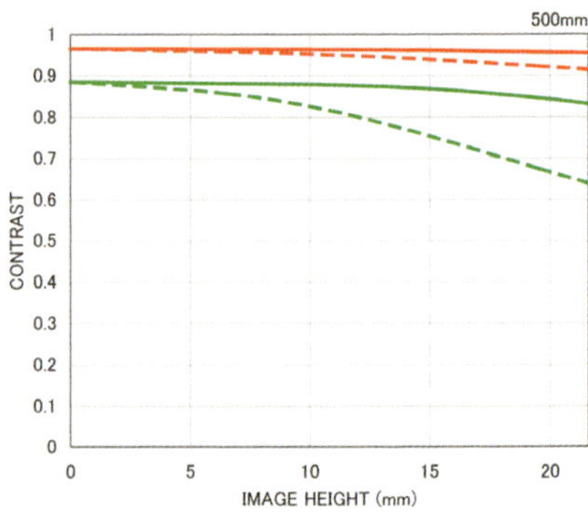

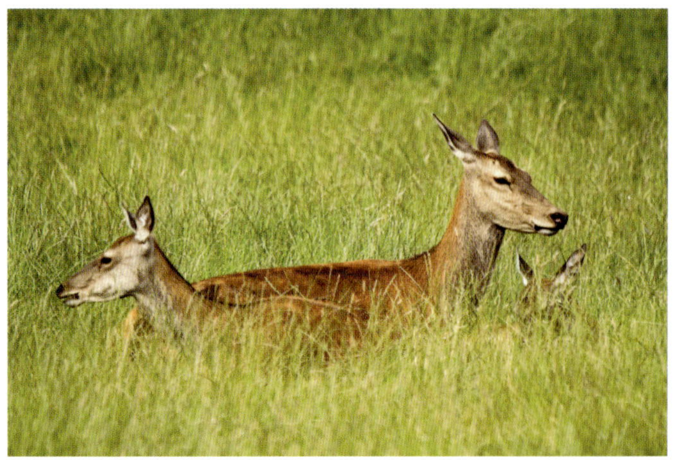

DEER
The 500mm f/4.5 gives you sufficient working distance to capture wildlife images like this without scaring your subject away.

Depth of field (m): 500mm f/4.5 APO EX DG HSM

Circle of confusion: 0.3333mm

Focused at Aperture		4.5	5.6	8	11	16	22	32
4m	Near	3.99	3.99	3.98	3.97	3.96	3.95	3.93
	Far	4.01	4.01	4.02	4.03	4.04	4.05	4.07
6m	Near	5.98	5.97	5.96	5.94	5.92	5.89	5.85
	Far	6.02	6.03	6.04	6.06	6.08	6.12	6.17
8m	Near	7.96	7.95	7.93	7.90	7.86	7.81	7.73
	Far	8.04	8.05	8.07	8.10	8.14	8.21	8.30
10m	Near	9.94	9.92	9.89	9.85	9.78	9.70	9.58
	Far	10.06	10.08	10.11	10.16	10.23	10.32	10.47
20m	Near	19.75	19.70	19.57	19.40	19.16	18.83	18.39
	Far	20.26	20.32	20.46	20.65	20.93	21.34	21.96
50m	Near	48.46	48.12	47.38	46.38	45.03	43.26	40.98
	Far	51.65	52.04	52.93	54.25	56.24	59.32	64.31
infinity	Near	1560	1280	905	640	453	321	227
	Far	inf	inf	inf	inf	inf	inf	inf

Verdict

This lens requires good handling technique—especially with moving subjects—and sufficiently regular usage to justify the substantial investment needed. Photographers prepared to meet those conditions will be well rewarded.

800mm f/5.6 EX DG APO HSM IF CONV

Lens construction: 12 elements in 9 groups
Angle of view: 3.1°
Diaphragm blades: 9
Min. aperture: f/32
Min. focusing distance: 700cm (275.6in)
Max. magnification: 1:8.8
Filter: 46mm rear (drop-in)
Dimensions: 156.6mm (W) × 521mm (L)
(6.2in × 20.5in)
Weight: 4900g (172.8oz)
Mounts: Sigma, Canon, Nikon (D)

Note: The appearance of lenses may differ depending on the camera mount.

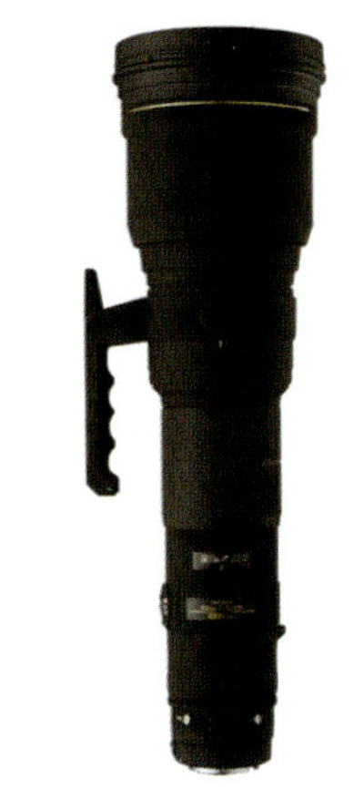

Like all Sigma's prime telephoto lenses, this lens makes use of Extraordinary Low Dispersion glass at the light-gathering end, which will feel a long way away when it is mounted on the camera. This is a large lens to carry around, with a weight to match, so it is most suited to those situations where you need extraordinary reach because you can't get as close to the subject as you would like: watching birds or wildlife from a hide, or sports with a fixed perimeter that distances you from the action, such as baseball or cricket.

LENS CONSTRUCTION

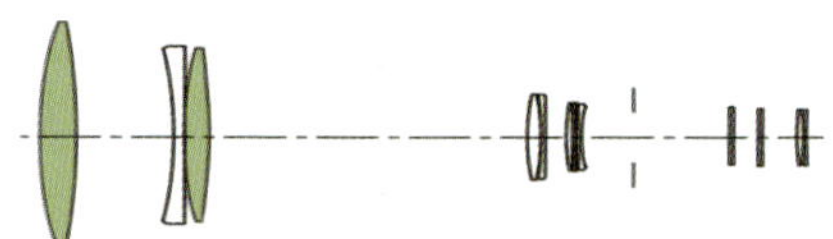

ELD glass

When mounted on a monopod, it is actually quite easy to maneuver, with the base of the handgrip on the tripod ring offering several

198

positions for fitting either tripod or monopod. However, tripod heads with quick-release plates are best avoided, given the substantial weight involved, unless the whole setup is to remain fixed in one place.

Image quality is excellent across the board, but your results will depend as much upon technique as optical quality. Lenses of this weight and length are in a different league if you are not used to them, bearing in mind that this has the same effective field of view on APS-C as a 1280mm on full-frame. That's effectively a 2560mm f/11 manual-focus monster if you add the 2x converter.

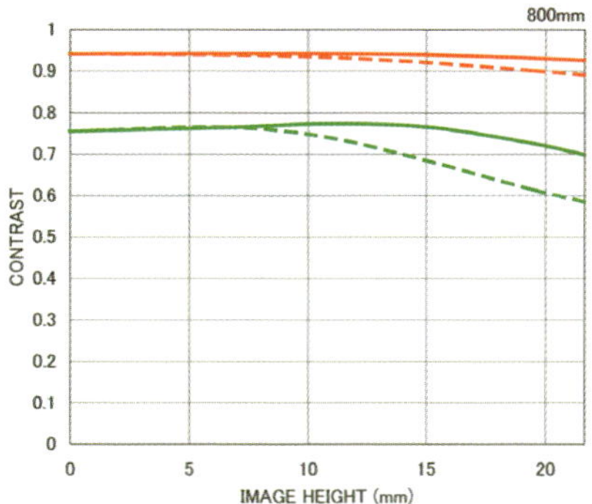

DROP-IN FILTER
A 46mm filter can be inserted near the rear of the lens, as shown below.

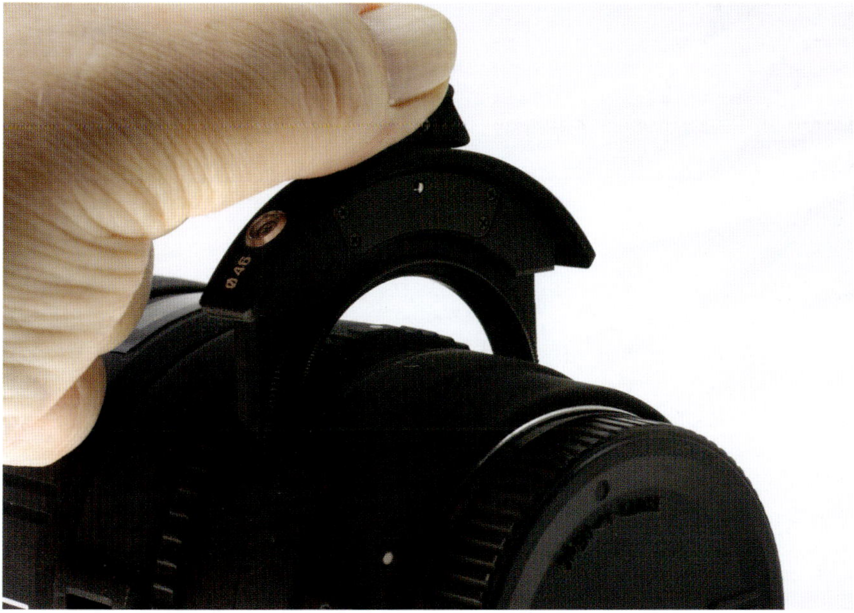

Depth of field (m): 800mm f/5.6 EX DG APO HSM

Circle of confusion: 0.3333mm

Focused at Aperture		5.6	8	11	16	22	32
7m	Near	6.98	6.98	6.97	6.96	6.94	6.91
	Far	7.02	7.02	7.03	7.05	7.07	7.09
12m	Near	11.95	11.94	11.91	11.87	11.82	11.74
	Far	12.05	12.07	12.09	12.13	12.19	12.27
20m	Near	19.87	19.82	19.75	19.65	19.51	19.31
	Far	20.13	20.18	20.26	20.37	20.52	20.75
30m	Near	29.71	29.60	29.44	29.22	28.91	28.48
	Far	30.30	30.41	30.58	30.83	31.19	31.71
100m	Near	96.9	95.8	94.1	91.9	88.9	85.0
	Far	103.4	104.6	106.7	109.8	114.4	121.7
infinity	Near	3092	2265	1603	1134	803	568
	Far	inf	inf	inf	inf	inf	inf

Verdict

A specialized lens for specific situations, with a price tag large enough to make you think twice. Nevertheless, the Canon equivalent is more than double the price, including image stabilization, and at the time of writing Nikon don't even produce anything this long.

200

Motion

Capturing a sense of motion essentially comes down to either freezing the action or exaggerating it through blur. In both cases, the key issue is the choice of shutter speed in relation to the speed of movement of the subject across the frame. This means that the camera-to-subject distance and the choice of lens also play a part.

With shutter speeds of up to 1/4000 or even 1/8000 sec now commonplace, freezing action is hardly difficult. However, it is often best to allow just a touch of blur to convey a better sense of movement. A good example would be the wheels of a race car, which rotate at a faster speed than the vehicle as a whole moves across the frame. The shutter speed needs to be fast enough to freeze the car, but slow enough to blur the wheels.

In the image below, the camera's fastest possible shutter speed of 1/4000 sec was ignored in favor of 1/1000 sec. Note how the front wheel shows distinct blur while the rest of the vehicle is comparatively sharp. Opting for a slightly slower shutter speed also means you can use a slower ISO speed for better quality and/or a slightly narrower aperture, creating better depth of field.

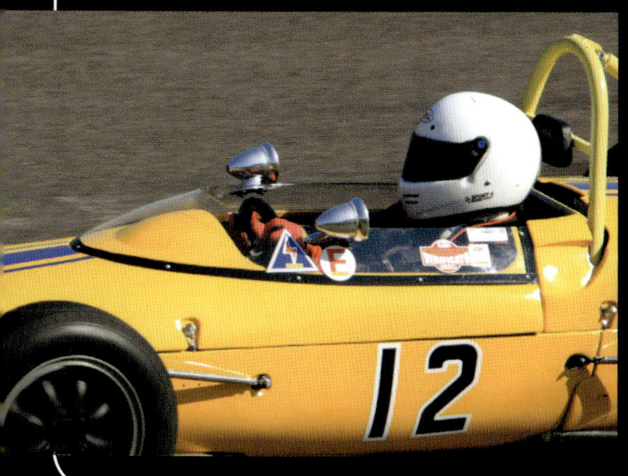

AUTO RACING

Settings
Focal length: 93mm (cropped)
ISO: 200
Aperture: f/5.6
Shutter: 1/1000

Bokeh

"Bokeh" is the term commonly used to describe the out-of-focus background caused by using wider apertures in situations where depth of field is limited.

These rosebud images were shot using apertures of (from left to right) f/32, f/18, f/8, and f/3.5 using Sigma's 180mm Macro lens on a Canon EOS 40D. You can easily see that there are two issues to bear in mind. The first is the out-of-focus blur in the background, and the second is what happens to small highlights. Highlights can take on a similar quality to that encountered with flare, as seen in the third image,

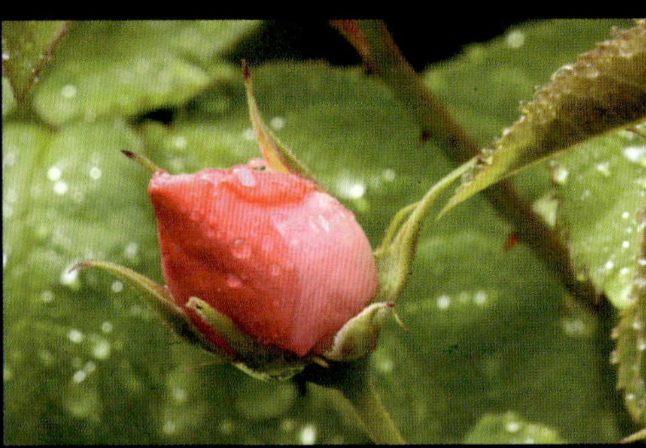

1/13 at f/32

ROSEBUD

Settings
Focal length: 180mm
ISO: 200

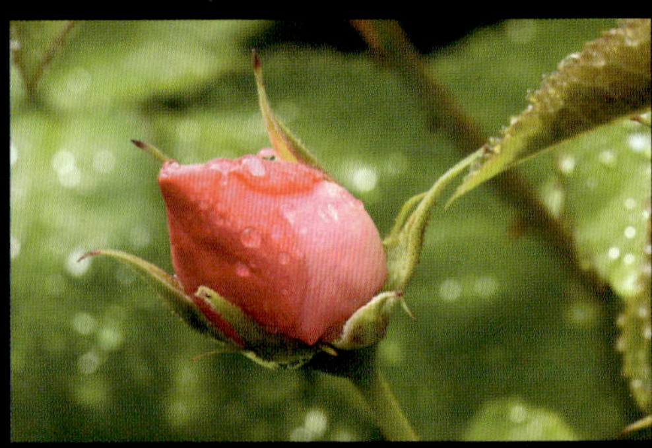

1/30 at f/18

shot at f/8. The most pleasing result, to my mind at least, is the image captured at f/3.5.

The image of the meerkat (right) had a very unsightly background, but fortunately it was about 3m (10ft) behind the subject. A Sigma 500mm f/4.5 lens, used wide open, saw to it that the backdrop was completely indistinguishable.

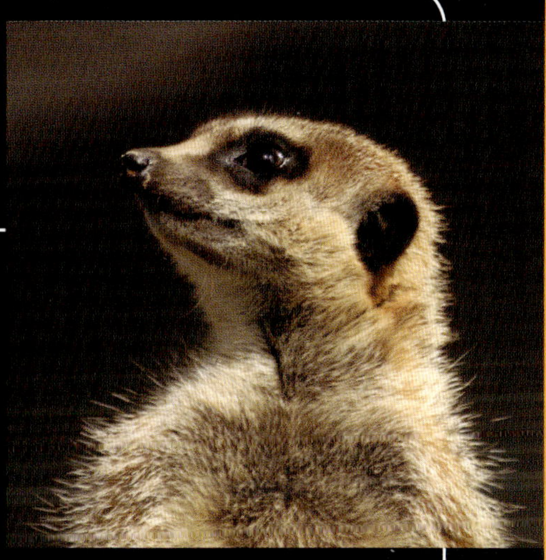

MEERKAT

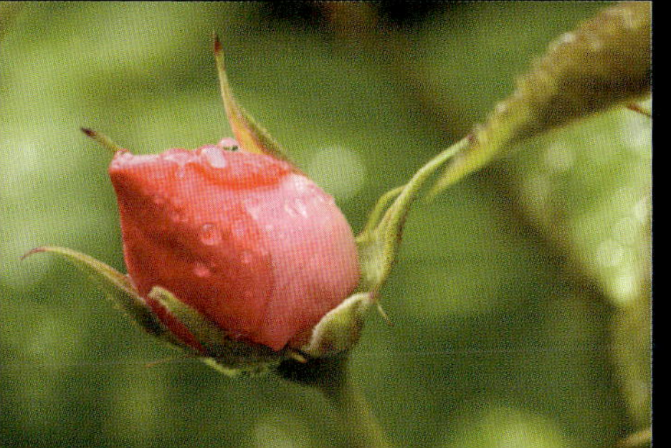

1/160 at f/8

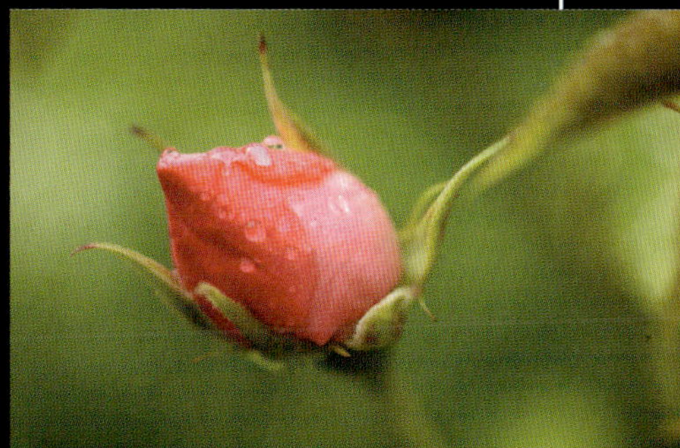

1/800 at f/3.5

Face-to-face

There is something extremely powerful about eye contact that can make all the difference to a photo. One look at this goose's countenance and there is absolutely no doubt who it is chasing after—it's you! Whether your subject is animal or human, it is usually important that their eyes are in sharp focus. Better still, try to include catchlights in the eyes—small bright reflections, usually from the lighting source, that give added life to the subject. The depth of focus in this shot of the charging goose was limited to about 2.5cm (1in), so timing and quick reactions were essential. The ability to judge when a shot is about to unfold, and anticipate the camera settings required, means you can focus (forgive the pun) on framing and the precise moment to trip the shutter.

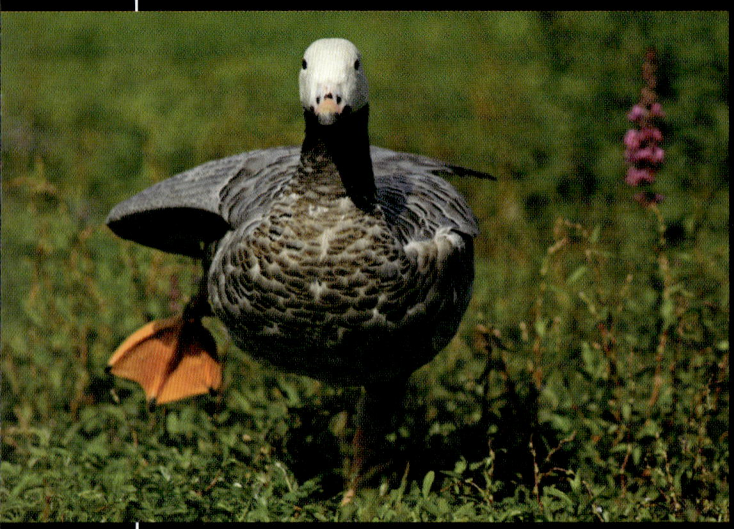

SPRINT

Settings
Focal length: 300mm +
1.4× converter
ISO: 200
Aperture: f/4
Shutter: 1/2000

The critical moment

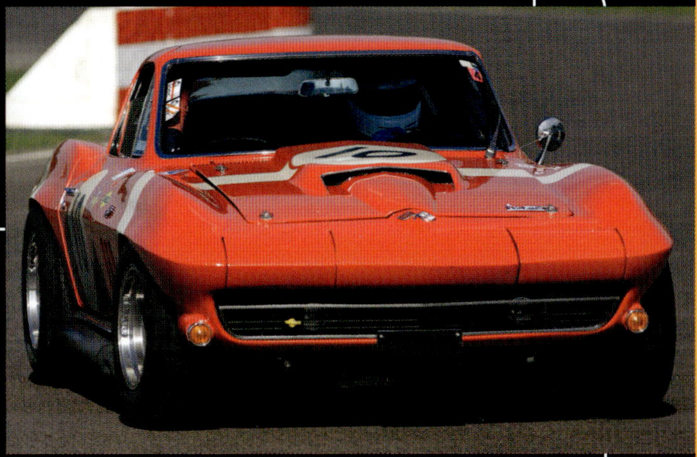

RAW POWER

When capturing a moving subject, watch out for times when the subject suddenly changes direction. These brief moments provide an opportunity to catch the subject when its speed is temporarily arrested, or at least reduced, a fraction of a second before it lurches off on a new trajectory. Such moments convey a huge amount of energy, despite the slight reduction in speed, because they capture all the latent momentum of the maneuver.

This image has been cropped, but only slightly. Filling the frame with a moving subject is as much about positioning as it is about quick reactions. For this shot, I was in exactly the right place to capture this Chevrolet Corvette Sting Ray just as it was exiting a chicane. Its speed was momentarily reduced and the side of the car was just visible as its wheels were angled for the approaching sprint onto the home straight.

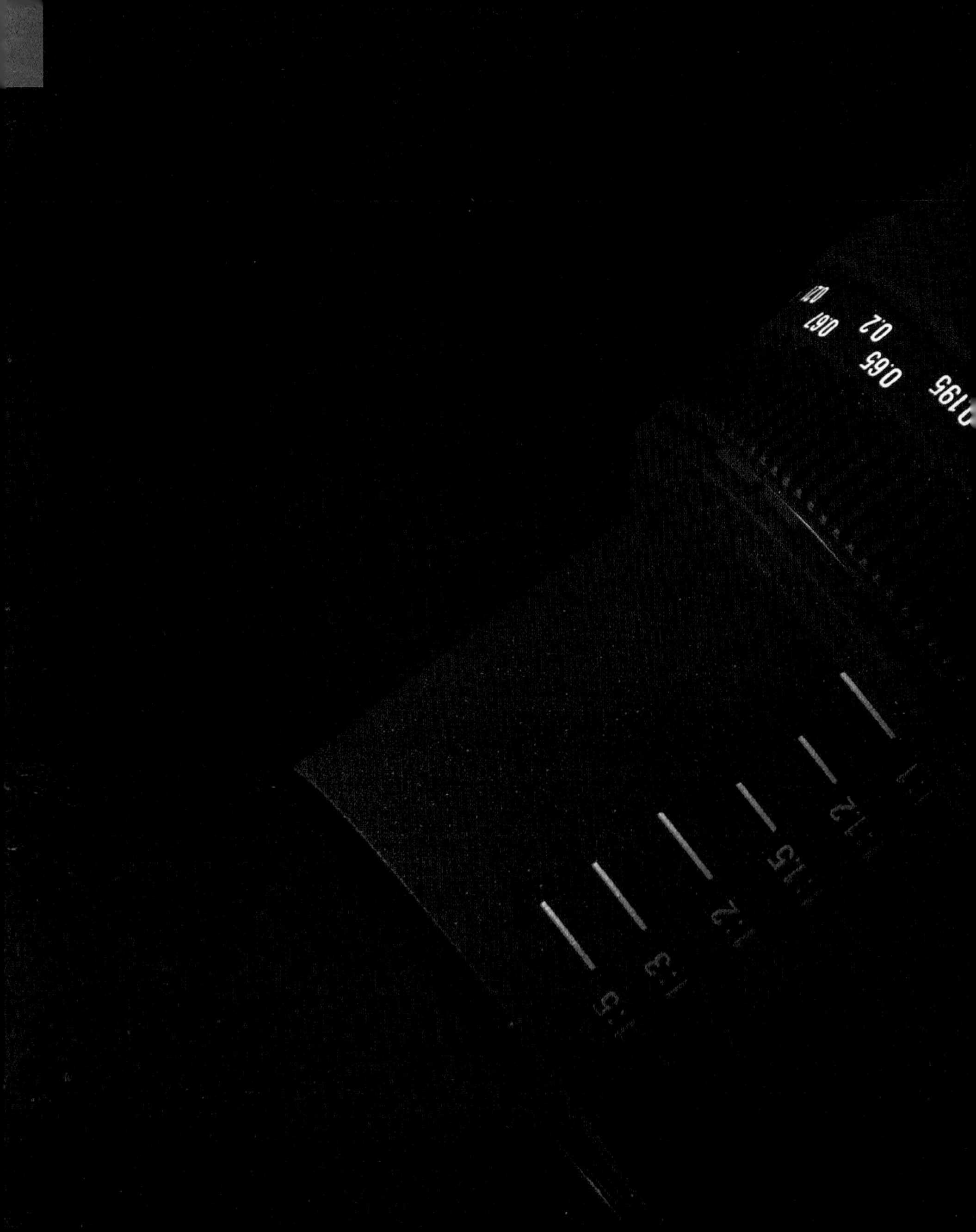

Chapter **10**

True macro lenses

The term "true" macro is used here to differentiate those lenses that provide 1:1 magnification from those that incorporate the term "macro" in their designations, but that offer magnifications less than life-size.

With the kind of magnification we are talking about here, there is more to consider than the camera and lens: technique, lighting, and camera support each play a vital role too. Technique doesn't just include the issues of focusing and determining the optimum exposure—both of which a modern DSLR will do for you with a very high success rate. It also includes using your background knowledge and experience to make decisions that will affect the final image, such as the placement of flash units and reflectors, whether to use mirror lockup, and when not to opt for the smallest aperture your lens will cater for. These decisions cannot be programmed into a camera.

The issue of which aperture to use is of particular importance with macro lenses, partially because the final image gives the viewer such a detailed representation of the subject, but also because macro lenses typically provide far narrower minimum apertures than is normally the case—f/45 on the 105mm f/2.8 EX DG Macro, for instance.

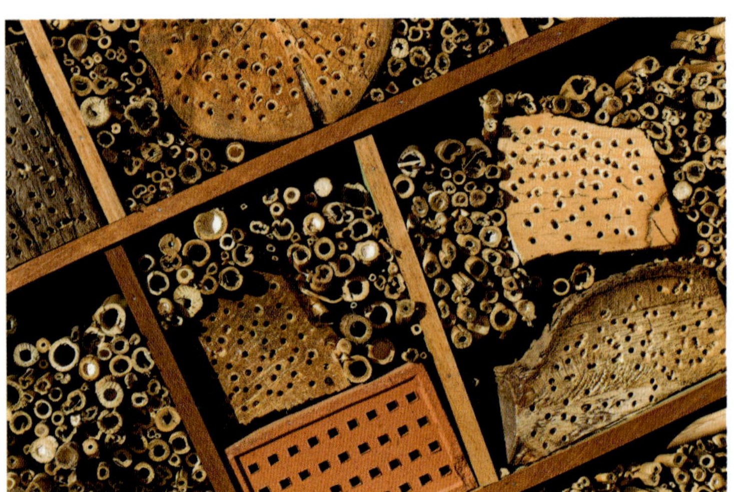

INSECT TOWER
Any subject with variety of shape and texture becomes fair game for close-ups, such as this tower for breeding insects.

While it is true that most lenses perform at their best when apertures two or three stops narrower than their maximum are selected, there is also a slight fall-off in performance toward the narrowest apertures, due to diffraction. The light waves passing through the lens also have to pass through the hole or "aperture" created by the diaphragm blades before they form the image. As long as light waves travel in a straight line, they are not an issue—that is why the center of an image is always the sharpest part of the photo. When light waves bend because they encounter an obstacle, it is known as refraction. Most people will have encountered this, without necessarily knowing what it is called—just think of looking up while you are below the surface of a swimming pool and remember all those fractured images.

But when light waves are made to change direction—as with those hitting the outer parts of a lens that has been shaped to refocus them at a certain point, along with all the other light waves—there is a loss of quality. Similarly, light waves passing over the edge of the aperture blades will be slightly bent, resulting in a small degree of diffusion and loss of sharpness. This loss of sharpness is known as diffraction. The smaller the aperture, the higher the proportion

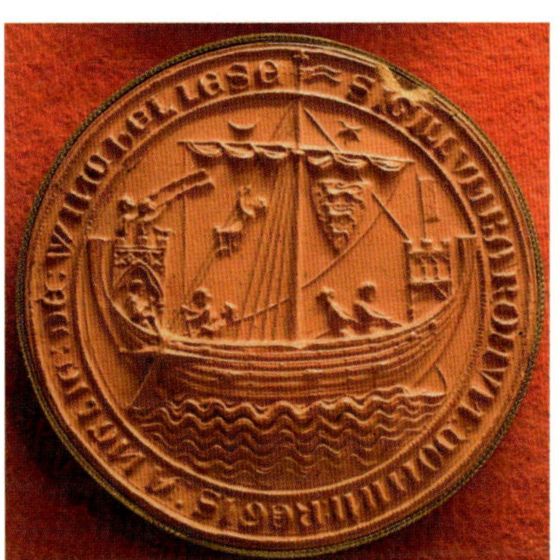

CINQUE PORTS SEAL
Flat subjects can be captured at relatively wide or medium apertures, thus avoiding diffraction.

of light waves that will be affected—which is why, for absolute detail and huge enlargements, the narrowest apertures may need to be avoided.

As with so many aspects of photography, it is a trade-off: less depth of field, but extremely sharp in-focus areas, or greater depth of field with slightly less resolution across a wider area. The factors that determine your choice will be the size at which the final image will be displayed, and the distance between the viewed image and the viewer.

Close-up photography

When exploring the topic of close-ups in general, you will encounter a number of terms relating to different techniques and technology. These are not always used in exactly the same way, but the following broad definitions should help you to decipher the information you find. Remembered that language is constantly evolving; the meanings of words change and new ones enter our vocabulary all the time—never more so than in the last decade and its technological rollercoaster ride.

The term "close-up" itself is usually reserved for an image of a single subject, which homes in on the subject to the exclusion of its surroundings. In photographic terms, it may be used to describe an image captured somewhere near the minimum focusing distance of the lens in use.

Macro photography

Linguistically speaking, the term "macro" comes from the Greek word for large or long, but it is also commonly used as the opposite to "micro," as in macrocosm. Macro photography used to be defined as images of a subject that were rendered life-size on the film or sensor—in other words, with a magnification ratio of 1:1. Over a period of time, the term has started to be used more loosely, to include lenses that perhaps captured an image at half-size, but to which lens a life-size converter could be added. There are many lenses that now use the designation "macro," but which only offer magnification

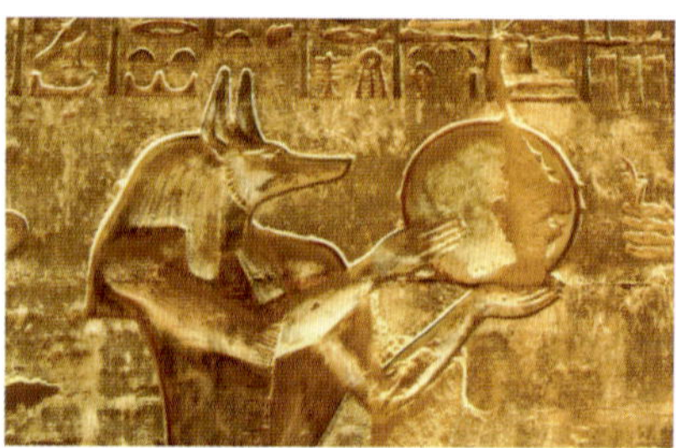

ANCIENT EGYPT
Extremely fine detail is shown in this temple decoration, despite a high ISO setting of 3200.

TREE RINGS
Unless the conditions force you to do otherwise, it is best to use a low ISO setting to capture Mother Nature's detail.

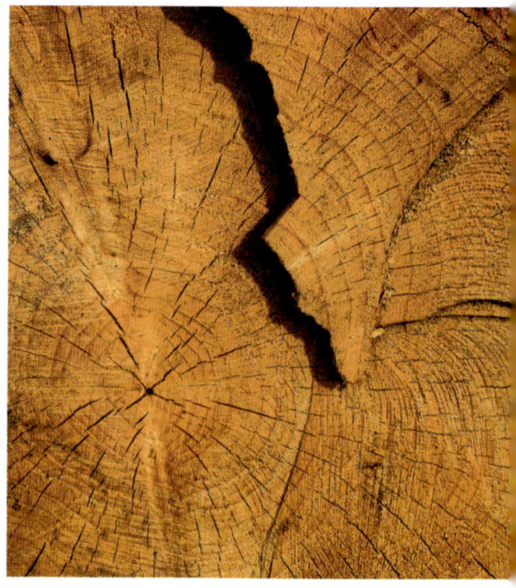

210

to perhaps 1:5, or one-fifth life-size. This is partly due to marketing, but is more to do with the fact that these lenses are designed and constructed specifically so that they perform at least as well at very close focusing distances as they do in everyday shooting. In this guide, the term "true macro" has been used to denote lenses that offer 1:1 magnification. Sigma currently offer five different models that meet this specification.

Micro photography

The term "micro" is also derived from Greek, this time from the word meaning "small." In general usage, it is often reserved for magnifications greater than life-size. In some contexts it indicates detail that may be so small that it is invisible to the naked eye. Micro photography has many exponents, who usually make use of bellows attachments between the camera and the lens in order to increase magnification. True macro lenses are sometimes used for this purpose, though higher levels of magnification can be achieved by reversing a wide-angle lens. Reversed enlarging lenses are also commonly used in this fashion. A variation on the terminology, photomicrography is the term applied specifically to taking photographs through a microscope.

DIFFERENTIAL FOCUS
Although it is tempting to capture everything in focus, sometimes it is more effective to use a wide aperture.

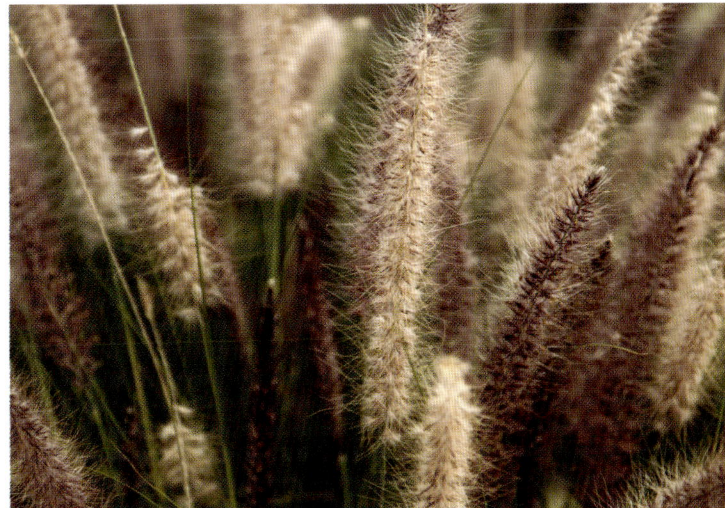

211

50mm f/2.8 EX DG Macro

Lens construction: 10 elements in 9 groups
Angle of view: 46.8°
Diaphragm blades: 7
Min. aperture: f/45
Min. focusing distance: 18.8cm (7.4in)
Max. magnification: 1:1
Filter: 55mm
Dimensions: 71.4mm (W) × 66.5mm (L)
(2.8in × 2.6in)
Weight: 320g (11.3oz)
Mounts: Sigma, Canon, Nikon (D), Sony, Pentax (not SFX or SF7)

Note: The appearance of lenses may differ depending on the camera mount.

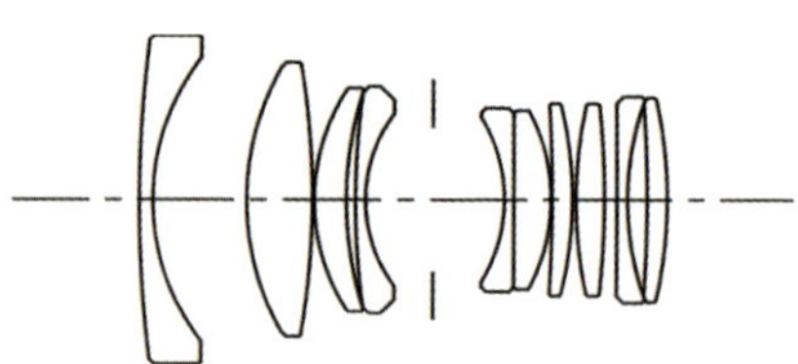

This lens is compact and extremely well made, with the finish we have come to expect from all EX designs. In addition to the usual AF/MF switch, it has a second switch to limit the focusing distance. Slide the Limit/Full switch to Full and the lens can make use of its full focusing range, from 18.8cm (7.4in) to infinity.

However, at close focusing distances, the AF system will "hunt," so if the camera-to-subject distance is over 25cm (9.8in), you can switch to Limit, which will stop the lens from trying to focus at its nearest normal limits. From infinity to 25cm

LENS CONSTRUCTION

(9.8in), the focusing ring rotates through approximately 90°, but from 25cm (9.8in) down to 18.8cm (7.4in), it rotates through an additional 125°, so switching to limited focusing prevents a great deal of travel and

Depth of field (m): 50mm f/2.8 EX DG Macro

Circle of confusion: 0.3333mm

Focused at Aperture		2.8	4	5.6	8	11	16	22	32	45
0.2m	Near	0.195	0.194	0.194	0.194	0.193	0.193	0.192	0.191	0.189
	Far	0.195	0.196	0.196	0.196	0.197	0.197	0.198	0.200	0.202
0.3m	Near	0.298	0.297	0.296	0.294	0.292	0.289	0.285	0.279	0.272
	Far	0.302	0.303	0.304	0.306	0.308	0.312	0.317	0.325	0.337
0.6m	Near	0.59	0.59	0.58	0.57	0.56	0.54	0.52	0.50	0.47
	Far	0.61	0.62	0.62	0.63	0.65	0.67	0.71	0.77	0.87
1m	Near	0.97	0.95	0.94	0.91	0.88	0.84	0.79	0.72	0.65
	Far	1.04	1.05	1.08	1.11	1.06	1.25	1.39	1.68	2.36
infinity	Near	24.24	17.78	12.59	8.92	6.33	4.49	3.19	2.28	1.63
	Far	inf	inf	inf	inf	inf	inf	inf	inf	inf

makes focusing much faster for day-to-day subjects. The top side of the lens barrel is marked with easy to read magnification ratios from 1:5 up to 1:1, and lens extension at life-size is just 3.7cm (1.5in). A shallow screw-in lens hood (not of petal design) is provided.

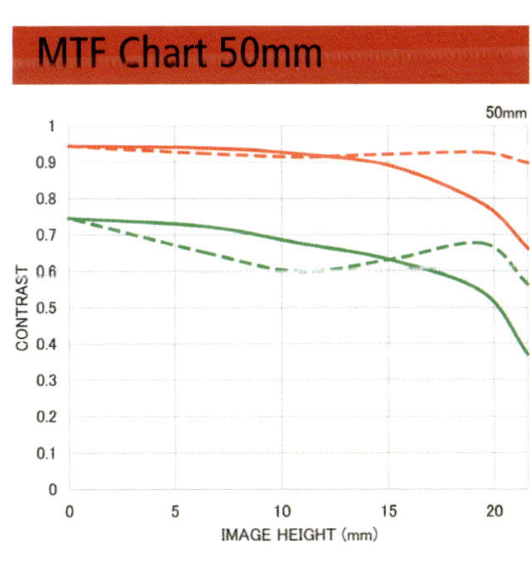

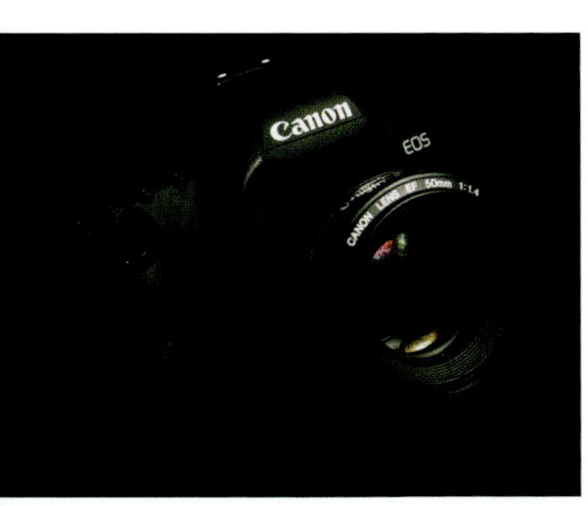

PRODUCT SHOT
This lens has been used extensively to shoot product images for the Expanded Guide series.

This lens, along with the 105mm Macro, boasts the narrowest aperture of any Sigma lens at f/45 (f/32 for Nikon and Pentax versions), providing a whole centimeter (0.4in) of depth of focus at maximum magnification. This may not sound very much if you are unfamiliar with macro work, but if you are, you will recognize that this is a major selling point. Diffraction, of course, comes into play at such extreme apertures; resolution is not quite as good when the lens is stopped right down to its maximum, but in some circumstances it is well worth sacrificing a slight loss of resolution in favor of superb depth of field.

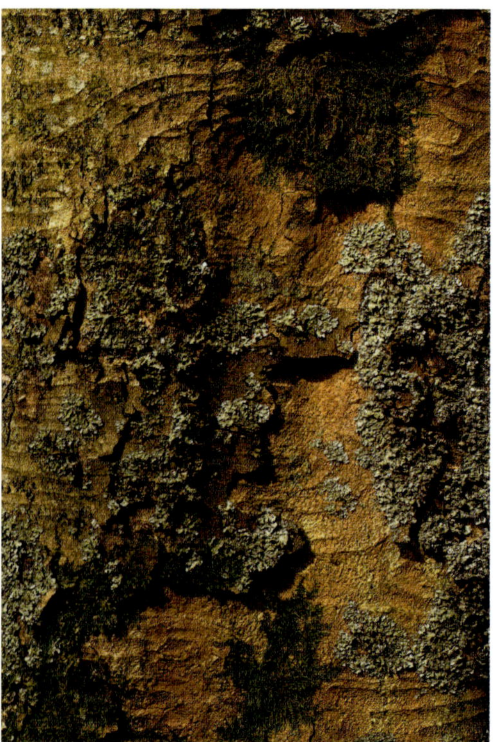

TREE BARK
The 50mm f/2.8 Macro is ideal as a general-purpose lens that also permits highly detailed close-ups of everyday subjects.

Verdict
If your macro work does not require a longer working distance between camera and subject, this lens will make an excellent investment. Being so small and light, it is ideal for taking out into the field and makes an ideal partner for Sigma's EM-140 ring flash. It is also a first-rate lens for general-purpose photography when you want to travel light.

70mm f/2.8 EX DG Macro

Lens construction: 10 elements in 9 groups
Angle of view: 34.3º
Diaphragm blades: 9
Min. aperture: f/22
Min. focusing distance: 25.7cm (10.1in)
Max. magnification: 1:1
Filter: 62mm
Dimensions: 76mm (W) × 95mm (L)
(3in × 3.7in)
Weight: 525g (18.5oz)
Mounts: Sigma, Canon, Nikon (D), Sony, Pentax (not SFX or SF7)

Note: The appearance of lenses may differ depending on the camera mount.

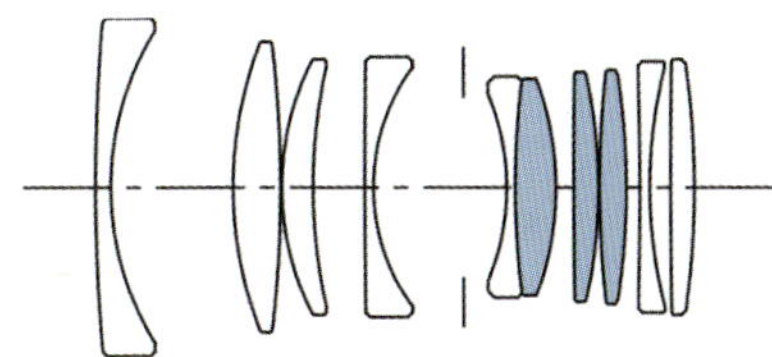

This the second of Sigma's five true macro lenses, all of which provide true excellence in terms of image quality. A focus-limiter switch is provided to create two separate ranges: 0.55m (21.7in) to infinity or 0.257m (10.1in) to 0.48m (18.9in) for close-up work. The focusing ring has to travel though an arc of approximately 190º when moving from the closest focusing distance to infinity, so limiting its scope means faster focusing. But focusing with this lens isn't just fast—it is also very accurate and copes well with both low light and low contrast.

LENS CONSTRUCTION

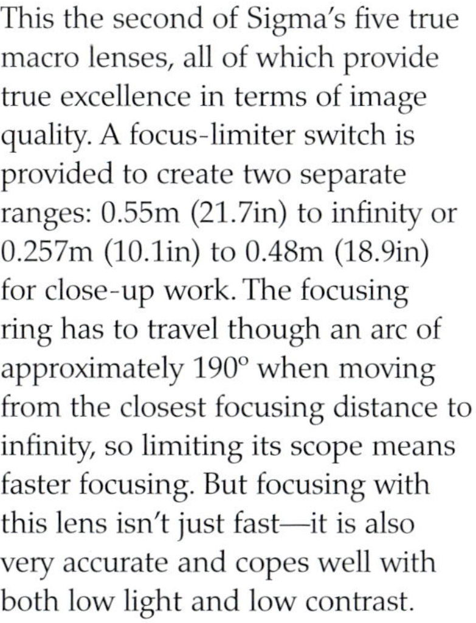

SLD glass

The build and finish are typical of the EX range and give you a sense of confidence that your images will live up to this lens's promise. In one sense it is a shame that there is no

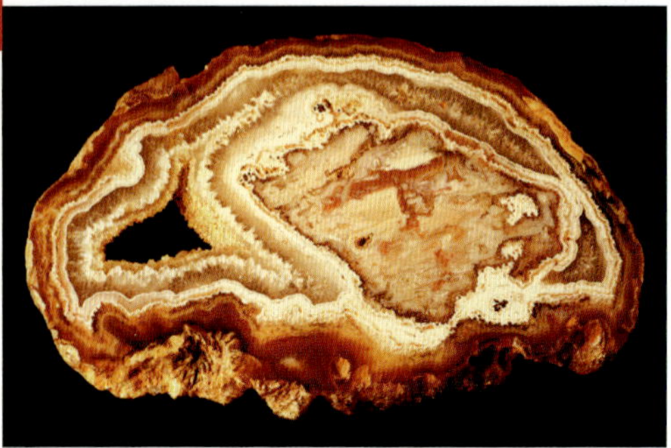

AGATE
Stunning close-ups like this slice of agate can be captured with the minimum of effort and equipment at home when the weather makes outdoor photography impossible.

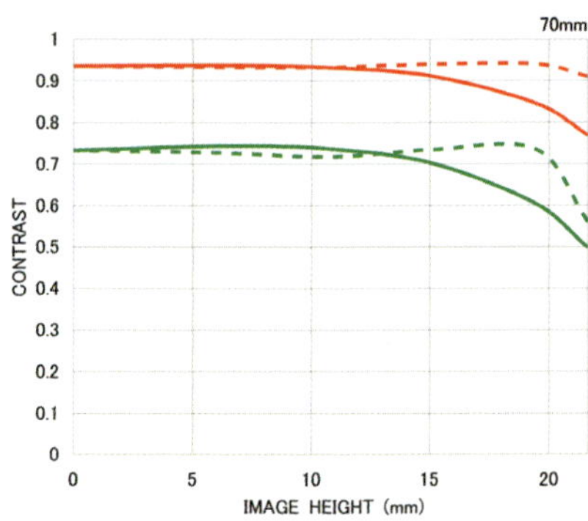

full-time manual override of the focusing, as there is with most of the HSM lenses, as the focusing ring falls beautifully to the thumb and forefinger of the supporting hand.

The magnification ratios marked on the barrel, from 1:5 to 1:1, are only visible with the focus set at less than the 0.55m (21.7in) limiter position.

The front element is not as deeply recessed as many true macro lenses around this focal length, so multiple flash/lighting setups need to be arranged carefully so that stray light doesn't cause unwanted flare.

Finally, the lens comes with a conventional screw-in (though the instruction sheet says bayonet) lens hood. Sadly, this can't be carried

Verdict
A good size and weight for handholding, with or without ring flash. Superb image quality on full-frame and staggering on APS-C, I have no hesitation in recommending this lens, or indeed any of the true macro lenses, for macro work or as everyday lenses when image quality is important. Whatever you pay for this or any of the true macro lenses, you will be rewarded handsomely.

reversed on the front of the lens— although it fits beautifully when reversed, as if designed to do so, there is no way to secure it in place.

216

105mm f/2.8 EX DG Macro

Specifications (based on Sigma mount)

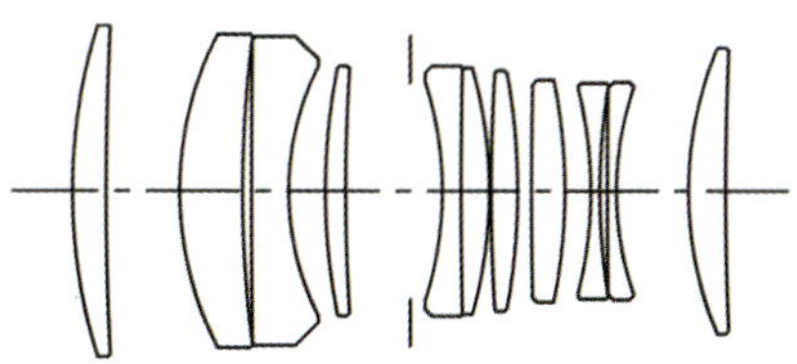

Lens construction: 11 elements in 10 groups
Angle of view: 23.3°
Diaphragm blades: 8
Min. aperture: f/45
Min. focusing distance: 31.3cm (12.3in)
Max. magnification: 1:1
Filter: 58mm
Dimensions: 74mm (W) × 97.5mm (L)
(2.9in × 3.8in)
Weight: 460g (16.2oz)
Mounts: Sigma, Canon, Nikon (D), Sony, Pentax (not SFX or SF7), Four Thirds

Note: The appearance of lenses may differ depending on the camera mount.

The focusing ring on this lens rotates through a huge arc approximately 270°—from the minimum focusing distance of 31.3cm (12.3in) to infinity. The maximum lens extension is 51mm (2in), revealing two sets of magnification ratio markings—one for AF in white and another in gold for manual focus. Both sets of markings run from a quarter life-size (1:4) to full life-size (1:1).

The lens has a push/pull focusing ring that utilizes Sigma's "clutch" mechanism for switching from autofocus to manual focus, or vice versa. This needs to be operated in

LENS CONSTRUCTION

addition to the AF/MF switch on your camera, or, with Sigma SA and Canon AF versions, the AF/MF switch on the lens itself. When the focus limiting switch on the side of the lens is changed from Full to Limit, the focusing arc is

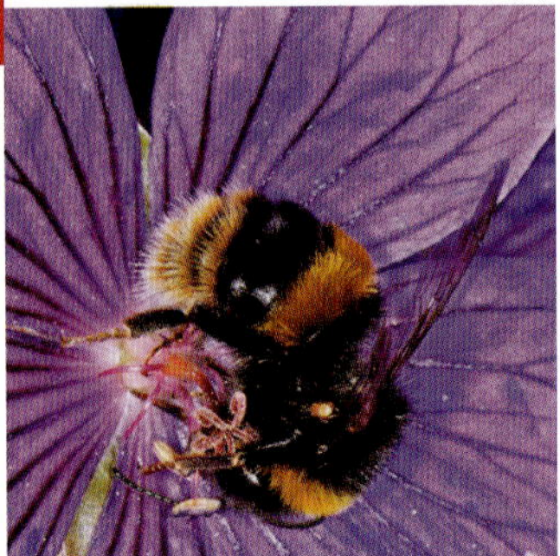

BEE
This macro shot was lit with a Sigma EM-140 ring flash.

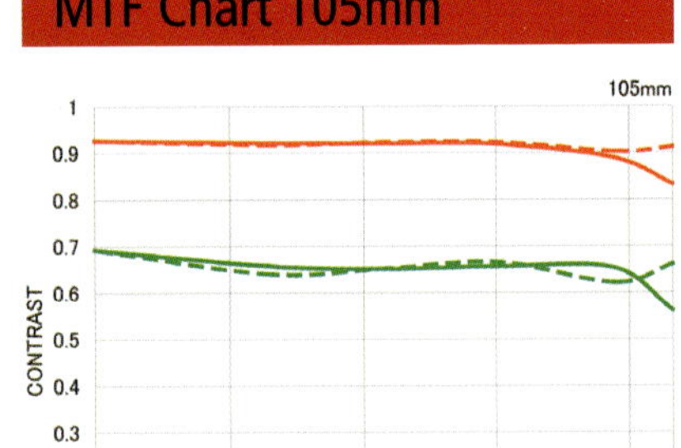

reduced to approximately 130°. If this is applied with focus set at greater than 40cm (15.7in), focus covers a range from 40cm and a magnification ratio of 1:2 (half life-size) to infinity. If the focus limiting switch is applied when the lens is focused at less than 40cm, focus will be limited to a range between the closest focusing distance of 31.3cm (12.3in)—a magnification ratio of 1:1—and just under 40cm (1:2).

The long extension at high magnifications reduces the amount of light passing through the lens and thus the effective aperture. TTL metering will adjust to this, but metering with a light meter will require you to calculate the revised aperture. The front element is deeply recessed and the lens hood (which is not reversible) can be left at home for macro or everyday shooting.

The instruction leaflet for the lens contains specific instructions for certain makes of camera which are too lengthy to reproduce here. Check these when examining a demo lens at your camera retailer.

Warning!

Before attaching the lens to the camera, make sure that the focus ring's "clutch" mechanism setting is positioned at AF. To do this, simply slide the push/pull focusing ring toward the front of the lens.

Verdict

Another staggeringly sharp lens with excellent contrast. Working distance with subjects like the bee shown above is still quite short, which can have implications for lighting, so you may also want to consider the possibility of acquiring Sigma's EM-140 ring flash.

150mm f/2.8 EX DG Macro HSM IF APO CONV

Lens construction: 16 elements in 12 groups
Angle of view: 16.4º
Diaphragm blades: 9
Min. aperture: f/22
Min. focusing distance: 38cm (15in)
Max. magnification: 1:1
Filter: 72mm
Dimensions: 79.6mm (W) × 137mm (L)
(3.1in × 5.4in)
Weight: 895g (31.6oz)
Mounts: Sigma, Canon, Nikon (D), Four Thirds

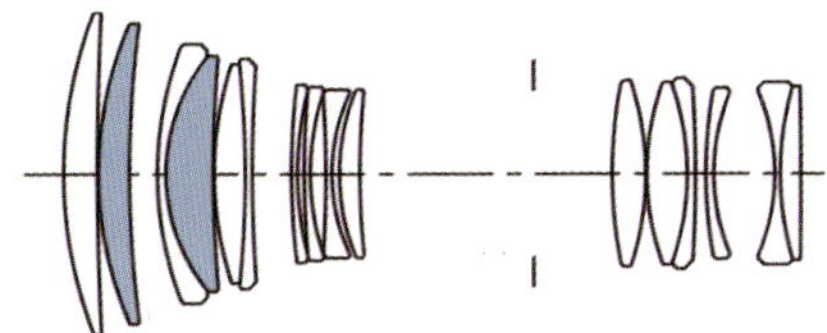

Note: The appearance of lenses may differ depending on the camera mount.

A glance at the MTF chart on the following page tells you everything you need to know about this lens: superb contrast and resolution across the range. Bitingly sharp and a joy to handle, this lens makes a superb choice for both close-ups and day-to-day use. Balance and handling are excellent when shooting handheld. It has a hinged tripod collar which can be removed while the lens is attached to the camera, and that allows quick rotation of the camera to permit vertical shooting when using a tripod. With life-size magnification

LENS CONSTRUCTION

SLD glass

and a moderate working distance, this lens is a flexible choice for those who like their nature photography up close and personal.

As this lens is of IF (inner focus) design, there is no extension of the lens barrel, so magnification ratios are marked on the focusing ring instead of the lens barrel. But it is also a superb performer when used for candids and for isolating detail, even when used wide open. A 1.4× or 2× converter can also be slipped into your pocket when you're out for the day, extending the lens's flexibility even more.

As well as the obvious AF/MF switch, there is also a three-position switch (Sigma, Canon, and Nikon

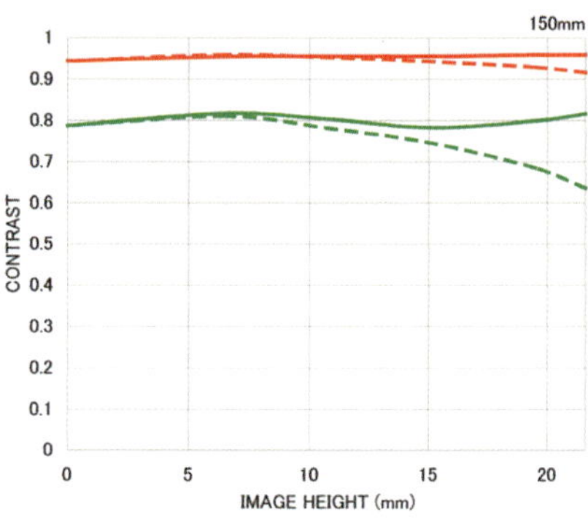

versions) for setting the focusing range. This can be set to Full, when it covers the full focusing range from 38cm (15in) to infinity, or to one of two limited range settings. The first

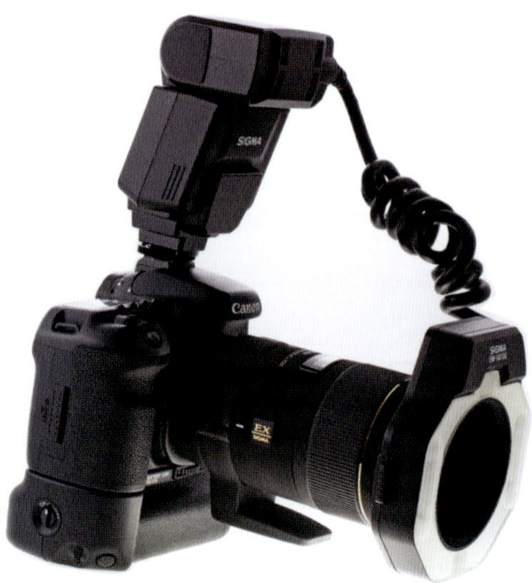

RING FLASH
The 150mm f/2.8 Macro with Sigma EM-140 ring flash attached.

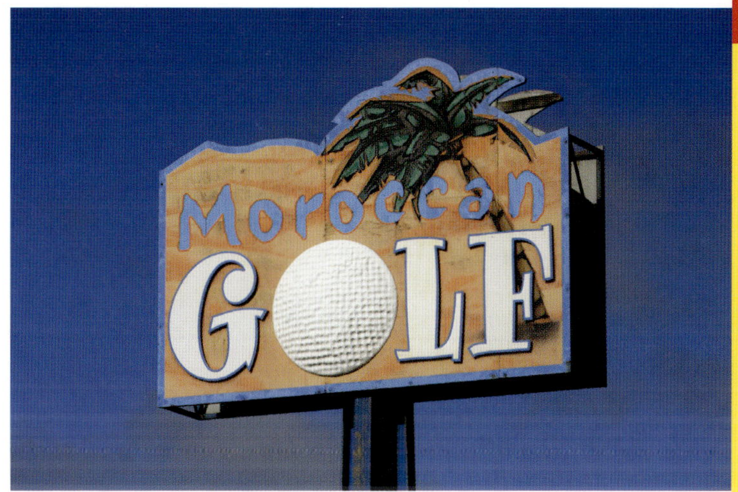

of these permits focusing between 52cm (20.5in) and infinity, while the second is for subjects between 38cm and 52cm from the focal plane.

While the HSM autofocus generally proved both silent and very responsive in testing, on the Full setting, the AF would sometimes "hunt," even in high-contrast lighting situations, due partly to the extensive arc through which the focusing ring must travel. Once it had locked onto the subject, however, focusing on other subjects at a similar distance was fast and positive.

Verdict

Awesome. This is one of the sharpest lenses I have ever used. It is beautifully balanced when used handheld, even with a ring flash attached. For distance work, especially at wide apertures on an APS-C body, images are incredibly crisp and high in contrast. The only things on my wish-list would be a better focus-limiter switch and a focus-limit range of perhaps a meter (3.3ft), rather than 52cm, to infinity, as this would reduce focus "hunting" when switching from close range to distant subjects in everyday (as opposed to macro) situations.

180mm f/3.5 EX DG Macro HSM IF APO CONV

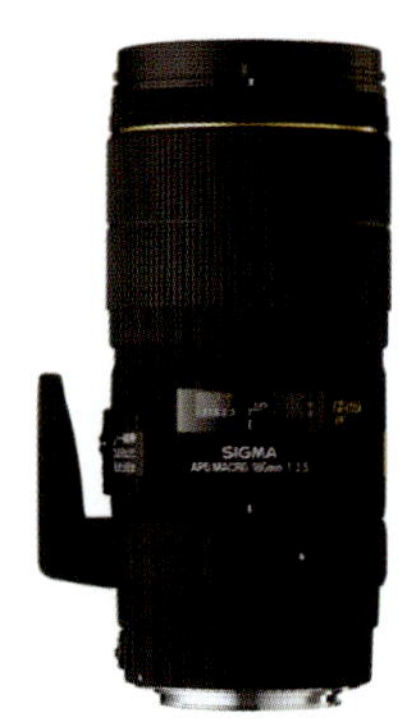

Specifications (based on Sigma mount)

Lens construction: 13 elements in 10 groups
Angle of view: 13.7°
Diaphragm blades: 9
Min. aperture: f/32
Min. focusing distance: 46cm (18.1in)
Max. magnification: 1:1
Filter: 72mm
Dimensions: 80mm (W) × 182mm (L)
(3.1in × 7.2in)
Weight: 965g (34oz)
Mounts (HSM): Sigma, Canon, Nikon (D)
Mounts (non-HSM): Sony, Pentax (not SFX or SF7)

Note: The appearance of lenses may differ depending on the camera mount.

With the longest focal length in Sigma's range of true macro lenses, this model provides just a little more working distance than the 150mm version. As the focusing mechanism is entirely internal, there is no lens extension to worry about when working at very short camera-to-subject distances. The HSM versions allow full-time manual focusing without necessarily switching the body/lens (depending on camera manufacturer) to manual focus. This means you can use autofocus but still fine-tune the focus manually,

LENS CONSTRUCTION

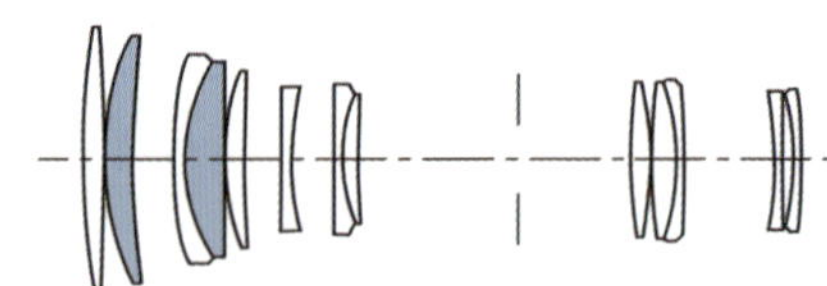

SLD glass

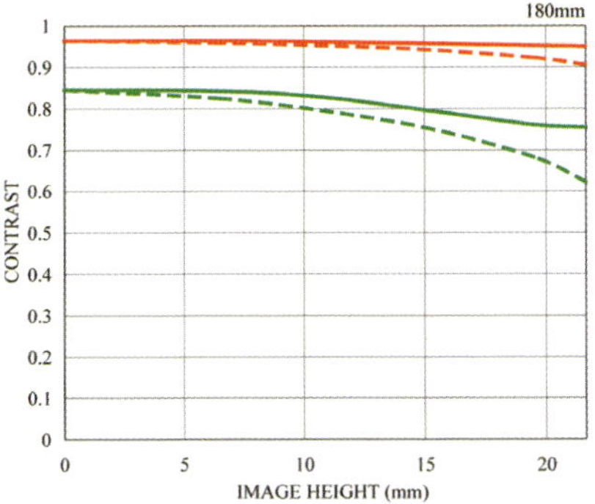

Verdict

With no huge difference in cost—or image quality, for that matter—the choice between this and the 150mm f/2.8 Macro is really down to which combination of weight, working distance, and maximum aperture you prefer. For predominantly tripod work, the 180mm is probably a better bet than the 150mm, though the latter is more flexibile and better for handheld use.

provided you keep partial pressure on the shutter release after first focusing using AF.

Working distance can be increased by using either the 1.4× or 2× APO EX teleconverter. The former allows you to use the lens as a 252mm f/5 lens (with Canon, Nikon and Sigma cameras*) while maintaining the camera's autofocus function from infinity to 1.2m (47.2 in). At distances closer than 1.2m (47.2 in), the lens automatically switches to MF. When used with the 2× APO EX teleconverter, the 180mm f/3.5 lens becomes a 360mm f/7 lens with manual focus function only, regardless of camera mount.

*When the 1.4× APO EX teleconverter is used with this lens on Minolta or Pentax cameras, the lens must be focused manually.

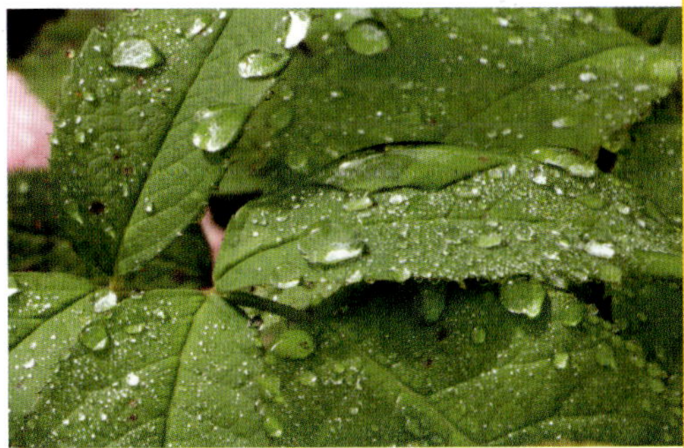

RAINDROPS
Sometimes the simplest of close-up subjects can provide plenty of options. These raindrops could also be magnified singly or in different combinations, accentuating their reflections.

Striking color

Images that rely on color rarely do so in isolation: shape and line usually play a part, too, as in the image below of the steps leading down the side of a jetty into the waters of a harbor on the island of Jersey. In this instance, the colors are complementary, but contrasting color can work just as well.

By excluding both the top and bottom of the steps, the lines are kept simple and there is an element left open to interpretation: do the steps lead down into the sea, or do they lead up out of it?

Most visitors to Gorey on the island of Jersey flock straight to Mont Orgueil Castle, which dominates every view, so attractive cameos like these steps are easily missed.

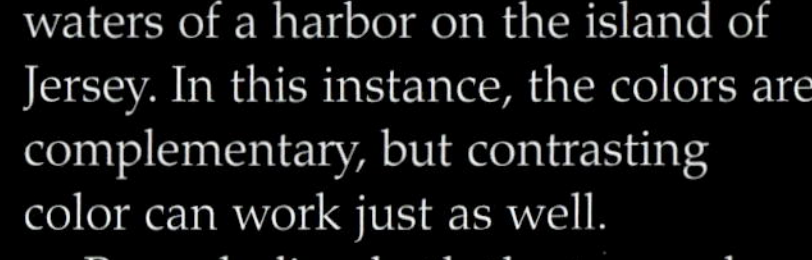

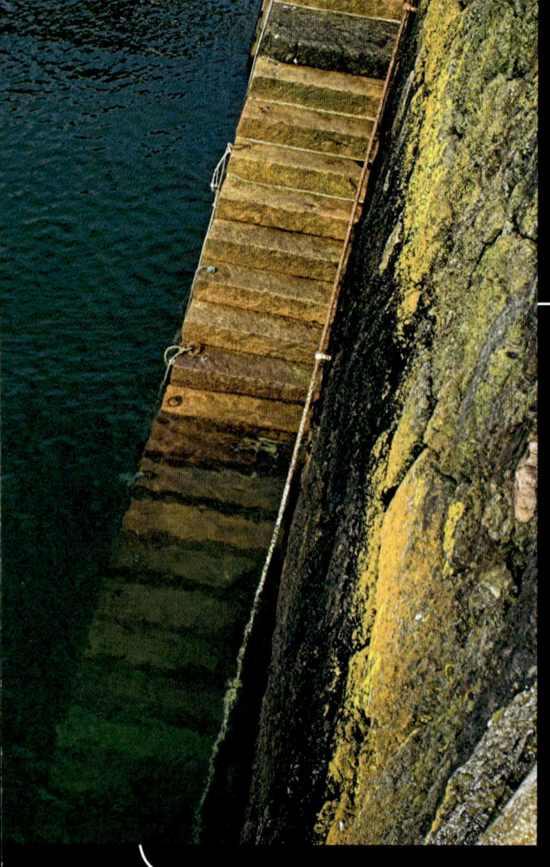

HARBOR STEPS

Settings
Focal length: 28mm
ISO: 400
Aperture: f/11
Shutter: 1/320

Absence of color

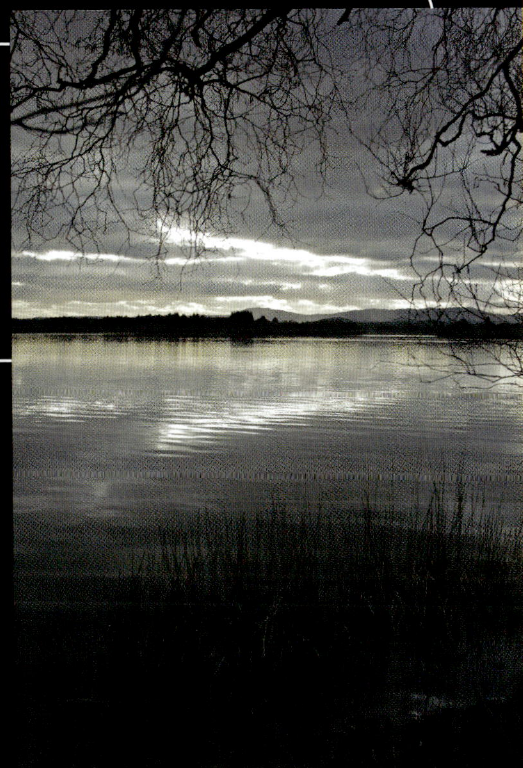

Sometimes an image barely contains any color at all, such as this shot of a lakeshore that relies almost entirely on a range of steely grays that add to the mood. It is Scotland's only lake (the rest being lochs), late on a winter afternoon. The image relies almost entirely on a limited range of tones with the aid of silhouetted elements both in the foreground and in the distance.

In this particular example, two graduated neutral density filters were used to keep all the tones within a workable range. The first graduated ND filter was used on the sky so that its tones matched those of the water. (Note that in these situations, although the water mirrors the sky, the exposure for the two are likely to be a couple of stops apart.) The second graduated ND filter was used inverted on the reeds in the foreground so that their detail gradually, and almost imperceptibly, becomes apparent.

White background

Smaller subjects are easy to shoot in pack-shot style using a light tent, light cube, or similar construction—in this case, the highly portable Lastolite ePhotomaker. All of these function in the same way, by placing the subject on a white base and surrounding it with white translucent material, which diffuses any light source(s). A high key image can then be captured with minimal shadows.

By using off-camera flash, especially a wireless setup with two or more flash units, strong, shadowless lighting is easily obtained—particularly if one flash unit is directed upward through the base material. This can be achieved by placing the base of the light-tent on a sheet of transparent plastic or similar material, supported at the corners, and placing a flash unit below and slightly in front of the subject, pointing upward at an angle.

Test shots are usually required to obtain the most favorable exposure, especially if you are blending flash and ambient lighting, and to determine the best positioning of the flash units.

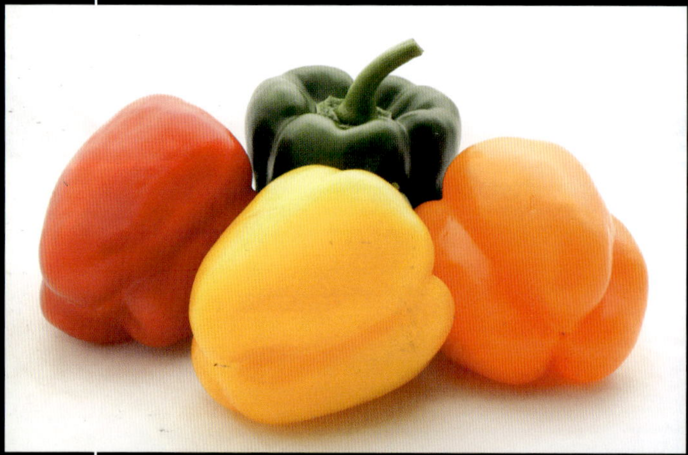

PEPPERS

Settings
Focal length: 50mm
ISO: 100
Aperture: f/22
Shutter: 0.3 sec

Black background

By setting the subject against a black velvet background and using diffused flash, with all the key elements on one plane to reduce the depth of field required, this Montbretia is captured in all its elegant simplicity. Such setups are relatively easy to create at home, but they can be achieved in the field too, by carrying a portable background along with the means to hold a plant stem steady.

Outdoors, the biggest problem with a shot like this is usually movement of the subject in a breeze, rather than lighting, so a small improvised roll-up windbreak can be equally useful.

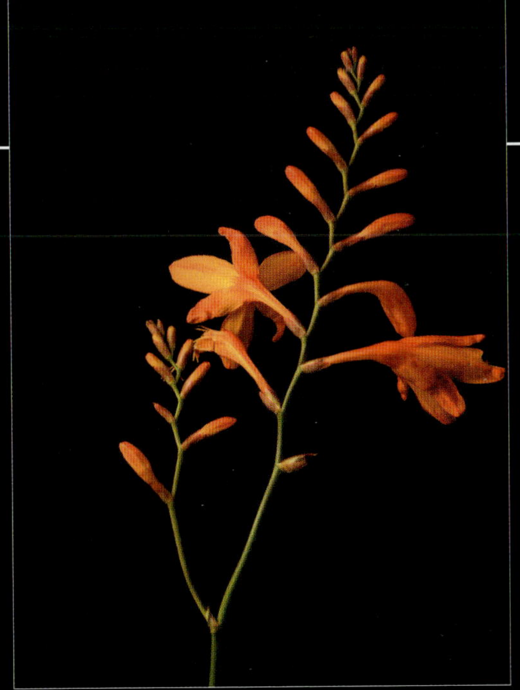

MONTBRETIA

Settings
Focal length: 50mm
ISO: 100
Aperture: f/11
Shutter: 1/200

Discontinued lenses

With one exception (see page 55), the lenses listed below are not featured in this book and can no longer be bought new, but examples may be found at used camera stores or on internet auction sites.

Lens	Max. mag.	Filter	Dia. × Length (mm)	Wgt (g)
15–30mm f/3.5–4.5 EX ASP DG DF	1:6	gel	87 × 130	615
17–35mm f/2.8–4 EX DG ASP	1:4.5	77	83.5 × 86.2	560
17–35mm f/2.8–4 EX ASP HSM	1:11.5	82	89 × 83.5	400
18–50mm f/2.8 EX DC	1:5	67	74.1 × 84.1	445
18–125mm f/3.5–5.6 DC	1:5.3	62	70 × 77.7	385
20–40mm f/2.8 EX DG	1:4.6	82	89 × 107.8	600
24–135mm f/2.8–4.5 ASP IF	1:4.5	77	83.6 × 90.9	530
28–70mm f/2.8–4 High-speed Zoom	1:6.5	58	67.5 × 60.0	245
28–80mm f3.5–5.6 ASP Macro HF	1:5.4	55	69.5 × 71.4	255
28–80mm f/3.5–5.6 Mini Zoom Macro II ASP	1:5.4	55	69.5 × 69.5	255
28–105mm f/2.8–4 DG ASP IF	1:5.5	72	77 × 79.5	405
28–105mm f/3.8–5.6 UC-III ASP IF	1:5.6	62	71 × 72.5	275
28–105mm f/2.8–4 ASP IF	1:5.5	72	77 × 79.5	405
28–135mm f/3.8–5.6 ASP IF Macro	1:2	62	75 × 75	410
28–200mm f/3.5–5.6 DG Compact ASP Macro	1:3.8	62	70 × 75.2	380
28–200mm f/3.5–5.6 Compact ASP Macro	1:3.8	62	70 × 75.2	380
28–300mm f/3.5–6.3 Macro	1:3	62	74 × 83.7	460
50–150mm f/2.8 EX DC APO HSM	1:5.3	67	76.3 × 135.1	770
50–500mm f/4–6.3 EX APO RF / RF HSM	1:5.2	86	94 × 218	1650
70–200mm f/2.8 EX DG APO MACRO HSM	1:3.5	77	86.6 × 184.4	1380
70–200mm f/2.8 EX DG APO IF / APO IF HSM	1:7.8	77	86 × 183	1220

70–200mm f/2.8 EX APO IF / APO IF HSM	1:7.8	77	86 × 183	1220
70–300mm f/4–5.6 APO Macro Super II	1:4	58	76.6 × 119.5	530
70–300mm f/4–5.6 DL Macro Super II	1:4	58	76.6 × 119.5	530
80–400mm f4.5–5.6 EX DG APO OS	1:5	77	95.0 × 189.5	1750
80–400mm f4.5–5.6 EX OS	1:5	77	95.0 × 189.5	1750
100–300mm f/4 EX IF / IF HSM	1:5	82	92.4 × 224	1480
100–300mm f/4.5–6.7 DL	1:5.9	55	70 × 99	410
120–300mm f/2.8 EX APO HSM IF	1:8.6	105	112.8 × 268.5	2600
135–400mm f/4.5–5.6 DG APO ASP	1:5.3	77	88.5 × 181.1	1210
135–400mm f/4.5–5.6 APO ASP	1:5.3	77	88.5 × 181.1	1210
170–500mm f/5–6.3 APO ASP	1:6.6	86	92.5 × 229.5	1320
300–800mm f5.6 EX APO HSM IF	1:6.9	46	156.5 × 541.5	5870

15–30mm f/3.5–4.5 EX DG ASP IF
This lens is listed here as discontinued, but at the time of writing it was still available new from many dealers, so it is also reviewed in full on pages 55–7.

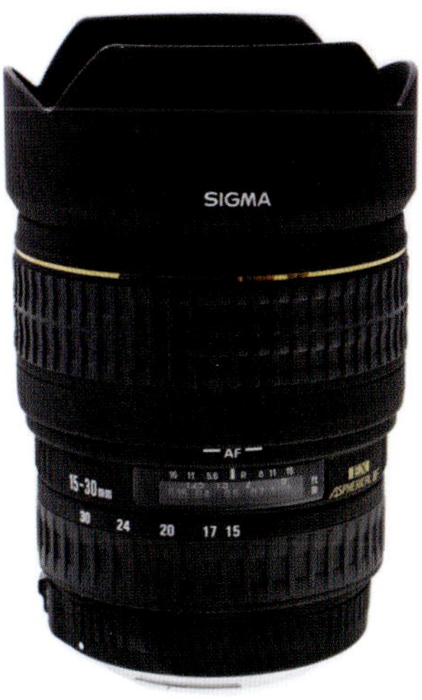

Useful websites

Sigma USA
www.sigmaphoto.com

Sigma UK
www.sigma-imaging-uk.com

Sigma Japan
www.sigma-photo.co.jp/english/index.htm

Canon USA
www.usa.canon.com

Canon UK
www.canon.co.uk/

Nikon USA
www.nikonusa.com

Nikon UK
www.nikon.co.uk

Pentax USA
www.pentaximaging.com

Pentax UK
www.pentax.co.uk

Sony USA
www.sony.com

Sony UK
www.sony.co.uk

DXO Mark: Image Quality Database
www.dxomark.com/index.php/eng/
Image-Quality-Database

Hyperfocal Distance Calculator
www.cambridgeincolour.com/tutorials/
hyperfocal-distance.htm

Online Depth of Field Calculator
www.dofmaster.com/dofjs.html

FILTERS

www.leefilters.com
www.tiffen.com
www.cokin.com
www.formatt.co.uk
www.hoya-online.co.uk

DIGITAL FILTERS

www.tiffen.com/dfx_essentials
www.niksoftware.com

NEWS & RUMORS

www.canonrumors.com
www.dpreview.com
www.photorumors.com
www.photographybay.com
www.ephotozine.co.uk

PUBLICATIONS

Photography books
www.ammonitepress.com

*Black & White Photography
& Outdoor Photography* magazines
www.pipress.com

Index

Contact us for a complete catalog or visit our website:
Ammonite Press, 166 High Street, Lewes, East Sussex, BN7 1XU, United Kingdom
Tel: +44 (0)1273 488006 Fax: +44 (0)1273 472418
www.ammonitepress.com